■ The New Mexico State Constitution

The Oxford Commentaries on the State Constitutions of the United States
G. Alan Tarr, Series Editor

Professor G. Alan Tarr, Director of the Center on State Constitutional Studies at Rutgers University, serves as General Editor for this important new series which in its entirety will cover each of the 50 states. Each volume of The Oxford Commentaries on the State Constitutions of the United States contains a historical overview of the state's constitutional development, plus a section-by-section analysis of the state's current constitution. Other features included in the volumes are the text of the state's constitution, a bibliographic essay, table of cases, and index. This series provides essential reference tools for those investigating state constitutional development and constitutional law.

The New Mexico State Constitution

Chuck Smith

Foreword by Stephanie Gonzales

THE OXFORD COMMENTARIES ON THE STATE CONSTITUTIONS OF THE UNITED STATES
G. Alan Tarr, Series Editor

OXFORD
UNIVERSITY PRESS

OXFORD
UNIVERSITY PRESS

Oxford University Press, Inc., publishes works that further Oxford University's objective of excellence in research, scholarship, and education.

Oxford New York
Auckland Cape Town Dar es Salaam Hong Kong Karachi Kuala Lumpur Madrid Melbourne Mexico City Nairobi New Delhi Shanghai Taipei Toronto

With offices in
Argentina Austria Brazil Chile Czech Republic France Greece Guatemala Hungary Italy Japan Poland Portugal Singapore South Korea Switzerland Thailand Turkey Ukraine Vietnam

Previously published in 1996 by Greenwood Press

Published by Oxford University Press, Inc.
198 Madison Avenue, New York, New York 10016

Library of Congress Cataloging-in-Publication Data

Smith, Chuck, 1941-
The New Mexico State Constitution / Chuck Smith and Stephanie Gonzales.
p. cm. — (The Oxford commentaries on the state constitutions of the United States)
Includes bibliographical references and index.
ISBN 978-0-19-977915-4 (hardback)
1. Constitutions—New Mexico. 2. Constitutional law—New Mexico.
3. Constitutional history—New Mexico. I. Gonzales, Stephanie.
II. New Mexico. Constitution. III. Title.
KFN40011911.A6 S648 2011
342.78902—dc22 2011003232

Note to Readers
This publication is designed to provide accurate and authoritative information in regard to the subject matter covered. It is based upon sources believed to be accurate and reliable and is intended to be current as of the time it was written. It is sold with the understanding that the publisher is not engaged in rendering legal, accounting, or other professional services. If legal advice or other expert assistance is required, the services of a competent professional person should be sought. Also, to confirm that the information has not been affected or changed by recent developments, traditional legal research techniques should be used, including checking primary sources where appropriate.

(Based on the Declaration of Principles jointly adopted by a Committee of the American Bar Association and a Committee of Publishers and Associations.)

Dedicated to **Professor Harry P. Stumpf**
my teacher and mentor, who over the years taught thousands of students
at the University of New Mexico the
importance of state courts and state constitutions.

CONTENTS

■ SERIES FOREWORD

In 1776, following the declaration of independence from England, the former colonies began to draft their own constitutions. Their handiwork attracted widespread interest, and draft constitutions circulated up and down the Atlantic seaboard, as constitution-makers sought to benefit from the insights of their counterparts in sister states. In Europe, the new constitutions found a ready audience seeking enlightenment from the American experiments in self-government. Even the delegates to the Constitutional Convention of 1787, despite their reservations about the course of political developments in the states during the decade after independence, found much that was useful in the newly adopted constitutions. And when James Madison, fulfilling a pledge given during the ratification debates, drafted the Federal Bill of Rights, he found his model in the famous Declaration of Rights of the Virginia Constitution.

By the 1900s, however, few people would have looked to state constitutions for enlightenment. Instead, a familiar litany of complaints was heard whenever state constitutions were mentioned. State constitutions were too long and too detailed, combining basic principles with policy prescriptions and prohibitions that had no place in the fundamental law of a state. By including such provisions, it was argued, state constitutions deprived state governments of the flexibility they needed to respond effectively to changing circumstances. This—among other factors—encouraged political reformers to look to the federal government, which was not plagued by such constitutional constraints, thereby shifting the locus of political initiative away from the states. Meanwhile, civil libertarians concluded that state bills of rights, at least as interpreted by state courts, did not adequately protect rights and therefore looked to the federal courts and the federal Bill of Rights for redress. As power and responsibility shifted from the states to Washington, so too did the attention of scholars, the legal community, and the general public.

During the early 1970s, however, state constitutions were "rediscovered." The immediate impetus for this rediscovery was former President Richard Nixon's appointment of Warren Burger to succeed Earl Warren as Chief Justice of the United States Supreme Court. To civil libertarians, this appointment seemed to signal a decisive shift in the Supreme Court's jurisprudence, because Burger was expected to lead the Court away from the liberal activism that had characterized the Warren Court. They therefore sought ways to safeguard the gains they had achieved for defendants, racial minorities, and the poor during Warren's tenure from erosion by the Burger Court. In particular, they began to look to state bills of rights to secure the rights of defendants and to support other civil-liberties claims that they advanced in state courts.

This "new judicial federalism," as it came to be called, quite quickly advanced beyond its initial concern to evade the mandates of the Burger Court. Indeed, less than two decades after it originated, it has become a nationwide phenomenon. For when judges and scholars turned their attention to state constitutions, they discovered an unsuspected richness. They found not only provisions that paralleled the federal Bill of Rights but also constitutional guarantees of the right to privacy and of gender equality, for example, that had no analogue in the U.S. Constitution. Careful examination of the text and history of state guarantees revealed important differences between even those provisions that most resembled federal guarantees and their federal counterparts. Looking beyond state declarations of rights, jurists and scholars discovered affirmative constitutional mandates to state governments to address such important policy concerns as education and housing. Taken altogether, these discoveries underlined the importance for the legal community of developing a better understanding of state constitutions.

Yet the renewed interest in state constitutions has not been limited to judges and lawyers. State constitutional reformers have renewed their efforts with notable success: since 1960, ten states have adopted new constitutions and several others have undertaken major constitutional revisions. These changes have usually resulted in more streamlined constitutions and more effective state governments. Also, in recent years political activists on both the left and the right have pursued their goals through state constitutional amendments, often enacted through the initiative process, under which policy proposals can be placed directly on the ballot for voters to endorse or reject. Scholars too have begun to rediscover how state constitutional history can illuminate changes in political thought and practice, providing a basis for theories about the dynamics of political change in America.

Chuck Smith's fine study of the New Mexico Constitution is the twenty-third volume in the series The Oxford Commentaries on the State Constitutions of the United States, which reflects this renewed interest in state constitutions and will contribute to our knowledge about them. Because the constitutional tradition of each state is distinctive, the volume begins with the history and development of the New Mexico Constitution. It then provides the full text of New Mexico's current constitution, with each section accompanied by commentary that explains the provision and traces its origins and its interpretation by the courts and other governmental bodies. For readers with a particular interest in a specific aspect of New Mexico constitutionalism, the book offers a bibliography of the most important sources dealing with the constitutional history and constitutional law of the state. Finally, the book concludes with a table of cases cited in the history and constitutional history, as well as a subject index.

G. Alan Tarr

■ FOREWORD

> The American government resembles a burro; but on this burro lawyers will ride, not priests.
>
> PADRE ANTONIO MARTINEZ (1793–1867), Taos, New Mexico

Some have suggested that part of the peculiar genius of the American system of government is that, within the framework of the U.S. Constitution, each one of the 50 states is allowed considerable freedom to undertake its own experiment in democracy. Certainly it has proved to be the case that, since achieving statehood in 1912, New Mexico has conducted a notably unique democratic experiment, one that has prospered and endured. But, as Professor Chuck Smith so effectively explains, New Mexico's experiment has succeeded despite being burdened with a flawed and cumbersome state constitution.

New Mexico's state constitution, a "nineteenth-century product," as it has been called by the great New Mexico historian Dorothy Cline, represented the culmination of the Land of Enchantment's 62-year struggle to join the union. This protracted effort for admission lasted longer than that of any other U.S. territory. And, for us today, what is especially instructive about the story of this document is how it so perfectly captures the essential tensions of New Mexico civic life—a continual tug-of-war between cultures and legal doctrines, between traditional communities and economics, between lofty principles and practical politics.

Four years after being occupied by the U.S. Army, New Mexico initiated its first attempt at statehood. But applying for admission to the union as a "free" state—just as that union was intensifying its slide toward catastrophe over the slavery question—helped doom the 1850 statehood initiative, making it the first of what was to become a series of abortive efforts.

By 1912 New Mexico could no longer be denied. Surely the instrument shaped by the 1910 Constitutional Convention helped smooth the way for admission. Here was a document that was clearly the result of compromise and coalition-building, special interest pandering, and plain old hardball politics. Its framers, perhaps unlike those of 1850, were acutely sensitive to the national political climate of the time. The result: New Mexico at last fulfilled the dream of statehood—but at a price. Ever since, New Mexicans have been saddled with a basic law so unwieldy that they have subsequently found themselves amending it 126 times.

Herein lies a wonderful irony about New Mexico and its special peoples, an irony of which the rest of the country might do well to take note.

Today we who live in New Mexico's multilingual community of cultures watch in uneasy fascination as a bitter national debate erupts over the question of "multiculturalism." And we witness in horror the latest upsurge of anti-immigrant sentiment, fueled by a new class of demagogues who would muffle Lady Liberty's call to history's "huddled masses yearning to breathe free."

We feel like telling people across America, "come see how we do it in New Mexico—flawed constitution and all! If we can make democracy work, so can you! We came into the United States as a conquered land. Then we joined ranks to resist secessionist invaders from that infernal place called Texas. Our Hispanic and native peoples have resolutely defended their respective heritages, while at the same time working with the immigrants from the East to forge an often difficult, sometimes turbulent, marriage of these traditions with the democratic values of 1776 and 1787."

The marriage has worked. And like any healthy relationship, it has definitely not been boring.

Thus, it is in a spirit of pride for my state, its history and traditions, its varied cultures and peoples, that I say to Professor Smith, "que bueno!" By giving us this well-reasoned and remarkably insightful treatment of the New Mexico State Constitution, tracing its development and surveying in depth all of its component parts, Professor Smith has not only provided other academicians with a first-rate piece of scholarship, but he has also presented the people and policymakers of New Mexico with a tool of immense value.

As we in New Mexico continue building upon our unique experiment in representative government, *The New Mexico State Constitution: A Reference Guide* will take an honored place on our bookshelves. I am certain that it will play a significant part in all future discussions of constitutional revision and reform.

The Honorable Stephanie Gonzales
New Mexico Secretary of State

■ INTRODUCTION

This is a book of resources about the basic law of the state of New Mexico, its constitution. Written in 1910, the constitution is a relatively new component in the government of the region. New Mexico has existed as an identifiable political entity for almost four hundred years. The Spanish from lower Mexico began to explore the area in 1538. And in 1598, Juan de Oñate y Salazar initiated a tenuous foothold for the Spanish Crown and founded the province of Nuevo Mexico. He established its capital at the Tewa village of Ohke north of presentday Espanola. In 1609 a new capitol was established at Santa Fe and construction begun on the Palace of the Governors, which can still be seen there. The next year, Gaspar de Villagra published a history of the founding of New Mexico. The Spanish were latecomers to the region; evidence of human existence in what is now New Mexico was left by the Sandia people between 12,000 and 10,000 B.C. These people were succeeded by others who developed agriculture and highly artistic pottery and baskets. Eventually, the Anasazi created the distinctive architecture of the multi-storied, apartment-like villages that the Spanish called pueblos. When the Spanish arrived the Pueblo Indians lived in such farming villages scattered along the Rio Grande and it tributaries. Other more nomadic people, such as the Apaches, Comanches, and Navajos, also lived in the region. People had lived, developed political systems, and governed themselves on this land for at least 13,000 years without a constitution.

Government with a strong constitutional orientation came to the region when the U.S. Army occupied Santa Fe in 1846. From that time New Mexico has been governed under the provisions of the U.S. Constitution. But not until 1912 did New Mexico join the Union as a state with its own constitution. Over the past 25 years scholars and legal practitioners have increasingly stressed the importance of state constitutions. As the fundamental law of a state, constitutions establish the structure and organization of the government, assign authority within the government, describe the procedure for making public policy, define the limits on government power, and enumerate basic human rights that the government cannot transgress. Each state constitution also is a reflection of characteristics of the state. Provisions of the New Mexico Constitution reflect its diverse multicultural heritage and the needs posed by its distinctive topography and climate. The constitution also has shortcomings. Many of its provisions are too detailed to serve well as a basic law, and reflect the framers' elitist distrust of democratic institutions. The constitution has served the state for more than 80 years, but not particularly well. A continuing process of frequent piecemeal amendment has been necessary to meet the changing needs of the state.

In writing this book I relied heavily on several sources, the most important of which were the annotation of the New Mexican Constitution in Volume 1 of *New Mexico Statutes Annotated 1978* and the serial publication of the New Mexico Legislative Council Service, *Piecemeal Amendment of the New Mexico Constitution.* The staff of Secretary of State Stephanie Gonzales assisted me by providing up-to-date details about constitutional amendments and legislative acts. In the middle of writing the book I moved 1,300 miles away from New Mexico. From this great distance, Ed Erazo, reference librarian at New Mexico State University, helped me greatly by tracking down many details, locating resources, and verifying citations. My friend Dan Bauer, a doctoral candidate at New Mexico State University, also assisted me checking on information in the library. My colleague at West Virginia State College, Professor Gerald Beller, read the final draft of the book, and made useful comments and suggestions. And Professor Ida Kramer provided valuable criticism and suggestions for the constitutional history section. I am grateful to the Honorable Stephanie Gonzales, who serves with distinction as the Secretary of State of New Mexico and generously agreed to write the foreword to this book.

My family and friends have supported and encouraged me while I worked on this book, as they have with all of my scholarly efforts, and I thank them for this. My sisters Linda Feagin and Ginger Smith continually supply me with good cheer and are the best friends anyone could ever have. My son Chris McDavid's frequent e-mail and telephone messages keep me in a positive frame of mind. And the friendship of my favorite New Mexican, Sonny Acosta, keeps my life happy and balanced.

PART ONE

The History of the New Mexico Constitution

The New Mexico Constitution, and statehood itself, resulted from a protracted struggle. In 1848, most of what is now New Mexico was ceded by the Treaty of Guadalupe Hidalgo to the United States as part of the territory Mexico lost in the Mexican-American War. In 1850, Congress declared New Mexico a territory. It took New Mexico 62 more years, however, to gain statehood; this was a considerably longer time than all the other territories seeking admission to the Union during that time—from California in 1850 to Oklahoma in 1907. After it came under the control of the United States, New Mexico held five constitutional conventions and produced four constitutions. The last of these, the Constitution of 1910, was amended to congressional specifications and was approved by Congress and the president in 1912. That constitution has served the state throughout its statehood.

New Mexico's constitutional history is a story replete with intrigue, murders, rebellion by native peoples, factional feuds, fraudulent land schemes, and bitter partisan conflict. Within the region, various factions opposed statehood throughout the territorial period. The statehood movement did not grow steadily, but grew strong and then weak in a series of cycles.[1] Outside of the territory,

[1] For detailed discussion of internal opposition to statehood, see Howard Roberts Lamar, *The Far Southwest 1846–1912: A Territorial History* (New Haven, CT: Yale University Press, 1966), pp. 86–88; Robert W. Larson, *New Mexico's Quest for Statehood, 1846–1912* (Albuquerque: University of New Mexico

statehood for New Mexico was widely opposed; it became a point of contention in the sectional struggle over slavery, an issue in presidential and congressional elections, and subject to the racial, ethnic, and religious prejudices of influential U.S. senators and many eastern newspapers.[2]

ACQUISITION PERIOD, 1846–1853

The Kearny Code

The constitutional history of New Mexico began shortly after the commencement of the Mexican-American War when, in July 1846, General Stephen Watts Kearny led the U.S. Army into Santa Fe. The American forces established themselves in New Mexico with dispatch. By late September, Kearny had established a civilian government and issued the "Organic Law of the Territory," known as the Kearny Code.[3] Kearny said the code was composed of laws

> taken from the laws of Mexico, retained as in the original—a part with such modifications as our laws and Constitution made necessary; a part from the laws of Texas and also of Texas and Coahuila, a part from the statutes of Missouri; and the remainder from the Livingston Code.[4]

The Kearny Code, with its accompanying Bill of Rights, introduced significant American constitutional values into New Mexico. The Code also

---

Press, 1968), pp. 119–120, 183–184, 211–212, 301–304; and the seven-part article by Marion Dargan, "New Mexico's Fight for Statehood, 1895–1912, I: The Political Leaders of the Latter Half of the 1890's and Statehood," *New Mexico Historical Review* 14 (January 1939): 1–33; "New Mexico's Fight for Statehood, 1895–1912, II: The Attitude of the Territorial Press," *New Mexico Historical Review* 14 (April 1939): 123–142; "New Mexico's Fight for Statehood, 1895–1912, III: The Opposition Within the Party (1888–1890)," *New Mexico Historical Review* 15 (April 1940): 133–187; "New Mexico's Fight for Statehood, 1895–1912, IV: The Opposition Within the Territory During the Nineties," *New Mexico Historical Review* 16 (January 1941): 70–103; "New Mexico's Fight for Statehood, 1895–1912, V: The Silencing of the Opposition at Home," *New Mexico Historical Review* 16 (October 1941): 379–400; "New Mexico's Fight for Statehood, 1895–1912, VI: Advertising the Backyard of 'the United States,'" *New Mexico Historical Review* 18 (January 1943): 60–96; and "New Mexico's Fight for Statehood, 1895–1912, VII: The Part Played by the Press of the Southwest," *New Mexico Historical Review* 18 (April 1943): 148–175.

[2] Dorothy I. Cline, *New Mexico's 1910 Constitution, A 19th Century Product* (Santa Fe: The Lightning Tree, 1984), p. 11.

[3] The text of the Kearny Code can be found with the historical documents in Volume 1, Pamphlet 3, "Territorial Laws and Treaties," of *New Mexico Statutes Annotated 1978* (Charlottesville, VA: The Michie Company, 1978) and in Richard N. Ellis, *New Mexico Historic Documents* (Albuquerque: University of New Mexico Press, 1975), pp. 3–9.

[4] As quoted by Loomis Morton Gandway, "New Mexico and the Sectional Controversy, 1846–1861," *New Mexico Historical Review* 18 (1943): 207. The Livingston Code was the initial law drafted for the Louisiana territory after it was acquired from France.

inaugurated such radically different political concepts as a strong legislature, the jury process and common law, and the even less familiar concepts of the separation of church and state, a standing paid militia, and a secular public school system.[5] These changes were welcomed by the American traders and businessmen who had slowly filtered into the region after Mexico gained its independence from Spain in 1821. The political institutions and concepts in the Kearny Code, however, were alien to, and not readily accepted by, the Spanish-Mexican population, "a people whose culture was still medieval in many ways."[6]

Nor were Kearny's actions well received in Washington. Members of Congress protested Kearny's usurpation of congressional power over the territories, and President Polk halted the establishment of a civilian government. Moreover, in 1847, Native Americans and Mexicans, who opposed the American government, rebelled in the Taos Uprising.[7] The insurrection was quelled by the army, but the uprising added to the Washington government's mistrust of the territory's population. In spite of the provisions for a civil government in the Kearny Code, the army continued to govern New Mexico until 1850, when Congress bestowed territorial status on New Mexico.[8]

The 1850 Constitution

Soon after the United States annexed New Mexico, a formal movement for statehood was organized. Support for statehood, however, was limited. The support that did exist came from those native New Mexicans for whom statehood was a chance to achieve long-desired home rule, and from more recently arrived Anglos who were interested in the federal and state offices that would be created.[9] Two questions complicated the resolution of New Mexico's status: (1) Would Negro slavery be allowed in New Mexico? (2) How could the claim of the State of Texas to much of eastern New Mexico be settled?[10] In March of 1848, the Texas legislature claimed all of New Mexico east of the Rio Grande, and named the region Santa Fe County.[11] These controversies kept the status and boundaries of New Mexico uncertain for the next two years. The issues of slavery, boundaries, and statehood, moreover, were of importance far beyond New Mexico, and the

[5] Lamar, op. cit, pp. 65–66.

[6] Ibid, p. 66.

[7] Cline, op. cit., p. 12; Lamar, op. cit., pp. 67–70; Larson, op. cit., pp. 6–7.

[8] For an American soldier's first-hand account of New Mexico at the time the territory was established, see George Archibald McCall, *New Mexico in 1850: A Military View* (Norman: University of Oklahoma Press, 1968).

[9] Lamar, op. cit., p. 77.

[10] Larson, op. cit., pp. 13–18.

[11] Lamar, op. cit., p. 89.

answers to these questions were to be determined on the national political stage.

The concept of slavery was not foreign to New Mexicans. They were quite familiar with peonage and the enslavement of Indians.[12] Nevertheless, when the antislavery question increasingly became the focus of disputes in Congress, both natives and Anglos declared for a free state to express their bitter animosity toward Texas.[13]

In Washington, President Zachary Taylor sought to avoid the slavery issue by seeking admission of both New Mexico and California as states as soon as possible. To accomplish this, he sent agents to both regions to encourage the local statehood movements.[14] In New Mexico this responsibility was assigned to Indian agent James Calhoun. A second agent, Brevet Lieutenant Colonel George A. McCall, had orders from the War Department to actively encourage the formation of a civil government.[15]

These men found deeply rooted factionalism in New Mexico. The territoryalists, by and large, had close ties to the military and federal patronage, and controlled the only printing press in Santa Fe. Those who favored statehood possessed little influence beyond the environs of Santa Fe. The statehood faction, however, slowly began to win over some influential territorialists by promising them seats in Congress and by arguing that statehood was the surest route to winning the boundary dispute with Texas.[16]

The uneasy truce between the territorialists and the statehood party resulted in a public meeting in Santa Fe on April 20, 1850. There the two parties drafted resolutions in favor of statehood and requested that the military governor call a constitutional convention. The call was issued and twenty delegates were elected on May 6; they assembled in Santa Fe on May 15 to draft a state constitution.[17] The former territorialists won an overwhelming majority of the convention delegates. The constitution they drafted reflected their Anglo-Saxon legal and political traditions and their antislavery stand, but the statehood party gained some concessions for the Spanish-speaking inhabitants.[18]

The Constitution of 1850 provided a three-branch government with a bicameral legislature and divided the state into three judicial districts. Slavery was rejected forever. The land claims of Texas were rejected, and a counterclaim was made to what is now the northern panhandle of Texas, the Oklahoma panhandle, southern Colorado, and southern Utah. The framers' dissatisfaction with

[12] Larson, op. cit., p. 46.

[13] Lamar, op. cit., p. 77.

[14] Ibid., p. 74.

[15] Larson, op. cit., pp. 27–28.

[16] Ibid., pp. 29–30.

[17] Ibid., p. 31.

[18] Ibid., p. 33.

military rule was reflected in clear subordination of the military to civil control, forbidding a standing army, disallowing the quartering of troops in private homes without the owner's consent or unless provided by law during war, protections for citizens from military law, and the denial of the vote to soldiers of the U.S. Army stationed in New Mexico. The spiritual domination of the Catholic Church was challenged by guaranteeing freedom of conscience, denying preference in law to any religious group or mode of worship, forbidding any religious test for holding public office or employment, and establishing tax-supported public schools; however, divorce could be obtained only by a special act of the legislature. Spanish civil law consistent with common law and the constitution would remain in effect. The right to vote was given to all male residents (including the Indians of the Pueblos, but not "uncivilized Indians"), provided that at least six months before any election they renounced allegiance to Mexico and pledged to support the Constitution of the United States.[19] The election for ratification of the constitution and the officers of the new state was held on June 20, 1850; the vote in favor of ratification was 8,371, with only 39 ballots cast against.[20]

The question of statehood, however, was decided by national political considerations. Before news of the constitution and its ratification reached Washington, President Taylor died. The new president, Millard Fillmore, favored the compromise measures proposed by Henry Clay in the Senate rather than Taylor's plan. As a consequence of his support for the Clay compromises, President Fillmore sent the New Mexican constitution to Congress without recommendations concerning its passage. In the Senate, a proposal of statehood for New Mexico made by Whig Senator William H. Seward from New York did not receive a single positive vote.[21] In his efforts to avoid disunion over the question of slavery, Senator Clay had proposed a series of resolutions; among them were a proposal to settle the boundary claims between Texas and New Mexico, and the admission of New Mexico as a territory. An amended version of the Clay proposals concerning the boundary dispute passed in the Senate on August 9, 1850, and a bill creating the Territory of New Mexico was enacted by the Senate on August 15.[22]

TERRITORIAL PERIOD, 1850–1910

The Territory of New Mexico created by Congress was much larger than the present state; it also included what is now Arizona. Furthermore, in 1853, the Gadsden Purchase added the broad strip of land that now forms the frontier of

[19] Ibid., pp. 33–35.

[20] Ibid., p. 38.

[21] Lamar, op. cit., p. 81.

[22] 9 Statutes 446, Chap. 49 (1850); Larson, op. cit., pp. 50–54.

New Mexico and Arizona with Mexico.[23] During the 1850s, there were several attempts to divide the territory and create Arizona. In 1863, Congress passed the Arizona Organic Act; it was signed into law by President Abraham Lincoln on February 20.[24]

After congressional rejection of the 1850 Constitution and the subsequent attainment of territorial status, statehood promoters continued to send petitions, messages, and delegations to Congress, and to hold conventions and write constitutions. Two constitutional conventions were called in the 1860s but both adjourned for lack of a quorum. These conventions failed in part because of the political instability in the region that accompanied the Civil War, and because of a continuing distrust between the Anglo and Mexican elements of the population.[25]

The 1872 Constitution

The deep ethnic divisions in the territory continued after the war and were frequently manifested through bitter partisan disagreements between Democrats and Republicans, both in and out of government. It is surprising, then, that the especially divisive 1872 session of the territorial legislature ended with a few days of compromise, during which several important tax and property laws were enacted. Then, in an unprecedented climax, the Republican leadership, with the support of some Democrats, drafted a new state constitution. The 1872 Constitution was modeled on the Constitution of Illinois, and its proponents claimed that it was the "best in the United States."[26] This constitution was the most liberal ever written for New Mexico. Looking forward to the time when railroads would reach New Mexico, the legislators included progressive restrictions on them. The constitution made provisions for homestead laws and a system of free public schools for all children. It also ensured that public lands or money would not be used to support sectarian schools or for any sectarian purpose. In several provisions, the constitution assured a strict separation of church and state; while these values may have been accepted elsewhere in the United States, in New Mexico they were perceived to be a challenge to the authority of the Catholic Church. Democrats opposed to the constitution claimed the religious provisions were proof of anti-Catholicism. The Democrats also charged that the main interest of the statehood leadership was their hope of personal gain by winning state and congressional offices for themselves. The vote for ratification

---

[23] J. J. Wagoner, "The Gadsden Purchase Lands," *New Mexico Historical Review* 26 (1953): 18–43; and Lamar, op. cit., p. 110. The texts of the Treaty of Guadalupe Hidalgo and the Gadsden Treaty are among the resources included in Ellis, op. cit.

[24] 12 Statutes 664, Chap. 56 (1863); Larson, op. cit., pp. 87–89; Lamar, op. cit., pp. 432–434; and Ellis, op. cit., pp. 51–52.

[25] Cline, op. cit., p. 13; and Larson, op. cit., pp. 91–92.

[26] Larson, op. cit., p. 100.

was held on June 3, 1872. Voter turnout for the ratification election was low in most of the territory. At most, no more than one-third of eligible voters participated, and newspaper reports indicated that the constitution failed to be ratified in almost every county. Territorial officers did not publish an official return. They probably wished to diminish the setback for statehood caused by the rejection of the constitution. But the attainment of statehood had received a significant rebuff, and it was seventeen years before another major attempt to gain statehood was undertaken.[27]

The 1889 Constitution

In the last two decades of the nineteenth century, railroads came to New Mexico and brought about a sharply increased population and expansion of the economy. The mere presence of the railroads caused territorial property values to increase from $41 million in 1880 to $231 million in 1890.[28] During this period, unscrupulous Anglo lawyers, known as the Santa Fe Ring, made extensive use of the uneasy status of property titles based on Spanish land grants to build their personal wealth through fraudulent land claims. A study of territorial court dockets between 1871 and 1890 shows that the largest bloc (641, or more than 20 percent) of the 3,633 criminal cases concerned land fraud charges.[29] Members of the Santa Fe Ring believed that their vast land holdings would increase in value when New Mexico became a state. After the rejection of the 1872 Constitution, the Santa Fe Ring became the most vocal force for statehood.[30] Others in the territory also favored changing New Mexico's territorial status, but not on the terms of the "land grabbers."[31] Outside of the territory, statehood was frequently criticized as only an attempt to gain two more Democratic seats in the U.S. Senate. The February 2, 1889, issue of *The Chicago Tribune* argued that New Mexicans were "not Americans, but 'Greaser' persons ignorant of our laws, manners, customs, language, and institutions."[32] During this period the negative conception of New Mexico held by easterners was based on two widely circulated ideas: The region was an uninhabitable desert, and the people were unfit to govern themselves.[33]

---

[27] Ibid., pp. 95–115.

[28] Lamar, op. cit., p. 110.

[29] Victor Westphall, *The Public Domain in New Mexico, 1854–1891* (Albuquerque: University of New Mexico Press, 1965), p. 107.

[30] The Santa Fe Ring is treated in detail by Lamar, op. cit., pp. 136–170; and Larson, op. cit., pp. 135–146.

[31] Larson, op. cit., p. 146.

[32] Quoted by Larson, ibid., p. 148.

[33] Dargan, op. cit., "New Mexico's Fight for Statehood, 1895–1912, VI: Advertising the Backyard of 'the United States,'" p. 63.

In 1885, President Grover Cleveland appointed the first Democratic governor of New Mexico in 25 years: Edmund G. Ross. Best remembered as the radical Republican senator from Kansas who, in 1863, cast the deciding vote against the impeachment of President Andrew Johnson, Ross moved to New Mexico after he became a political pariah in Kansas. He was willing to use the power of the federal government to reconstruct New Mexico just as the post-Civil War radicals tried to reconstruct the South. A Free Soiler and advocate of liberal homesteading laws, Ross was soon in a bitter struggle with the Santa Fe Ring and range cattlemen.[34] Although he had the support of the Cleveland administration, his attack on fraudulent land holdings led powerful New Mexicans to oppose his reforms. His central reform program, tax-supported public schools, was hampered by local Republican officials, territorial legislators of his own party, the Santa Fe Ring, and the Republican Party hierarchy.[35] Ross turned to statehood as the only way to modernize New Mexico; however, extensive efforts in late 1888 and 1889 to have Congress pass an enabling act for statehood failed.[36] Nevertheless, Ross so dramatized New Mexico's Byzantine politics and corrupt land system that the need for reform became widely recognized. Moreover, the Republican Party and the Santa Fe Ring began their own statehood movement because they wanted to ensure that a hostile administration in Washington would never again disturb the internal affairs of New Mexico as Ross had.[37]

In the 1889 session of the legislature, Santa Fe Ring Republicans joined the Spanish-speaking Republicans to defeat a progressive public school bill. In return the Spanish-speaking Republicans supported the Santa Fe Ring's call for a constitutional convention.[38] Partisan controversy erupted at once, Democrats claimed that the apportionment of the delegates for the convention favored Republican counties. When the election of delegates did take place, Republicans in control of the canvassing board insured that as many of their candidates as possible won seats.[39]

Only 51 of the 73 delegates elected attended the convention. They did represent a cross section of the business, cultural, and political interests of New Mexico; however, the dominant Republican delegates chose to bulldoze their views through the convention. This was to be expected; the Santa Fe Ring was

---

[34] Larson, op. cit., pp. 141–143.

[35] Lamar, op. cit., p. 179.

[36] Larson, op. cit., pp. 147–155.

[37] Lamar, op. cit., p. 185.

[38] Ibid., p. 187.

[39] Ibid., pp. 187–188; and Larson, op. cit., pp. 156–158, provide detailed accounts of the dispute over apportionment.

well represented (fourteen of the delegates were the owners and attorneys for 9 million acres of land grants).[40]

The most persistent dilemma of the day, the question of schools, had to be addressed by the convention. Congress would require the new state to provide public schools, and the English-speaking population was demanding them. But the Catholic Church had enjoyed the position of primacy in education for three centuries, and Catholic leaders were suspicious of public schools. Rumors were circulated among the Catholic population that children would be denied any but a secular education. While the convention was in session, the Archbishop of Santa Fe published a letter calling for state support for parochial schools. Nevertheless, the delegates ignored this appeal and provided that the public school system would be "under the absolute control of the state, and free from sectarian or church control; and no other or different schools shall ever receive any aid or support from public funds."[41] In anticipation of the expected Catholic dissatisfaction with the school article, the framers drafted an "irrevocable" article that provided for religious freedom, and several other references to religious freedom were included. The constitution also limited laws granting divorces. But the framers also snubbed Hispanics by requiring that citizens be able to understand English to qualify to vote or serve on a jury. The 1889 Constitution established three branches of government with a bicameral legislature, and provided a workable amendment procedure. This was a less progressive charter than the 1872 Constitution; it included provisions reflecting the growing public concern about monopolies, but those provisions were weak compared to the antirailroad provision of the 1872 Constitution. The Santa Fe Ring protected its interests by providing that taxes on property were never to exceed one percent, while allowing a higher rate on mining and industry. They also provided that the state would assume all the debts of the territory, and promised payments at face value for the militia warrants, debts incurred largely for defense against the Indians. At the time, the warrants were selling for 60 to 75 percent of their face value and most were owned by A. A. Staab, a charter member of the Santa Fe Ring.[42]

The ratification campaign was a bitter fight. The new constitution and statehood were largely supported by the local newspapers throughout the territory and by owners of large land holdings. The principal claims of opponents were that increased taxation would accompany statehood and that Spanish-speaking people would control the state. Hispanics were dissatisfied with the lack of support for church schools and the provisions that discriminated against Spanish-speaking people.[43] The Democrats raised four additional objections to the constitution: Appellate judges were to be appointed; the governor was to be

---

[40] Lamar, op. cit., p. 188.

[41] Larson, op. cit., p. 159.

[42] Ibid., p. 161; and Lamar, op. cit., pp. 188–189.

[43] Larson, op. cit., p. 155.

suspended from office during impeachment proceedings; the state tax on property was limited to one percent; and the apportionment of legislators was unjust.[44] Opponents named it the "Tom-Cat constitution," identifying it with Thomas Catron, a leading Republican politician, member of the Santa Fe Ring, and owner of vast tracts of land.[45] During the fight for ratification, resistance to statehood continued in Congress and was fed by various eastern newspapers. An official delegation of 29 New Mexicans sent to Washington to lobby for statehood failed to get the needed support from key members of Congress.[46] Given these factors and the mutual suspicions between the factions and parties in the territory, the outcome of the October 7, 1890 ratification election was as expected. The constitution was rejected by a vote of 16,180 against ratification, and 7,493 in favor.[47]

The defeat of the "Tom-Cat," "land-grabbers" constitution confirmed the existence of deep divisions among the people of New Mexico and reinforced the belief of some members of Congress that New Mexicans were not interested in statehood. The proponents of statehood realized that New Mexicans had to settle their internal problems and conflicts before statehood could be gained. Some leaders in both parties started the long process of reform of the public schools, tax policy, and the land-grant system.[48] During the 1890s and the first few years of the new century, both parties promoted various attempts to reinitiate the statehood process. But each party opposed the efforts of the other, each fearing that the other would gain political capital for achieving statehood; so that partisan support for statehood was "a sort of hothouse plant, easily chilled when there was any prospect of advantage for the other party."[49]

DRAFTING AND RATIFYING THE 1910 CONSTITUTION

Railroad building at the end of the nineteenth century continued to bring dramatic changes in New Mexico between 1900 and 1910. Railroads opened the previously isolated territory to regional and national markets, revolutionized

---

[44] Ibid., p. 167.

[45] Lamar, op. cit., p. 189. William A. Keleher, identified Catron as "the one man, who more than any other, dominated New Mexico's political and business affairs for fifty years," *The Fabulous Frontier* (Albuquerque: University of New Mexico Press, 1962), p. 117. In 1894, it was estimated that Catron owned nearly 2 million acres, and was part owner or attorney for 4 million more; see Lamar, op. cit., pp. 149–150; and Keleher, op. cit., pp. 130–131.

[46] Larson, op. cit., p. 162.

[47] Lamar, op. cit., p. 191.

[48] Ibid., pp. 191–192.

[49] Dargan, op. cit., "New Mexico's Fight for Statehood, 1895–1912, IV: The Opposition Within the Territory During the Nineties," p. 83. The various forces working for and against statehood are examined in the other articles in the series by Dargan; see note 1. A detailed history of the politics of statehood between 1889 and 1907 is also presented by Larson, pp. 169–252.

commerce, and brought a boom in land sales. In 1900, the population was 195,000, and almost all of these people were native-born with Spanish surnames who lived in the communities along the Rio Grande or the rivers in northern New Mexico. By 1910, the population had almost doubled; 132,300 people had moved into New Mexico. These people came from Texas and the East; they spoke English and, no matter what their ethnic origin or race, became known as Anglos.[50] These new immigrants brought an interest in national affairs that was uncharacteristic of native New Mexicans. And because Washington was now less than a week away by train, those in the national government gained an improved knowledge of the territory.[51] The resulting winnowing down of the Hispanic majority and modification of New Mexico's unique cultural and ethnic complexion made statehood more palatable to the national government. Congress passed an Enabling Act in 1910 that called for a constitutional convention and a ratification election for the new constitution. The Act also included the unusual stipulation that statehood required presidential approval.

The Convention

The Enabling Act authorized a convention of 100 delegates, to be chosen in a partisan election. Appeals for a nonpartisan convention were futile. In many counties both parties began to raise their concerns and put forward candidates who supported the party's position. The dominant issue in elections in most counties was whether the constitution would include provisions for direct legislation, that is, the mechanisms of initiative, referendum, and recall. This was not merely a local concern. These mechanisms were among the key reforms of the Progressive movement sweeping across the nation, and how this issue was resolved in the constitutions being written in New Mexico and Arizona was the focus of national attention.[52]

The convention convened on October 3, 1910. It was controlled by Republicans, who held 71 of the seats, the Democrats held 28, and there was a single Socialist delegate.[53] The Republicans were dominated by the conservative "Old Guard," made up, for the most part, of the influential territorial leaders,[54] and dominated by members of the Santa Fe Ring, which was still composed of

---

[50] Cline, op. cit., p. 23.

[51] Lamar, op. cit., p. 196.

[52] Larson, op. cit., pp. 272–273.

[53] Thomas J. Mabry, "New Mexico's Constitution in the Making—Reminiscences of 1910," *New Mexico Historical Review* 19 (1944): 168–184. Mabry was a Democratic delegate to the convention. His folksy reminiscence provides vignettes of the delegates and political maneuvering during the convention, as well as an off-the-cuff analysis of the significant issues at the convention.

[54] Jack E. Holmes, *Politics in New Mexico* (Albuquerque: University of New Mexico Press, 1967), p. 49.

lawyers and land speculators who continued "to exploit large and small land owners, usually Hispanics, but also Anglos and Indians."[55] After the failure to gain statehood in 1889, the Santa Fe Ring and lesser land rings continued to acquire substantial tracts of choice lands that were supplied with adequate water; to invest in timber and mines; to process questionable land sales; and to act as agents in managing land grants. They pursued statehood in the belief that they would gain control of the state government and thereby clear their land titles, which would add greatly to the value of their land holdings. Thirty-two of the delegates were lawyers, most with ties to the land rings. It is little surprise that the land-holding group was seen to be the most powerful special interest at the convention.[56]

To achieve statehood the convention had to frame a constitution that was acceptable not only to the territory's voters, but also to a conservative president, William Howard Taft, and a wary Congress. The Old Guard was determined to avoid drafting a document that seemed controversial or experimental. The reforms adopted by Progressives and civic reformers in neighboring Colorado and some other states were seen by the Old Guard as dangerous and radical. This view set the stage for an acrimonious fight between the Old Guard of the Republican Party and the mostly progressive Democratic delegates.

The Democrats were largely favorable toward providing for initiatives and referenda, recall elections, merit system for public employment, nonpartisan ballots for judges, government regulation of corporations and utilities, and other proposals to reorganize economic and political institutions. Even though the Republican Old Guard controlled enough delegates to ride roughshod over the convention, other interests did exert some pressure on the convention. Women were on the march either as suffragettes or prohibitionists. The prohibitionists vowed to contact every delegate in order to secure a prohibition clause in the constitution. At the national level, President Taft warned against a progressive constitution for New Mexico. But, Theodore Roosevelt, in a tour of the West, warned the people of Arizona and New Mexico against the dangers of an iron-clad constitution that defied easy amendment. His view was championed by the "irreconcilables," a faction of Democrats who would accept nothing less than a progressive constitution. Another important interest group was the sizable Spanish-speaking delegation, whose concern was to protect their customs, culture, and rights.[57]

As soon as it began, the Republican majority took firm control of the convention. Thomas Catron, who was considered the most likely choice for chairman of the convention, had placed fifth in a field of five delegates elected by Santa Fe

---

[55] Cline, op. cit., p. 20.

[56] Reuben W. Heflin, "New Mexico Constitutional Convention," *New Mexico Historical Review* 20 (1946): 62. Heflin was a Democratic delegate to the convention.

[57] Larson, op. cit., p. 275; and Mabry, op. cit., p. 178.

County; therefore he relinquished his claim for the position. Charles A. Spiess, a former Catron law partner, easily won election to the chair in a strict party-line vote.[58] Other Republican leaders among the delegates were Albert B. Fall, Holm O. Bursum, George W. Armijo, Charles Springer, and Jose D. Sena.

The Republicans used rules limiting debate to turn back every progressive reform proposed by the Democrats. Each of the convention's 27 committees included Democrats, but also had a Republican chairman and majority. Each committee submitted a draft of its work to the Republican caucus where it was reviewed before being reported to the convention. Because all Republicans were committed to these reports in caucus, substantial changes in the original report were seldom made, despite the partisan debate which often ensued during the plenary sessions of the convention. The Old Guard also imposed so-called "gag" rules on the convention. These rules prevented roll call votes so that there was no record of the votes of individual delegates; they also provided that a delegate could only speak twice on the same subject, and that any member could end debate by calling the previous question.[59] The delegates were seated in county delegations, which spread the Democratic minority throughout the hall, thereby decreasing their ability to respond quickly to Republican proposals. The majority also refused to allow a verbatim record of the convention; the journal only included committee reports, key votes, and the like. The Republicans also dispensed with the reading of the journal, and copies were available only to the officers of the convention. Therefore, one of the Democratic delegates argued "the official Journal, as published after the convention had adjourned, is by no means a reliable report of what happened on the floor."[60]

Direct legislation, the most contentious issue of the convention, was settled to the Republicans' satisfaction. In order to avoid too negative a response to the most popular issue of the day, the Republicans adopted a diluted referendum measure that provided a mechanism for the people to abrogate some legislative acts, but it exempted many categories of legislation (see Article IV § 1). The progressive ideal of an easily amended constitution was rejected outright, and the amendment procedure made it extremely difficult to change the constitution. The constitutional protections of Spanish-speaking citizens were made even more difficult to amend, a provision intended to overcome the apprehensions of the native population that the Anglos might discriminate against them.[61] These protections were also part of a compromise in which Spanish-speaking delegates agreed to give women the vote in school elections.[62] Even though the

---

[58] Larson, op. cit., pp. 275–276.

[59] Ibid., p. 277.

[60] Edward D. Tittmann, "New Mexico Constitutional Convention: Recollections," *New Mexico Historical Review* 27 (1952): 168–184. Tittman was a Democratic delegate to the convention.

[61] Larson, op. cit., pp. 278–279.

[62] Tittmann, op. cit., p. 182.

Women's Christian Temperance Union and Anti-Saloon League waged a vigorous lobbying campaign, a prohibition provision was not written into the constitution. Proponents of women's suffrage gained only the right for women to vote in school elections.[63]

Legislative apportionment was another divisive issue. Using their numerical superiority and playing on the desire of delegates from sparsely populated counties for at least one representative in the legislature,[64] Republicans gerrymandered the districts so effectively that in the first election of state officials, they won two-thirds of the seats in both houses of the legislature. This legislative majority ensured that Republicans would represent New Mexico in the U.S. Senate, even though Democrats were elected as governor and members of the U.S. House of Representatives.

Charles A. Spiess, chairman of the convention, characterized the new constitution as "one of the grandest documents ever written for a people."[65] Spiess's hyperbolic assessment of the constitution's long-term value for the people of New Mexico is questionable. The constitution clearly reflected the Republican-dominated convention's interest in limited government. It was designed to protect the corporations in the state and encourage others to come. The convention rejected the initiative mechanism, adopted a form of referendum which was unworkable, provided for the partisan election of judicial officials, created a plural executive by dividing executive power among eight state officials, and severely limited the taxing, borrowing, and spending powers of the state. The constitution included extensive, statute-like provisions for the administration and operation of the state government and its political subdivisions.

The thoroughly conservative constitution was designed to protect the political and economic interests of the Santa Fe Ring and corporations by creating a weak state government and a fragmented executive. As such, as Cline has argued, the constitution was more suited to the nineteenth than the twentieth century.[66] Many of its details could have been left to future legislative provisions or judicial interpretation, in order to allow for reasonable adjustments to meet the problems posed by a growing state. The provisions for amending the constitution were so difficult to fulfill that it was, for any practical purpose, impervious to change. The convention had produced a document designed to preserve the conservative policies of its authors against future change.

---

[63] Larson, op. cit., p. 280.

[64] Tittmann, op. cit., pp. 179–180.

[65] *Proceedings of the Constitutional Convention of the Proposed State of New Mexico* (Albuquerque, NM: Press of the Morning Journal, 1910), p. 288. This source is available on microfilm at the Special Collections Division of the library of the University of New Mexico in Albuquerque.

[66] Cline, op. cit.

Ratification and Statehood

The enthusiastic territorial secretary, Nathan Jaffa, praised the constitutional convention for producing a model document, so "progressive as to meet all demands of republican government."[67] The beleaguered Democrats, who lost every battle at the convention, did not agree. They held a party convention in Santa Fe on December 19, 1910, and compiled a list of thirteen objections to the constitution. Chief among the objections was the difficulty entailed in amending the constitution. Democrats also raised objections to the inequitable apportionment of the legislature, the impractical referendum provision, and the omission of provisions for initiative and recall. Their party, however, was weak, lacked funds, and was divided on ratification; thus many Democrats, unwilling to postpone statehood any longer, begrudgingly endorsed the constitution. The fight against ratification was carried on by the leader of irreconcilables, Harvey Fergusson.[68] The Republicans had money, were organized statewide, and had the support of most of the press. They presented the constitution as steering the state on a safe course between radical "socialist" and reactionary politics. Newspapers called it safe and sane.[69]

The constitution was approved by the people on January 21, 1911, by an overwhelming three-to-one majority (31,742 for ratification, 13,399 against). Statehood now needed only the approval of Congress and President Taft. But an unexpected roadblock was encountered. Soon after New Mexicans ratified their new constitution, a convention in Arizona drafted and ratified a liberal constitution which included such Progressive measures as provisions for direct legislation and the regulation of child labor. Liberals in the U.S. Senate tied approval of New Mexico statehood with that of Arizona and President Taft vetoed the measure because of his opposition to the liberal provisions of the Arizona Constitution. Several months of political dealing and maneuvering were necessary before Congress finally passed a second resolution for statehood for New Mexico. That resolution required that the constitution be changed to provide a more realistic formula for amendment. Therefore, less than a year after it was drafted, and before New Mexico became a state, the constitution was amended for the first of

---

[67] Nathan Jaffa, *Report of the Secretary of the Territory, 1909–1910, and Legislative Manual* (Santa Fe, 1911), p. 11.

[68] Larson, op. cit., pp. 283–284. Fergusson led the Democrats at the constitutional convention and was considered to be the most accomplished and dynamic orator at the gathering. When New Mexico became a state he was elected to the U.S. House of Representatives. Some of his arguments against ratification can be found in "Addresses on the Making of a Constitution by H. B. Fergusson and Frank W. Chancy," *Bulletin of the University of New Mexico, Sociological Series,* 1, no. 1 (1910).

[69] Larson, op. cit., pp. 285–286.

many times. The amendment, known as the "blue ballot" amendment because it was printed on blue paper, was ratified by the people on November 7, 1911.[70]

Long-delayed Statehood

New Mexico achieved statehood 62 years after it was made a territory; no other territory took so long to become a state. Many factors contributed to this delay, some of which were the result of national political considerations rather than developments in the territory. Statehood was delayed because of the sectional struggle over slavery and by the boundary dispute with Texas. Moreover, political trends in New Mexico were frequently contrary to prevalent national attitudes. During the 1890s, New Mexico was identified with Free Silver and Populism and lost the support of conservatives in Washington. In the first years of the twentieth century there was a shift toward conservatism in New Mexico at the time when most of the country was embracing the Progressive spirit. Statehood was further complicated by the prejudice of many easterners toward the Indian and Spanish-speaking Catholic populations of New Mexico. The easterners also thought of New Mexico as a vast, arid wasteland which would support only a small population.

Internal dissension and periodic loss of interest in statehood in the territory also contributed to the long wait to join the Union. Partisan disputes regularly tied support for statehood to considerations of which political party would be credited with winning statehood. Furthermore, the land-grabbers' identification with the statehood movement alienated many New Mexicans. Throughout the territorial period a sizable number of New Mexicans preferred territorial status to statehood. Many feared that higher taxes would be necessary to support a state government. Some Anglos and Hispanics feared that members of the other group would win dominance in a state government. And the opposition of the Catholic hierarchy to secular state schools further aggravated the distrust of other New Mexicans and the predominantly Protestant nation.[71]

Finally, the many barriers to statehood were overcome. On January 6, 1912, the last of the requirements of the Enabling Act of 1910 was met when President Taft approved the new constitution and proclaimed New Mexico a state. A little more than a month later, Arizona was proclaimed a state; 64 years after the signing of the Treaty of Guadalupe Hidalgo, the region was brought fully into the United States.[72]

---

[70] Ibid., pp. 278–300.

[71] Ibid., pp. 301–304.

[72] Ibid., p. 304.

CALLS FOR CONSTITUTIONAL REFORM

Attempts to meet the shortcomings and defects in the constitution by amending it started soon after New Mexico became a state. From 1912 through 1949, the legislature proposed 76 amendments to the constitution; 29 of them were ratified by the people. In 1949, Governor Thomas Mabry initiated what would become a twenty-year movement to rewrite the constitution. He criticized the "patchwork system" of constitutional reform and suggested the need for a constitutional convention.[73] Mabry, a framer of the constitution, was reacting to the unprecedented problems for the state government that came with the growth brought on by World War II. The rise of boom towns, a rapidly growing population, mushrooming scientific and military facilities, dwindling populations in rural counties, and the emergence of greater Albuquerque, the state's first metropolitan area, all brought ever-increasing demands on government for more services and more regulations.

In 1951, Governor Edwin Mechem, a Republican elected on a "good government" platform, called on the legislature to create a State Reorganization Committee to study the government and make recommendations for reforms. A year later the committee called for centralizing administrative authority in the governor; establishing comprehensive personnel, budget, and finance programs; and consolidating executive agencies with similar functions into a smaller number of departments.[74] The legislature enacted some of these recommendations; however, others could only be achieved through constitutional reform. The committee report increased interest and support for a constitutional convention, but not enough to impel the legislature to call for one.

In 1963, newly elected Governor Jack Campbell called for "essential changes" in the constitution, and the legislature established the Constitutional Revision Commission. Fourteen months later, the commission submitted a report to the governor. It recommended a constitutional convention, and suggested that the constitution be changed to provide for frequent legislative reapportionment, a postlegislative audit of the state's budget, a judicial commission, a court of appeals, and the appointment of district and supreme court judges. The constitutional commission also called for, and was given, a two-year extension to continue its work.[75] Further support for constitutional reform was manifested in 1965 and 1966, when voters ratified constitutional amendments that created a court of appeals and abolished justice of the peace courts and replaced them with magistrate courts. The commission continued to review the constitution,

---

[73] Dorothy I. Cline, "Constitutional Politics in New Mexico: 1910–1976," in F. Chris Garcia and Paul L. Hain (eds.), *New Mexico Government* (Albuquerque: University of New Mexico Press, 1976), p. 224.

[74] *Report. New Mexico State Reorganization Committee* (Santa Fe: The Capitol, June 30, 1952).

[75] *1964 Report of the Constitutional Revision Commission* (Santa Fe: The Capitol, September 29, 1964).

and in 1966 submitted its report to newly elected Governor David Cargo.[76] It again recommended calling a constitutional convention. The bulk of the commission's report was a proposed constitution and a rationale for retaining or changing the various provisions of the 1910 Constitution.[77]

THE 1969 CONSTITUTIONAL CONVENTION

The 1967 legislature put the question of calling a convention on the general election ballot. The convention easily won the approval of the voters on November 8, 1968. The legislature, however, provided scanty resources for the convention. It was limited to one 60-day session, one delegate was elected from each of the state's 70 legislative districts, only a $20.00 per diem was provided for the delegates, and provisions for resources and staff were extremely limited. Unlike the 1910 convention, only a few of the delegates were political or economic leaders. The partisan composition of the convention was 48 Democrats, 21 Republicans, and one independent.[78]

The delegates attempted to create a short, concise, well-integrated document that laid out the broad outline of government based on the principle of representative democracy, and avoided the detailed, statute-like material of the type found in the 1910 Constitution. Many unnecessary provisions were eliminated, and articles and sections were rearranged or synthesized. The 1910 Constitution's 24 articles, expressed in more than 24,000 words, were compressed into 14 articles comprised of 15,000 words.

The most controversial issues considered by the convention were proposals for fundamental changes in the executive and judicial articles. The delegates drafted changes in the executive branch by eliminating five statewide elective offices, and allowing the governor to reduce the number of executive departments and establish a cabinet. The convention rejected the proposed appointive system for selecting judges and retained their selection by election. The arguments of the proponents of the appointment plan were weakened with the daily appearance of news concerning President Nixon's appointment of Clement Haynesworth for a seat on the U.S. Supreme Court.[79]

Other important reforms in the draft constitution's legislative article provided for reapportionment after each federal census, longer legislative sessions, interim committees, and a salary for legislators. The revised executive article extended the term of elected officials from two to four years, provided that candidates for

---

[76] *Report of the Constitutional Revision Commission State of New Mexico, 1967.* Adopted November 5, 1966, Harry L. Patton, Chairman (Santa Fe: The Capitol, 1967).

[77] These proposals are discussed in the seven articles in "Student Symposium: The New Mexico Constitutional Convention 1969," *Natural Resources Journal* 9 (1969): 422–480.

[78] Cline, "Constitutional Politics in New Mexico: 1910–1976," pp. 227–228.

[79] Ibid., pp. 232–233.

governor and lieutenant governor run on the same ticket, provided for the election of the land commissioner and auditor, while it eliminated the secretary of state, attorney general, and treasurer as elected officials. The provisions for municipalities allowed cities to operate under a charter and exercise those powers not denied by the legislature. The new education article mandated the legislature to provide bilingual, bicultural education with English as the basic language, and replaced the ten-member, elected state school board with a governor-appointed, nine-member board that would have control of school budgets. The article that provided for amending the constitution also required that a question for the calling of a constitutional convention be placed on the ballot every fourteen years.[80]

The 1969 Constitution was rejected by the voters by a narrow margin (63,387 against; 59,685 for). Opponents of the new constitution included Democrats fearful of losing their patronage base and longtime control of the government; legislators opposed to a strong executive; businesses fearful of losing the established relationships with the agencies and commission that regulated them; and executive officials afraid of losing their power base in elective politics.[81]

REFORM BY PIECEMEAL AMENDMENT

Piecemeal Amendment

The framers of the constitution designed a detailed charter document that they expected to meet most contingencies. Ironically, the dominant framers' resistance to the progressive measures made the constitution ill suited to the twentieth century. Its plethora of statutory details has necessitated extensive piecemeal amendments. Such amendments appeared on the first general election ballot in 1912 and showed up regularly on ballots throughout the century. Table 1 presents a list of all of the amendments proposed to the people and identifies those that were ratified. Amendments that are ratified are incorporated into the text of the constitution rather than being appended to the end in the order that they were adopted. The excessive detail of the constitution has required amendments for such innocuous things as changing the name of some state institutions and increasing the compensation for legislators and state officers.

The constitution was amended in a piecemeal manner 73 times between 1912 and 1969. After the entirely new, "modern" constitution, drafted in 1969, was rejected by the people, the process of piecemeal amendment continued.

[80] For a description of these changes and the other provisions of the 1969 Constitution, see Jeff Bingaman's *Comparison of Proposed and Present Constitution* (Santa Fe: Office of the Attorney General, 1969).

[81] Cline, "Constitutional Politics in New Mexico: 1910–1976," p. 234.

TABLE 1 *Constitutional Amendments Submitted to Voters, 1911–1994*

Amendment Number	Article & Section	Subject of the Amendment	Adopted or Rejected
		1911 Territorial Legislature	
Blue Ballot	19 § 1–5	Amendments to the constitution	11/07/1911
		1912 Legislature	
JR 9	21 § 5	Suffrage qualifications for holding office deleted	11/05/1912
		1913 Legislature	
JR 9	10 § 2	Terms of county officers changed from 4 to 2 years	11/03/1914
JR 10	8 § 1–7	Property tax	11/03/1914
JR 15	5 § 1	Terms of executive officers changed from 4 to 2 years	11/03/1914
		1917 Legislature	
JR 15	8 § 1	Property tax	rejected[a]
JR 16	6 § 12 & 25	Judicial districts	rejected[a]
JR 17	23	Prohibition imposed	11/06/1917[a]
		1919 Legislature	
JR 11	9 § 8	Restrictions on state indebtedness	rejected
JR 12	7 § 6	Absentee voting	rejected
JR 13	12 § 13	Placing state educational institutions under board control	rejected
	14 § 3	Creation of board control for institutions	
		1921 Legislature	
CA 1	7 § 2	Qualification for holding office	09/20/1921[a]
CA 2	2 § 22	Alien land ownership	09/20/1921[a]
CA 3	5 § 1	Executive offices	rejected[a]
CA 4	8 § 5	Head of family veteran tax exemptions	09/20/1921[a]
CA 5	11 § 19	Legislature to establish powers of corporation commission	rejected[a]
CA 6	20 § 3	Date terms of office elective officers begin	rejected[a]
CA 7	13 § 1–10	Public land, creating state land commission	rejected[a]
CA 8	8 § 2	Property tax limitations	rejected[a]
CA 9	9 § 12	Restrictions on municipal indebtedness	rejected[a]
CA 10	10 § 2	Terms of county officers, limited to 2 terms	rejected[a]
CA 11	9 § 16	State highway bond	09/20/1921[a]
		1923 Legislature	
CA 1	10 § 2	Terms of county officers, change to 4 years	rejected
CA 2	5 § 1	Terms of executive officers, change to 4 years	rejected
CA 3	2 § 14	Indictment and information, information provision added	11/04/1924
		1925 Legislature	
CA 1	4 § 10	Compensation of legislators, increase	rejected
CA 2	add new 24	Apportionment of money from state lands	rejected
		1927 Legislature	
CA 1	4 § 10	Compensation of legislators, increase	rejected
CA 2	add new 24	Terms of county and executive officers, change to 4-year terms for executive, 2-year terms for count	rejected
CA 3	21 § 11	Consent to exchange state lands	rejected

TABLE 1 *(Continued)*

Amendment Number	Article & Section	Subject of the Amendment	Adopted or Rejected
CA 4	add new 24	Contracts for development of minerals on state lands	11/06/1928
CA 5	4 § 19	Introduction of bills, 45th day	rejected
		1929 Legislature	
CA 1	21 § 11	Consent to exchange state lands	rejected
CA 2	12 § 6	Five-member state board of education, powers & duties	rejected
		1931 Legislature	
CA 1	21 § 11	Consent to exchange state lands	11/08/1932
CA 2	4 § 19	Introduction of bills, 45th day	11/08/1932
		1933 Legislature	
CA 1	23	Repeal prohibition	09/19/1933[a]
CA 2	9 § 11	Restrictions on school district indebtedness	09/19/1933[a]
CA 3	6 § 1, 12, 13, 16, 17, 23, 25, & 27	Judicial reform: restructure judicial districts, increase compensation for judges, and abolish probate courts	rejected[a]
CA 4	8 § 2	Property tax limitations, exceptions	09/19/1933[a]
		1935 Legislature	
CA 1	8 § 5	Head of family and veteran tax exemptions, increases	rejected
CA 2	5 12 § 6	Five-member state board of education, powers and duties	rejected
CA 3	25	Land exchanges between New Mexico and the U.S.	rejected
CA 4	2 § 15	Double jeopardy, degrees to be stricken	rejected
CA 5	2 § 14	Indictment and information	rejected
		1937 Legislature	
CA 1	7 § 1	Absentee voting	rejected
CA 2	9 § 17	Limitation on state institution building bonds	rejected
CA 3	10 § 2	Terms of county officers, remove 2-term limitation	rejected
CA 4	5 § 1	Terms of executive offices, remove 2-term limitation	rejected
CA 5	6 § 15	District judge pro tempore	11.08/1938
CA 6	4 § 10	Legislators' compensation	rejected
		1939 Legislature	
CA 1	9 § 17	Limitation on state institution building bonds	rejected
CA 2	7 § 1	Absentee voting	rejected
CA 3	4 § 5	Split legislative session, 30 and 30 days	11/05/1940
		1941 Legislature	
CA 1	4 § 3	Legislative apportionment	rejected
CA 2	4 § 10 & 28	Compensation of legislators, annual salary, appointment of other offices	rejected
CA 3	24	Contracts, agricultural leases, state lands	rejected
CA 4	12 § 13	Staggered terms, regents, educational institutions	rejected
CA 5	4 § 5	Split legislative sessions, 20 and 40 days	rejected
CA 6	12 § 14	N.M. educational institutions board	rejected

TABLE 1 *(Continued)*

Amendment Number	Article & Section	Subject of the Amendment	Adopted or Rejected
		1943 Legislature	
CA1	4 § 10	Legislators' compensation	11/07/1944
		1945 Legislature	
CA 1	4 § 5	Eliminate split session	11/05/1946
CA 2	8 § 3	Property tax exemptions	11/05/1946
		1947 Legislature	
CA 1	4 § 6	Special sessions called by legislature	11/02/1948
CA 2	4 § 9	Eliminate maximum compensation for legislative staff	11/02/1948
CA 3	2 §24	Right to work	rejected
CA 4	10 § 2	Terms of county officers, change to 4 years	rejected
CA 5	5 § 1	Terms of executive officers, change to 4 years	rejected
CA 6	5 § 7	Succession to governorship by lieutenant governor	11/02/1948
		1949 Legislature	
CA 1	7 § 1	Absentee voting	rejected
CA 2	6 § 17	Legislature to set salary of district judges	rejected
CA 3	5 § 4	Creating state highway commission	09/20/1949[a]
CA 4	6 § 23	Allow legislature to grant civil jurisdiction on probate courts	09/20/1949[a]
CA 5	8 § 5	Tax exemptions for heads of families and veterans to include community or joint property	09/20/1949[a]
CA 6	10 §4	Organization of city-county governments	09/20/1949[a]
CA 7	12 § 13	Board of regents, educational institutions, terms of office	09/20/1949[a]
CA 8	add new	Natural resources trust fund	rejected
CA 9	4 § 10	Legislators' compensation, annual salary	rejected
CA 10	4 § 3	Legislative apportionment	09/20/1949[a]
		1951 Legislature	
CA 1	21 § 1	Eliminate prohibition of sale of liquors to Indians	rejected
CA 2	12 § 6	State board of education increased to 9 members	rejected
	5 § 1	Delete references to superintendent of public instruction	
CA 3	6 § 11	Allow legislature to fix salary of supreme court justices	rejected
CA 4	6 § 17	Allow legislature to fix salary of district court judges	rejected
CA 5	9 § 12	Debt contracting power of municipalities, elections	rejected
CA 6	7 § 1	Absentee voting	rejected
CA 7	4 § 10	Legislators' compensation	rejected
CA 8	add new 25	Nonpartisan election of judges	rejected
		1953 Legislature	
CA 1	9 § 12	Debt contracting power of municipalities, elections	rejected[a]
CA 2	21 § 1	Eliminate prohibition of sale of liquors to Indians	09/15/1953[a]

TABLE 1 *(Continued)*

Amendment Number	Article & Section	Subject of the Amendment	Adopted or Rejected
CA 3	4 § 22	Governor's veto required within 20 days after passage	09/15/1953[a]
CA 4	4 § 4	Filling vacancies in legislature	09/15/1953[a]
CA 5	4 § 10	Legislators' compensation	09/15/1953[a]
CA 6	8 § 5	Tax exemptions for heads of families and veterans	09/15/1953[a]
CA 7	4 § 5	Annual legislative sessions	rejected[a]
CA 8	6 § 11	Allow legislature to fix supreme court justices' salaries	09/15/1953[a]
CA 9	6 § 17	Allow legislature to fix district judges' salaries	09/15/1953[a]
CA 10	7 § 4	Absentee voting	rejected[a]
CA 11	8 § 8	Natural resources investment fund	rejected[a]
		1955 Legislature	
CA 1	4 § 3	Legislative apportionment	09/20/1955[a]
CA 2	7 § 1	Absentee voting	rejected[a]
CA 3	5 § 14	State highway commission	09/20/1955[a]
CA 4	14 § 3	Legislature design control of state land institutions	09/20/1955[a]
CA 5	14 § 1, 3	Confirming certain institutions as state land institutions	09/20/1955[a]
CA 6	11	State corporation commission	rejected[a]
		1957 Legislature	
CA 1	7 § 1	Absentee voting	rejected
CA 2	12 § 6	Elected state board of education	11/04/1958
	5 § 1	Abolish elected state superintendent of public instruction	
CA 3	12 § 4	Investment of state permanent funds	11/04/1958
CA 4	4 § 32	Remission, debts due state	11/04/1958
CA 5	10 § 2	Term of county officers 4 years	rejected
		1959 Legislature	
CA 1	4 § 4	Staggered terms for state senators	11/08/1960
CA 2	4 § 5	Annual legislative sessions	rejected
CA 3	4 § 19	Time limit on bill introduction, set by legislature	11/08/1960
CA 4	14 § 1	Confirming institutions as state institutions	11/08/1960
CA 5	5 § 1	Terms of elected State officials, 4 years	rejected
CA 6	5 § 15	Location of executive offices	rejected
CA 7	12 § 11	Change names of certain state institutions	11/08/1960
CA 8	5 § 13	Division of counties into county-commission districts	11/08/1960
CA 9	4 § 2	Continuity of government in disaster	11/08/1960
		1961 Legislature	
CA 1	5 § 1	Terms of executive officers, 4 years	rejected[a]
	10 § 2	Terms of county officers, 4 years	
CA 2	5 § 14	Appointment procedure for state highway commission	rejected[a]
CA 3	17 § 1	Change wording of reference to state mine inspector	09/19/1961[a]
CA 4	7 § 1	State mine commission, legislature to prescribe qualifications	09/19/1961[a]

TABLE 1 *(Continued)*

Amendment Number	Article & Section	Subject of the Amendment	Adopted or Rejected
CA 5	12 § 5	Absentee voting	rejected[a]
CA 6	4 § 10	Current school fund, fines and forfeitures,	rejected[a]
CA 7	11 § 1 & 2	State corporation commission	rejected[a]
CA 8	4 § 5	Annual legislative sessions	rejected[a]
CA 9	7 § 2	Legislature to establish qualifications of public officers	09/19/1961[a]
CA 10	5 § 1 & 12	Delete state auditor & provisions relating to officers' salaries	rejected[a]
CA 11	6 § 26	Legislature to define qualifications of justices of peace, etc.	09/19/1961[a]
CA 12	4 § 28	Legislators to serve on state board of finance	rejected[a]
CA 13	5 § 1 & 2, 7 § 5	Election of governor and lieutenant governor on joint ticket	11/06/1962[a]
		1963 Legislature	
CA 1	13 § 3	Validating land titles prior to September 4, 1956	11/03/1964
CA 2	4 § 5	Annual legislative sessions	11/03/1964
CA 3	12 § 11	Western New Mexico University, name change	11/03/1964
CA 4	10 § 5	H-class county charter	11/03/1964
CA 5	7 § 1	Absentee voting and removal of voting restrictions for women and Indians	rejected
CA 6	9 § 10	School bond issues, remodeling and additions	11/03/1964
CA 7	9 § 12	Municipal bonds, special election, nonresident vote	11/03/1964
CA 8	4 § 18	Permitting tax legislation by reference	11/03/1964
CA 9	5 § 14	Director, state highway department	rejected
CA 10	11 § 5, 7, 8	Corporation commission, salaries, powers, and duties	11/03/1964
		1965 Legislature	
CA 1	4 § 10	Legislative compensation	rejected[a]
CA 2	12 § 7	State permanent fund investments	09/28/1965[a]
CA 3	9 § 11	Bonds for remodeling schools	09/28/1965[a]
CA 4	4	Weighting voting, state senate	rejected[a]
CA 5	6 § 1 & 2	Establishing court of appeal	09/28/1965[a]
CA 6	4 § 42	Establishing legislative auditor	rejected[a]
CA 7	19 § 5	Constitutional amendment procedure	rejected[a]
CA 8	16	District court water appeals	rejected[a]
CA 9	19 § 1	Constitutional amendment procedure	withdrawn
CA 10	6 § 1, 18 21, 26–27	Abolishing justice of the peace courts, and establish magistrate courts	11/08/1965[a]
		1967 Legislature	
CA 1	9 § 14	Permitting economic development loans	rejected[a]
CA 2	8 § 4	Public money deposits in savings and loan associations	11/07/1967[a]
CA 3	24	Geothermal steam development on public lands	11/07/1967[a]
CA 4	5 § 14	State highway commission	11/07/1967[a]
CA 5	16 § 5	District courts water appeals	11/07/1967[a]
CA 6	6 § 32	Judicial discipline and removal	11/07/1967[a]

TABLE 1 *(Continued)*

Amendment Number	Article & Section	Subject of the Amendment	Adopted or Rejected
CA 7	7 § 1	Absentee voting and removal of voting restrictions for women and Indians	11/07/1967[a]
CA 8	8 § 2	Electors for property tax	11/07/1967[a]
		1969 Legislature	
CA 1	8 § 1	Property tax, property classification	nullified[b]
CA 2	8 § 1	Property tax, personal exemption	nullified[b]
CA 3	12 § 4	Current school fund levy	nullified[b]
CA 4	10 § 6	Municipal home rule	nullified[b]
		1970 Legislature	
CA 1	10 § 6	Municipal home rule	11/30/1970
CA 2	7	Elective franchise	rejected
CA 3	5 § 1	Terms of executive officers, 4 years	11/30/1970
CA 4	12 § 4	Current school fund, state levy	rejected
CA 5	19 § 5	Amendment procedure	rejected
CA 6	12 § 13	Board of regents removal	rejected
CA 7	9 § 14	Student loan payment	rejected
CA 8	8 § 1	Taxation and revenue	rejected
		1971 Legislature	
CA 1	7 § 1	Lower voter age to 18	rejected[a]
CA 2	4 § 10	Legislative compensation, $40 per diem	11/20/1971[a]
CA 3	2 § 6	Right to bear arms	11/20/1971[a]
CA 4	20 § 17	Uniform system of textbooks	11/20/1971[a]
CA 5	9 § 14	Vietnam veterans scholarship	11/01/1971[a]
CA 6	8 § 1	Property tax, property classification	11/02/1971[a]
CA 7	8 § 3	Property tax, exempt water-user cooperative	rejected[1]
CA 8	19 § 5	Amendment procedure	rejected[3]
CA 9	20	Pollution control	11/02/1971[a]
CA 10	12 § 4	Current school fund, state levy	11/02/1971[a]
		1972 Legislature	
CA 1	2 § 18	Equal rights	11/07/1972
CA 2	8 § 3	Property tax exemptions	11/07/1972
CA3	2 § 12	Six-man juries	rejected
		1973 Legislature	
CA 1	7 § 2	Sex discrimination in qualifications	11/06/1973[a]
CA 2	8 § 5	Sex discrimination in veterans' property tax exemptions	11/06/1973[a]
CA 3	12	Local school board recall	11/06/1973[a]
CA 4	7 § 1	Qualifications for voting	rejected[3]
CA 5	10	Five-member board of county commissions, 4-year terms, in A-class counties	11/06/1973[a]
CA 6	8 § 8	Freeport personal property tax	11/06/1973[a]
CA 7	10 § 2	Age limitation on county officers, 2-year unlimited terms	rejected[3]
		1974 Legislature	
CA 1	4 § 10	Legislative compensation commission	rejected
CA 2	8	Tax levy or assessment prohibited by political subdivisions with appointed board	11/05/1974
CA 3	9 § 14	Loans to students of healing arts	11/06/1974

TABLE 1 *(Continued)*

Amendment Number	Article & Section	Subject of the Amendment	Adopted or Rejected
		1975 Legislature	
CA 1	10 § 2	Terms of county officers 2-year limitation removed	rejected
CA 2	5 § 1	Terms of state executive officers, 2 four-year term limitation	rejected
CA 3	8 § 3	Property tax, permit legislature to exempt certain interest in property owned by tax-exempt entity	rejected
CA 4	12	Appointive state board of education, state dept. of education	rejected
CA 5	10 § 7	Five-member board county commission, 4-year terms, B-class county	rejected
CA 6	8	Severance tax permanent fund	11/02/1976
		1976 Legislature	
CA 7	4	Legislature, number of members	11/02/1976
		1977 Legislature	
CA 1	6 § 32	Judicial conduct	11/07/1978
CA 2	6 § 15	Retired judges	11/07/1978
		1978 Legislature	
CA 3	8	Postponement of property taxes for elderly	rejected
CA 4	4 § 10	Annual legislative session	rejected
		1979 Legislature	
CA 1	10 § 7	Doña Ana County board of commissioners allowed 5 members	11/04/1980
CA 2	12 § 15	Albuquerque school district, 7-member board	11/04/1980
CA 3	2 § 13	Denial of bail	11/04/1980
CA 4	5 § 1	State officers, two consecutive terms	rejected
CA 5	1 § 14	Grand jury convention petition, signature increase	11/04/1980
		1980 Legislature	
CA 6	4 § 10	Legislative per diem and mileage increased	rejected
		1981 Legislature	
CA 1	6 § 4. 10, 12, 14, 16, 28 33, 35, & 36; 20 § 4	Merit selection of judges	rejected
CA 2	8 § 10	Severance tax permanent fund	11/02/1982
CA 3	8 § H	$3000 income tax exemption for national guard	rejected
		1982 Legislature	
CA 4	10 § 2	County sheriffs unlimited 2-year terms	rejected
CA 5	4 § 10	Legislative per diem and mileage increase	11/02/1982
CA 6	11 § 7	Yellow page amendment	11/02/1982
CA 7	9 § 10	County indebtedness for public works projects	11/02/1982
		1984 Legislature	
CA 1	10 § 8	State-mandated county services	11/06/1984
		1985 Legislature	
CA 1	12 § 4	Local school boards, recall	11/04/1986
CA 2	2 § 6	Right to keep and bear arms	11/04/1986
CA 3	5 § 13	Governing bodies, single-member districts	11/04/1986
CA 4	8 § 4	Public money deposits	11/04/1986

TABLE 1 *(Continued)*

Amendment Number	Article & Section	Subject of the Amendment	Adopted or Rejected
		1986 Legislature	
CA 5	12 § 4	Disposition of fines	11/04/1986
CA 6	4 new § 42	Interim hearing by senate on confirmations	11/04/1986
CA 7	12 § 6	State board of education, expand and enhance control	11/04/1986
CA 8	12 § 13	UNM board of regents, increase	11/04/1986
CA 9	10 § 2	County officers, 4 consecutive terms	rejected
CA 10	3 § 1	Workmen's compensation body	11/04/1986
CA 11	5 § 1	State executive officers, two consecutive four-year terms	11/04/1986
		1988 Legislature	
CA 1	4 § 10	Legislative retirement	rejected
CA 2	5 § 5	Gubernatorial removal of appointees	11/08/1988
CA 3	8 § 5	Head of family exemption	11/08/1988
CA 4	9 § 10	County bond issues	11/08/1988
CA 5	2 § 13	Bail for convicted persons	11/08/1988
CA 6	6 § 4, 8, 12, 16, 19, 26, 28, add 33, 34, 35, 36, 37, 38, 20 § 4	Judicial reform, provide for new judicial selection system	11/08/1988
CA 7	10 § 7	County commission, 5 members, staggered 4-year terms	11/08/1988
		1989 Legislature	
CA 1	12 § 7	Permanent school funds management	11/06/1990
		1990 Legislature	
CA 2	12 § 7	Permanent school funds investment	rejected
CA 3	4 § 10	Legislative per diem and salary	rejected
CA 4	9 § add 17	State financial obligations	rejected
CA 5	21 § add 17	Land exchange authority	rejected
		1991 Legislature	
CA 1	9 § 10	Change restrictions on county indebtedness	rejected
		1992 Legislature	
CA 2	add 2 § 24	Provide right for victims of crimes	11/03/1992
CA 3	10 § 2	Terms of county officers, change to 4 years	11/03/1992
	10 § 7	Allow 5-member boards of commissioners in all counties	11/03/1992
CA 4	4 § 10	Create citizens' legislative compensation commission	rejected
		1993 Legislature	
CA 1	12 § 14	Repeal recall election of school board members	rejected
CA 2	2 § 14	Number of signatures required for grand jury petition	11/08/94
CA 3	12 § 13	Adds student to some universities' board of regents	11/08/94
CA 4	5 § 14	Change name of state highway commission	rejected
CA 5	4 § 10	Change calculation for reimbursement of legislators	Withdrawn[d]
CA 6	9 § 10	Allow counties to borrow to purchase open space	rejected

TABLE 1 *(Continued)*

Amendment Number	Article & Section	Subject of the Amendment	Adopted or Rejected
CA 7	14 § 1	Change name of state hospital at Las Vegas	rejected
CA 8	add 20 § 22	Allow legislature to establish a lottery, games of chance	nullified[e]
CA 9	9 § 14	Allow state to provide land and infrastructure to private business; encourage economic development	11/08/95
		1994 Legislature	
CA 10	6 § 33	Require incumbent to receive 57 percent of the vote to win judicial retention election	11/08/94
CA 11	7 § 1	Remove obsolete voter qualifications and references	rejected
CA 12	8 § 10	Change method of distributing money from severance tax permanent fund	rejected
CA 13	12 § 2, 4, 7	Deposit land grant earnings in permanent school fund	rejected
CA 14	4 § 10	Provide legislators' reimbursement as allowed by IRS	rejected

[a] These amendments were considered for ratification by the people at special elections rather than at a general election.

[b] These amendments, proposed by the legislature, were nullified by the submission of the proposed constitution to the voters in 1969 (1969–70 *Opinion of Attorney General*, No. 69–151). The voters rejected the proposed constitution and these amendments were submitted to the people in 1970 and defeated.

[c] This amendment, proposed by the legislature, was nullified by the submission of the proposed constitution to the voters in 1969 (1969–70 *Opinion of Attorney General*, No. 69–151). The voters rejected the proposed constitution and another amendment addressing this subject was submitted to the people in 1970 and passed.

[d] This amendment proposed by the 1993 legislature, was withdrawn by the 1994 legislature, which reworded it and resubmitted it as amendment 14 on the 1994 general election ballot.

[e] The New Mexico Supreme Court issued a peremptory writ of mandamus ordering the state board of canvassing not to canvass the results of the election with regard to this amendment, because it violated the Article XIX § 1 provision that two or more amendments shall be voted on separately (*State ex rel. Clark v. State Canvassing Board*, 1995).

From 1969 through 1995, 98 amendments to the constitution were proposed and 53 of them were ratified.[82]

THE CONSTITUTION TODAY

The length of the New Mexico Constitution reflects one of its significant characteristics. State constitutions written before the Civil War were relatively short; their purpose was limited to serving as the state's basic law. The constitutions adopted during the last half of the nineteenth century, however, tended to legislate extensively.

[82] The amendments submitted by the legislature between the 1969 constitutional convention and 1990 are discussed in Richard H. Folmar's "Recent Constitutional Activity," in Paul H. Hain, F. Chris Garcia, and Gilbert K. St. Clair (eds.), *New Mexico Government*, third edition (Albuquerque: University of New Mexico Press, 1994).

When it was drafted, the New Mexico Constitution contained 21,227 words; fortunately, when it is amended the changes are incorporated into the text and repealed portions are deleted. Nevertheless, the constitution has grown to somewhat more than 27,200 words. New Mexico reached the threshold of the twenty-first century with a constitution that, some have argued, was suited to the nineteenth rather than the twentieth century. Without a new constitution the state will enter the new century continuing to adopt piecemeal amendments to adjust its obsolete or inefficient provisions to meet contemporary needs, much as it has through the twentieth century.

PART TWO

The New Mexico Constitution and Commentary

PREAMBLE

> We the people of New Mexico, grateful to Almighty God for the blessings of liberty, in order to secure the advantages of a state government do ordain and establish this constitution.

The preamble recognizes that the people of the state are the constitution makers. The Constitution of New Mexico, like the constitutions of almost every state, recognizes a dependence on God. Implicit in the second clause of the preamble is the concept that government derives its authority from the consent of the people; a principle that is guaranteed in Article II §§ 2 and 3. The preamble has not been the subject of judicial interpretation.

Article I

Name and Boundaries

> The name of this state is New Mexico and its boundaries are as follows: Beginning at the point where the thirty-seventh parallel of north latitude intersects the one hundred and third meridian west from Greenwich; thence along said one hundred and third meridian to the thirty-second parallel of north latitude; thence along said thirty-second parallel to the Rio Grande, also known as the Rio Bravo del Norte, as it existed on the ninth day of September, one thousand eight hundred and fifty; thence, following the main channel of said river, as it existed on the ninth day of September, one thousand eight hundred and fifty, to the parallel of thirty-one degrees forty-seven minutes north latitude; thence west one hundred miles to a point; thence south to the parallel of thirty-one degrees twenty minutes north latitude; thence along said parallel of thirty-one degrees twenty minutes, to the thirty-second meridian of longitude west from Washington; thence along said thirty-second meridian to the thirty-seventh parallel north latitude; thence along said thirty-seventh parallel to the point of beginning.

The boundary article expresses the state's territorial imperative. Congress established the boundaries of the Territory of New Mexico in 1850 (9 Statutes 446, Chap. 49). They encompassed most of the area that makes up the present states of New Mexico and Arizona. In 1853, the Gadsden Purchase added to the territory the broad strip of land that now forms the frontier of New Mexico and Arizona with Mexico. The western boundary of New Mexico was established by an 1863 Act of Congress, which separated the present-day state of Arizona from

New Mexico and established the Territory of Arizona (12 Statutes 664, Chap. 56). New Mexico's boundary lines have remained the same since 1863. There have been no litigated border disputes with its neighboring states. Interstate suits have been limited to water use disputes with Colorado and Texas. This article has not been subjected to judicial interpretation.

Article II

Bill of Rights

SECTION 1

Supreme law of the land. The state of New Mexico is an inseparable part of the federal union, and the constitution of the United States is the supreme law of the land.

This section reiterates the principle confirmed by the Civil War that the United States is an indissoluble union of states. It also emphasizes acceptance of the constitutional doctrine based in the U.S. Constitution's supremacy clause, that state constitutions and laws must conform to the national Constitution and laws.

SECTION 2

Popular sovereignty. All political power is vested in and derived from the people; all government of right originates with the people, is founded upon their will and is instituted solely for their good.

Here, popular sovereignty, the underlying principle of American republican government, is recognized as the source of political power in the state. This concept was introduced into New Mexican law in 1846 by the first clause of the Kearny Bill of Rights.

SECTION 3

Right of self-government. The people of the state have the sole and exclusive right to govern themselves as a free, sovereign and independent state.

This provision explicitly guarantees the popular sovereignty, claimed in Section 2 of this article.

SECTION 4

Inherent rights. All persons are born equally free, and have certain natural, inherent and inalienable rights, among which are the rights of enjoying and defending life and liberty, of acquiring, possessing and protecting property, and of seeking and obtaining safety and happiness.

This language recalls Thomas Jefferson's use in the Declaration of Independence of the ideas of John Locke. The provision of this section insures that each person may seek safety and happiness in any way that does not unreasonably interfere with the safety and happiness of another. These rights are not absolute, however, and are subject to reasonable regulation (*Otero v. Zouhar*, 1985). The specific mention of the right of the protection of property in this section may provide the basis for additional protection against unreasonable searches and seizures (*State v. Sutton*, 1991).

SECTION 5

Rights under Treaty of Guadalupe Hidalgo preserved. The rights, privileges and immunities, civil, political and religious guaranteed to the people of New Mexico by the Treaty of Guadalupe Hidalgo shall be preserved inviolate.

The reiteration of these rights is primarily of symbolic importance. It is symbolic because these rights, already insured by the Treaty itself, are not legally enhanced or made more secure by their inclusion in the constitution; however, their enumeration emphasizes their significance in the minds of New Mexicans. This section reflects the preeminent role people of Mexican heritage have played and continue to play in the life of New Mexico and reflects the unique status of New Mexico as a part of the territory ceded to the United States by Mexico in 1848. Articles VIII and IX of the Treaty are of particular importance to this section of the constitution. Those articles listed the rights of Mexicans who lived in the territories ceded to the United States. These enumerated rights provided that they could continue to reside where they resided, retain the property in their possession, remove their property and return to Mexico without taxation on that property, remain in the territory and retain Mexican citizenship, elect to become American citizens, enjoy liberty and property, and security in the free exercise of religion. These same rights were extended to the persons living in the territory ceded by Mexico in the Gadsden Treaty in 1853.

Federal and territorial courts determined the nature of protections conferred by the Guadalupe Treaty provisions largely before New Mexico became a state. In practice, through the period of 1860 to 1890, the legal status of lands granted by the Spanish and Mexican governments was unclear, and enforcement of U.S. law was exceedingly difficult.[1] Settlers from eastern states exploited Hispanic and Native American landowners, and ignored or bypassed land claims based on Spanish and Mexican land grants.[2]

New Mexico's territorial courts interpreted the Treaty to provide the inhabitants commonly known as "Pueblo Indians" with more extensive legal rights than accorded to most Native Americans in the nineteenth century. Through the Treaty they gained personal and property rights in the United States that they had in Mexico (*U.S. v. Juan Santistevan*, 1874). At the date of the Treaty, Pueblo Indians were citizens of Mexico and became citizens of the United States. Therefore, the New Mexico Territorial Supreme Court did not see Pueblo Indians as subject to laws for "wandering savages and administered by agents of the Indian department" (*U.S. v. Lucero*, 1869). This understanding was reflected in the Constitution of 1850, which granted the vote to Pueblo Indians.[3]

In more contemporary times, New Mexico courts have not accepted expansive, treaty-based claims made by descendants of the Mexicans who remained in the territory after it was ceded. For example, the courts rejected the claim that the Treaty confers proprietary right to have the Spanish language and culture preserved and continued in public schools at public expense (*Lopez Tijerina v. Henry*, 1969). The rights of Spanish-speaking citizens are also discussed in commentary on Article XII.

SECTION 6

Right to bear arms. No law shall abridge the right of citizens to keep and bear arms for security and defense, for lawful hunting and recreational use and for other lawful purposes, but nothing herein shall be held to permit the carrying of concealed weapons. No municipality or county shall regulate, in any way, an incident of the right to keep and bear arms.

---

[1] Dorothy I. Cline, *New Mexico's 1910 Constitution, A 19th Century Product* (Santa Fe: The Lightning Tree, 1985), p. 20.

[2] Robert W. Larson, *New Mexico's Quest for Statehood, 1846-1912* (Albuquerque: University of New Mexico Press, 1968); Victor Westphall, *The Public Domain in New Mexico* (Albuquerque: University of New Mexico Press, 1973).

[3] Larson, op.cit., p. 35.

These provisions and protections are more expansive than their federal counterpart in the Second Amendment of the U.S. Constitution.[4] In response to the movement toward regulation of firearms by Congress that began in the 1960s, New Mexicans twice amended this section to provide more explicit protection for the right to bear arms. The 1971 amendment inserted "No law shall abridge the right of the citizens to keep and" for "The people have the right to bear," it also deleted "their" before "security and defense" and inserted "for lawful hunting and recreational use and other lawful purposes." The last sentence of this section was added by the 1986 amendment.

This section does not prevent the state from enacting reasonable regulation of firearms. The courts have rejected constitutional challenges to the prohibition of carrying firearms into a liquor establishment (*State v. Dees*, 1983); and the prosecution of intoxicated persons brandishing firearms (*State v. Rivera*, 1993). This provision has influenced the development of New Mexico tort law; citing this section, the supreme court held that in view of the general policy of the state to permit firearms to be kept in the home, parents who keep a loaded firearm in their home and are without knowledge of their minor child's indiscreet or reckless use of the firearm, are not liable for a tort committed by the minor (*Lopez v. Chewiwie*, 1947).

Ordinances prohibiting the carrying of concealed weapons have generally been held to be a proper exercise of police power and do not deprive citizens of their right to bear arms; such laws only regulate that right. But an ordinance which purports to completely prohibit the right to bear arms is void (*City of Las Vegas v. Moberg*, 1971, decided before the 1986 amendment).

SECTION 7

Habeas corpus. The privilege of the writ of habeas corpus shall never be suspended, unless, in case of rebellion or invasion, or the public safety requires it.

This provision is an almost exact reiteration of the limits placed on Congress by Article I § 9 of the U.S. Constitution. The writ of habeas corpus is a legal device for questioning the lawfulness of a person's imprisonment or detention. The writ is issued by a court and demands that the person holding the prisoner justify his detention or release him. Habeas corpus proceedings are not the type of special statutory proceedings which authorize appeals from final judgment of the district court to the supreme court (*In re Forest*, 1941).

---

[4] Throughout this commentary, references to numbered constitutional amendments, as here to the Second Amendment, are to the U.S. Constitution. Amendments to the New Mexico Constitution are incorporated into the text and therefore not numbered.

SECTION 8

Freedom of elections. All elections shall be free and open, and no power, civil or military, shall at anytime interfere to prevent the free exercise of the rights of suffrage.

Free elections are a necessary component of a republic; this provision recognizes this principle and protects elections from interference from government powers. The Supreme Court of New Mexico has recognized a right to vote as a preeminent right, calling it "the supreme right guaranteed by the constitution of the state" (*State ex rel Walker v. Bridges*, 1921). Further protections of and provisions for free elections are provided in Article VII.

SECTION 9

Military power subordinate; quartering of soldiers. The military shall always be in strict subordination to the civil power, no soldier shall in time of peace be quartered in any house without the consent of the owner, nor in time of war except in a manner prescribed by law.

The democratic principle that the military should be subordinate to the representatives of the people is implicit in the provisions of the U.S. Constitution. In the Constitution of New Mexico, however, that principle is stated explicitly. The provision concerning the quartering of soldiers is an almost exact replication of the Third Amendment, and like it, has never been the subject of significant judicial interpretation.

SECTION 10

Searches and seizures. The people shall be secure in their persons, papers, homes, and effects, from unreasonable searches and seizures, and no warrant to search any place, or seize any person or thing, shall issue without describing the place to be searched, or the papers or things to be seized, nor without a written showing of probable cause, supported by oath or affirmation.

This section prohibits the state from making unreasonable searches or seizures. The touchstone of the determination of the legality of any search or seizure is its reasonableness (*State v. Clark*, 1976). Reasonableness is determined by the facts and circumstances of each case examined in light of general legal standards (*State v. Sanchez*, 1975; *State v. Sedillo*, 1968). A search that is unreasonable is not made reasonable by the discovery of the evidence of a crime (*State v. Baca*, 1974; *State v. Deltenre*, 1967).

There are generally three instances in which a search or seizure is lawful under this provision: (1) if conducted pursuant to a legal search warrant, or (2) conducted by consent, or (3) conducted incident to a lawful arrest (*State v. Torres*, Ct. App. 1970). A search is not unconstitutional if the state justifies it on two grounds and one of the asserted grounds is not sustained (*State v. Sedillo*, 1968).

No Good Faith Exception

Generally, the Constitution of New Mexico may provide standards that are more demanding than those of the federal Constitution (*State v. Deltenre*, 1967). The state's courts do not recognize the good-faith exception developed by the U.S. Supreme Court, which has held that evidence gathered by police acting in good faith, yet with a defective search warrant, may be used as evidence in a criminal prosecution (*U.S. v. Leon*, 1984). This good-faith exception is incompatible with the New Mexico Constitution's mandate that search warrants may be issued only upon probable cause (*State v. Gutierrez*, 1993).

The New Mexico Constitution protects more areas from warrantless searches than does the federal Constitution. The use of the word "homes," where the U.S. Constitution uses the word "houses," provides evidence that the state constitution may be interpreted to include open fields as areas requiring a warrant before they can be searched (*State v. Sutton*, 1991).

Forcible Entry

New Mexico case law requires that police acting under a valid search warrant must meet standards that soften the intrusion of police into the lives of citizens. A warrant does not provide officers with an unrestricted right of entry of the places to be searched. Before entry, an officer must give notice of the nature of authority and the purpose of the search; if entrance is denied, only then can forcible entry be made. Forcible entry without notice may be lawfully made only if exigent circumstances exist. Such circumstances might be the good-faith belief that the officer or someone else is in peril of bodily harm or that the person to be arrested is fleeing or there is an attempt to destroy evidence (*State v. Baca*, 1974). Officers armed with a warrant, who simultaneously identify themselves and enter a house are acting unreasonably (*State v. Sanchez*, 1975).

Probable Cause

For warrants to meet the probable cause requirement of the New Mexico Constitution, (1) a probability of criminal conduct must be shown, (2) less vigorous proof may be used than the rules of evidence require for a conviction, and (3) common sense should control. Appellate courts should show deference to the magistrate's determination of probable cause (*State v. Bowers*, 1974). Probable cause for the issuance of a warrant, however, can only be determined by a judge; a police officer does not have the authority to do so (*State v. Baca*, 1982).

Warrantless Arrests

Officers may make arrests without a warrant if the circumstances would allow a reasonable person to believe that an offense has been committed by the person being arrested (*State v. Truilljo,* 1973), or if the person arrested commits a crime in the presence of the officer (*State v. Ramirez,* 1968). The burden is on the state, however, to show the requisite probable cause to justify a warrantless arrest (*State v. Gorsuch,* 1974).

SECTION 11

Freedom of religion. Every man shall be free to worship God according to the dictates of his own conscience, and no person shall ever be molested or denied any civil or political right or privilege on account of his religious opinion or mode of religious worship. No person shall be required to attend any place of worship or support any religious sect or denomination; nor shall any preference be given by law to any religious denomination or mode of worship.

Like most state constitutions, the New Mexico Constitution provides more explicit provisions concerning religious freedom than does the U.S. Constitution. In addition to this section of the bill of rights, the constitution also provides specific protection for religious liberty in Article II § 5, Article VII § 3, Article XII § 9, Article XX § 13, Article XXI § 1. This section requires the state to take a neutral stance toward religion, neither directly advancing it nor inhibiting it, and it protects the practice of religion without unreasonable state interference.

The courts have held that this section is not violated by local ordinances prohibiting the Sunday sale of alcohol (*Pruey v. Department of ABC,* 1986). Neither is the free exercise of religion unconstitutionally restricted by ordinances regulating the placement and size of signs erected by religious organizations, so long as the message on the signs is not regulated (*Temple Baptist Church, Inc. v. City of Albuquerque,* 1982), nor by requiring a zoning special use permit for the operation of a parochial school (*City of Las Cruces v. Huerta,* 1984).

SECTION 12

Trial by jury; less than unanimous verdicts in civil cases. The right to trial by jury as it has heretofore existed shall be secured to all and remain inviolate. In all cases triable in courts inferior to the district court the jury may consist of six. The legislature may provide that verdicts in civil cases may be rendered by less than a unanimous vote of the jury.

This provision maintains the right to trial by jury as it existed in the Territory of New Mexico immediately before the adoption of the constitution (*State v.*

Holloway, 1914). The right to a jury trial as it existed at the time of the adoption of the constitution does not preclude reasonable changes in regulating juries and the procedure to be followed in securing that right (*Carlile v. Continental Oil Co.*, 1970). Although the right to trial by jury is constitutionally guaranteed, one relying on that right must assert it in appropriate form (*Knabel v. Escudero*, 1927). The legislature has provided that twelve member juries in civil cases may render a verdict with the agreement of ten jurors (38-5-17 NMSA 1978 [1987 Repl.]).

SECTION 13

Bail; excessive fines; cruel and unusual punishment. All persons shall, before conviction be bailable by sufficient sureties, except for capital offenses when the proof is evident or the presumption great and in situations in which bail is specifically prohibited by this section. Excessive bail shall not be required, nor excessive fines imposed, nor cruel and unusual punishment inflicted.

Bail may be denied by the district court for a period of sixty days after the incarceration of the defendant by an order entered within seven days after the incarceration, in the following instances:

A. The defendant is accused of a felony and has previously been convicted of two or more felonies, within the state, which felonies did not arise from the same transaction or a common transaction with the case at bar;
B. the defendant is accused of a felony involving the use of a deadly weapon and has a prior felony conviction, within the state. The period for incarceration without bail may be extended by any period of time by which trial is delayed by a motion for a continuance made by or on behalf of the defendant. An appeal from an order denying bail shall be given preference over all other matters.

This section provides those accused of crimes with the opportunity to post bail and that neither excessive fines nor cruel and unusual punishment may be imposed. Bail has several purposes. It relieves the accused of imprisonment, it honors the presumption of innocence until guilt is proved, enables the accused to prepare a defense to the charge, and it relieves the state of the burden of keeping the accused person pending trial. People released on bail remain in the custody of the law and under the power of the court. This section also makes provision for denying bail to those whose incarceration is judged to be in the public's interest.

A ban on "cruel and unusual punishment" was included in the English Bill of Rights of 1689. George Mason and James Madison saw that it was incorporated into the 1776 Virginia Declaration of Rights, from which it was incorporated verbatim into the Eighth Amendment. The phrase "cruel and unusual punishment" is seen to forbid inhuman practices and the imposition of punishments unauthorized by statute or disproportionate to the offense.

"Cruel and unusual punishment implies something inhuman and barbarous" (*State v. Peters,* 1967), and the term "unusual" refers to the punishment under consideration rather than the infrequency of its imposition (*State ex rel Serna v. Hodges,* 1976). The New Mexico courts have generally refused to use this provision to review whether the punishment for a given crime is too severe and proportionate to an offense and held that fixing penalties is a legislative function (*McCutcheon v. Cox,* 1962). Neither consecutive sentences of life imprisonment (*State v. Padilla,* 1973) nor execution as provided in the New Mexico Capital Felony Sentencing Act (*State v. Cheadle,* 1984) violate the constitution's prohibition of cruel and unusual punishment.

SECTION 14

Indictment and information; grand juries; rights of accused. No person shall be held to answer for a capital, felonious, or infamous crime unless on a presentment or indictment of a grand jury or information filed by a district attorney or attorney general or their deputies; except in cases arising in the militia when in actual service in time of war or public danger. No person shall be so held on information without having had a preliminary examination before an examining magistrate or having waived such preliminary examination.

A grand jury shall be composed of such number, not less than twelve, as may be prescribed by law. Citizens only, residing in the county for which a grand jury may be convened and qualified as prescribed by law, may serve on a grand jury. Concurrence necessary for the finding of an indictment by a grand jury shall be prescribed by law; provided, such concurrence shall never be by less than a majority of those who compose a grand jury, and provided; at least eight must concur in finding an indictment when a grand jury is composed of twelve in number. Until otherwise prescribed by law a grand jury shall be composed of twelve in number and eight must concur in finding an indictment. A grand jury shall be convened upon order of a judge of a court empowered to try and determine cases of capital, felonious, or infamous crimes at such times as to him shall be deemed necessary, or a grand jury shall be ordered to convene by such judge upon the filing of a petition thereof signed by not less than the greater of two hundred registered voters or two percent of the registered voters of the county, or a grand jury may be convened in any additional manner as may be prescribed by law.

In all criminal prosecutions, the accused shall have the right to appear and defend himself in person, and by counsel; to demand the nature and cause of the accusation; to be confronted with the witnesses against him; to have the charge and testimony interpreted to him in a language that he understands; to have compulsory process to compel the attendance of necessary witnesses in his behalf, and a speedy public trial by an impartial jury of the county or district in which the offense is alleged to have been committed.

Indictment and Information

This section raises various common law standards for the prosecution of crime to the level of constitutional guarantees. Indictment and information are formal, openly made charges that the accused has committed a crime. An indictment is the written accusation of a grand jury against one or more persons. Information is a written accusation of a crime presented by a public prosecutor without the intervention of a grand jury.

A 1924 amendment to this section allowed the state to use information as well as indictment as the means of accusing persons of crimes. But to insure the reasonableness of the charge brought by information, accused persons must be afforded the opportunity of a preliminary examination before a magistrate. The 1924 amendment also added the extensive description of the composition of a grand jury and the requirement that indictments require more than the assent of a simple majority of the grand jury. Finally, the amendment also provided that grand juries could be convened at the petition of registered voters. A 1980 amendment changed the number of petitioners to require a judge to convene a grand jury from 75 to "the lesser of two hundred registered voters or five percent of the registered voters." A 1994 amendment change that phrase to "the greater of two hundred registered voters or two percent of the registered voters." The history of the development of the grand jury is reviewed in *Buzbee v. Donnelly* (1981).

The state constitution's provision for prosecution of a felony by information does not violate either the grand jury provision of the Fifth Amendment or the due process clause of the Fourteenth Amendment (*State v. Reyes,* 1967). The constitutional requirement of a preliminary examination for defendants charged with information is unknown in common law; it is, however a matter of law and not discretionary with the judge (*Williams v. Sanders,* 1969).

Right to Counsel

The constitutional right to counsel extends to every critical stage of criminal proceeding including the lineup (*State v. Garcia,* 1969); custodial interview, trial, and appeal (*State v. Lewis,* 1969); and arraignment (*State v. Torres,* 1970). Persons charged with a crime who don't have financial means to procure counsel are entitled to a court-appointed lawyer (*State v. Dalrymple,* 1965); however, the accused person must show indigence before counsel will be appointed (*State v. Powers,* 1965).

Other Due Process Rights

This section also provides the right of accused persons to confront witnesses against them, the right to a speedy trial, and to an impartial jury. The right of a person accused of a crime to confront witnesses against him and to cross-examine them is fundamental to due process of law (*State v. Holly*, 1968). The constitutional right to a speedy trial has three purposes: (1) it protects the accused, who is held in jail while awaiting trial, against prolonged imprisonment; (2) it relieves him of long periods of time under public suspicion; and (3) prevents the hazards of trial after a great lapse of time because of loss of witness and dulling of memory (*Raburn v. Nash*, 1967). The constitution's requirement of an impartial jury means that it must not favor one side more than another, it must treat all alike, be unbiased, equitable, fair, and just (*State v. Verdugo*, 1968).

SECTION 15

Self-incrimination; double jeopardy. No persons shall be compelled to testify against himself in a criminal proceeding, nor shall any person be twice put in jeopardy for the same offense; and when the indictment, information or affidavit upon which any person is convicted charges different offenses or different degrees of the same offense and a new trial is granted the accused, he may not again be tried for an offense or degree of the offense greater than the one of which he was convicted.

Protection from Self-incrimination

The privilege against self-incrimination is a development of common law, where it was considered to be derived from natural law. It appears late in common law, evidently in response to the inquisitorial methods of interrogating accused persons in the late seventeenth century, see 21A *Am. Jur.2d*, Criminal Law § 702.

This privilege bars compelling communication or testimony from the accused, but does not extend to compulsion that makes the suspect or accused person the source of real or physical evidence (*State v. Jameson, 191 A*). Therefore, an accused person may be required to allow witnesses to view them for purpose of identification (*State v. White*, 1967), directed to talk for voice identification, and to walk for the purpose of supplying identifying characteristics (*State v. Ramirez*, 1967). Nor is the privilege violated by requiring a person to provide hair samples (*State v. Williamson*, 1968), or furnish handwriting samples (*State v. Archuleta*, 1971), or to be fingerprinted (*State v. Jameson, 191 A*), or provide blood samples (*State v. Richardson*, 1975), or undergo psychiatric examination (*State v. Kindall*, 1977).

Double Jeopardy

Several principles underlie the double jeopardy prohibition: (1) guilt should be determined by proving the crime to a single jury, rather than depending on the increased possibility of conviction resulting from multiple prosecution before many juries, (2) nor should the prosecutor be able to search for a desired sentence by bringing the same case before different judges, (3) furthermore, criminal trials should not be an instrument used by the government to harass individuals, and (4) judges should not impose multiple punishment for a single, legislatively defined crime (*State v. Tanton*, 1975). Protection from double jeopardy does not prohibit the prosecution of a defendant in both state and federal courts on charges arising out of a single action (*State v. Rogers*, 1977).

SECTION 16

Treason. Treason against the state shall consist only in levying war against it, adhering to its enemies, or giving them aid and comfort. No person shall be convicted of treason unless on the testimony of two witnesses to the same overt act, or on confession in open court.

This section defines what constitutes treason against the state. Then, like the federal Constitution and many other state constitutions, it sets the requirements for conviction for treason. This section has never been the subject of litigation.

SECTION 17

Freedom of speech and press; libel. Every person may freely speak, write and publish his sentiments on all subjects, being responsible for the abuse of that right; and no law shall be passed to restrain or abridge the liberty of speech or of the press. In all criminal prosecutions for libels, the truth may be given in evidence to the jury; and if it shall appear to the jury that the matter charged as libelous is true and was published with good motives and for justifiable ends, the party shall be acquitted.

This provision protects the freedom of expression, but recognizes that there are restraints on this liberty and that it must be exercised responsibly. The standard test for determining if expression in speech or press are harmful under this article is the standard of common law in force at the time of the adoption of the federal Constitution (*Curry v. Journal Publishing Co.*, 1937).

Statutes that provide punishment of all acts, peaceful or otherwise, which have as their objective the destruction of organized government, or acts antagonistic to or in opposition to such organized government, are laws that violate the protection of this section (*State v. Diamond*, 1921).

Most litigation using this section to challenge state regulation has concerned either the regulation of outdoor advertising signs or banning media coverage of trials. In general, reasonable restrictions on outdoor signs, that are not aimed at the content of the signs, do not violate this section (*Stuckey Stores Inc. v. O'Cheskey*, 1979; *Temple Baptist Church Inc. v. City of Albuquerque*, 1982). Media coverage of trials may be banned only when there is substantial evidence that such coverage will deny the defendant a fair trial; in making this decision the court must provide for objections (*State ex rel National Press Association v. Kaufman*, 1982).

SECTION 18

Due process; equal protection; sex discrimination. No person shall be deprived of life, liberty, or property without due process of law; nor shall any person be denied equal protection of the laws. Equality of rights under law shall not be denied on account of the sex of any person. The effective date of this amendment shall be July 1, 1973.

This section reiterates the requirements of due process of law and equal protection under the law that are imposed on the states by the Fourteenth Amendment. The section was amended by the people in 1971; the second sentence was added to explicitly protect against sexual discrimination under the law.

Due process of law not only embraces protection of the liberty of individuals in the enforcement of law, but also in the making of law. The legislature may not make law outside of its competency to do so (*State v. Henry*, 1933). Nevertheless, the supreme court has repeatedly held that courts should presume the constitutionality of a legislative act (*McGeehan v. Bunch*, 1975). Substantive due process challenges to statutes must meet demanding requirements. The party attacking the constitutionality of a statute or ordinance has the burden of establishing its invalidity (*City of Albuquerque v. Jones*, 1975). Where a statute is susceptible to two constructions, one supporting the statute and the other rendering it void, the court must adopt the construction which upholds its constitutionality (*Abeytia v. Gibbons Garage*, 1920). The constitutional questions concerning the validity of statutes will be decided only when it is necessary to dispose of the issues before the court (*Ratliff v. Wingfield*, 1951).

In order to show a statute unconstitutional, plaintiffs must show either an impairment of their rights (*State v. Hines*, 1967), or that, using acceptable rules of construction, it is impossible to determine what the legislature intended. Even though statutes may not be overbroad, they may allow some flexibility in their application (*New Mexico Municipal League v. New Mexico Environmental Improvement*, 1975).

In criminal prosecutions, it is in the courts' jurisdiction to do whatever is necessary under general rules of jurisprudence to insure due process protection for defendants (*State v. Valdez*, 1972). Where a claim of denial of due process is made there must be a showing of prejudice (*Deats v. State*, 1969), and not only must the state abuse its discretion, it must result in injury to the defendant (*State v. Nieto*, 1967).

In construing the meaning of the equal protection section of the New Mexico Constitution, courts are to be guided by the federal courts' construction of the Fourteenth Amendment (*Board of Trustees v. Montano*, 1971).

SECTION 19

Retroactive laws; bills of attainder; impairment of contracts. No ex post facto law, bill of attainder nor law impairing the obligation of contracts shall be enacted by the legislature.

This section replicates the requirements placed on the state by Article 1 § 10 of the national Constitution. These provisions are intended to insure the basic fairness of the substance of the laws passed by the legislature. Ex post facto laws are retroactive criminal laws that work to the disadvantage of an individual. A bill of attainder is a legislative act inflicting punishment, including deprivation of property, without judicial procedure on specified individuals or members of a specified group. Forbidding the impairment of contracts prevents the legislature from extending the time which debtors could take to meet their payments or to otherwise avoid contractual obligations. In New Mexico these prohibitions apply equally to legislative and judicial rule-making (*State v. Norush*, 1982).

SECTION 20

Eminent domain. Private property shall not be taken or damaged for public use without just compensation.

This section recognizes the government's power of eminent domain, taking private property for public use, but requires that the owner be given just compensation. It also provides that compensation should be paid for damages to property caused by government use. In general the holdings of the U.S. Supreme Court concerning the taking clause of the Fifth Amendment are used as guiding principles in construction of this section of the New Mexico Constitution.

Using this section, the state may appropriate private property for public use by an act of the legislature (*State ex rel Red River Valley Co. v. District Court*, 1935). There is no limit on the legislature's right to designate agencies that shall exercise the power of eminent domain, except as restricted by the constitution, and the question of the necessity or expediency of a taking lies with the legislature and is not a proper subject for judicial review (*State ex rel State Highway Commission v. Burks*, 1966). This section also confers on the property owner the right to recover just compensation (*Garver v. Public Service Co.*, 1966). A taking of property is not required in order for an owner to claim compensation, it is sufficient if there are consequential damages (*Board of County Commissioners v. Harris*, 1961).

SECTION 21

Imprisonment for debt. No person shall be imprisoned for debt in any civil action.

This section prevents imprisonment for debt. Imprisonment for failure to pay a civil contempt fine, however, is not imprisonment for failure to pay a debt (*Atlas Corp. v. DeVilliers*, 1972), nor is the imprisonment of a husband for contempt of court, for a definite term or until sum was paid to wife, for violation of a divorce action restraining order prohibiting removal of estate from the jurisdiction (*In re Canavan*, 1914).

SECTION 22

Alien landownership. Until otherwise provided by law no alien, ineligible to citizenship under the laws of the United States, or corporation, copartnership or association, a majority of the stock or interest in which is owned or held by such aliens, shall acquire title, leasehold or other interest in or to real estate in New Mexico.

This section of the constitution, as ratified in 1911, provided that no distinction should be made by law between resident aliens and citizens in regard to ownership or descent of property. In 1921, this section was amended to make such distinction, unless otherwise provided by law. The provisions for aliens to acquire or hold real estate by deed, will, inheritance, or otherwise were enacted by the legislature in 1975, see 45-2-111 NMSA 1978.

SECTION 23

Reserved rights. The enumeration in this constitution of certain rights shall not be construed to deny, impair or disparage other retained by the people.

This section insures the understanding that the rights specifically enumerated in the constitution are not inclusive, meaning that the rights enjoyed by the people are not limited to those listed in the constitution.

SECTION 24

Crime victims' rights. A. A victim of arson resulting in bodily injury, aggravated arson, aggravated assault, aggravated battery, dangerous use of explosive, negligent use of a deadly weapon, murder, voluntary manslaughter, involuntary manslaughter, kidnapping, criminal sexual penetration, criminal sexual contact with a minor, homicide by vehicle, great bodily injury by vehicle or abandonment or abuse of a child or that victim's representative shall have the following rights as provide by law:

(1) the right to be treated with fairness and respect for the victim's dignity and privacy throughout the criminal justice process;
(2) the right to timely disposition of the case;
(3) the right to be reasonably protected from the accused throughout the criminal justice process;
(4) the right to notification of court proceedings;
(5) the right to attend all public court proceedings the accused has the right to attend;
(6) the right to confer with the prosecution;
(7) the right to make a statement to the court at sentencing and at any post-sentencing hearings for the accused;
(8) the right to restitution from the person convicted of the criminal conduct that caused the victim's loss or injury;
(9) the right to information about the conviction, sentencing, imprisonment, escape or release of the accused;
(10) the right to have the prosecuting attorney notify the victim's employer, if requested by the victim, of the necessity of the victim's cooperation and testimony in a court proceeding that may necessitate the absence of the victim from work for good cause;
(11) the right to promptly receive any property belonging to the victim that is being held for evidentiary purposes by law enforcement agency or the prosecuting attorney, unless there is compelling evidentiary reason for retention of the victim's property.

B. A person accused or convicted of a crime against the victim shall have no standing to object to any failure by any person to comply with the provisions of Subsection A of Section 24 of Article 2 of the constitution of New Mexico.

C. The provisions of this amendment shall not take effect until the legislature enacts laws to implement this amendment.

This section was added to the Bill of Rights by an amendment ratified by the voters in 1994. It raises to a level of constitutional protection the rights of victims of serious crimes and is intended to balance the rights provided to those accused of crimes.

Article III

Distribution of Powers

SECTION 1

Separation of departments. The powers of government of this state are divided into three distinct departments, the legislative, executive and judicial, and no person or collection of persons charged with the exercise of powers properly belonging to one of these departments, shall exercise any powers properly belonging to either of the others, except as in this constitution otherwise expressly directed or permitted. Nothing in this section, or elsewhere in this constitution, shall prevent the legislature from establishing, by statute, a body with statewide jurisdiction other than the courts of this state for the determination of rights and liabilities between persons when those rights and liabilities arise from transactions or occurrences involving personal injury sustained in the course of employment by an employee. The statute shall provide for the type and organization of the body, the mode of appointment or election of its members and such other matters as the legislature may deem necessary or proper.

This article provides that the state government will be organized on the model deeply etched into the political culture of the United States: the separation of powers among the legislative, executive, and judicial branches of government. The national Constitution does not require such a structure for the states nor is it essential to a republican form of government, yet each of the 50 states has adopted this model.

None of the three separate departments of government is subordinate to another. Article II § 2 recognizes that the inherent powers of state government are vested in the people; Article III is not a grant of power to the three branches, but a limitation on their powers; none of the branches may add or detract from its clear mandate under this article (*State ex rel. Hovey Concrete Products Co. v. Mechem*, 1957). The legislature, however, may delegate authority to an administrative agency when that authority is restricted by specific legislative standards (*Montoya v. O'Toole*, 1980). Nor do legislative acts setting mandatory sentencing policies violate the doctrine of separation of powers (*State v. Mabry*, 1981). Court decisions may be modified by legislative enactments in any manner and to any degree, so long as the legislation conforms to constitutional standards (*Ferguson v. New Mexico State Highway Commission*, 1982).

The section was amended in 1981 by adding the last two sentences to protect the state workers' compensation agency from challenges that it is an executive agency usurping legislative or judicial powers in violation of this section.

Article IV

Legislative Department

SECTION 1

Vesting of legislative power; location of sessions; referendum on legislation. The legislative power shall be vested in a senate and house of representatives which shall be designated the legislature of the state of New Mexico, and shall hold its sessions at the seat of government.

The people reserve the power to disapprove, suspend and annul any law enacted by the legislature, except general appropriation laws; laws providing for the preservation of the public peace, health or safety; for the payment of the public debt or interest thereon, or the creation or funding of the same, except as in this constitution otherwise provided; for the maintenance of the public schools or state institutions, and local or special laws. Petitions disapproving any law other than those above excepted, enacted at the last preceding session of the legislature, shall be filed with the secretary of state not less than four months prior to the next general election. Such petitions shall be signed by not less than ten per centum of the qualified electors of each of three-fourths of the counties and in the aggregate by not less than ten per centum of the qualified electors of the state, as shown by the total number of votes cast at the last preceding general election. The question of the approval or rejection of such law shall be submitted by the secretary of state to the electorate at the next general election; and if a majority of the legal votes cast thereon, and not less than forty per centum of the total number of legal votes cast at such general election, be cast for the rejection of such law, it shall be annulled and thereby repealed with the same effect as if the legislature had then repealed it, and such repeal shall revive any law repealed by the act so annulled; otherwise, it shall remain in force unless subsequently repealed by the legislature. If such petition or petitions be signed by not less than twenty-five per centum of the qualified electors under each of the foregoing conditions, and be filed with the secretary of state within ninety days after the adjournment of the session of the legislature at which such law was enacted, the operation thereof shall be thereupon suspended and the question of its approval or rejection shall be likewise submitted to a vote at the next ensuing general election. If a majority of the votes cast thereon and not less than forty per centum of the total number of votes cast at such general election be cast for its rejection, it shall be thereby annulled; otherwise, it shall go into effect upon publication of the certificate of the secretary of state declaring the result of the vote thereon. It shall be a felony for any person to sign any such petition with any name other than his own, or to sign his name more than once for the same measure, or to sign such petition when he is not a qualified elector in the county specified in such petition; provided, that nothing herein shall be construed to prohibit the writing thereon of the name of any person who cannot write, and who signs the same with his mark. The legislature shall enact laws necessary for the effective exercise of the power hereby reserved.

This section assigns the legislative power to a bicameral legislature, composed of a senate and house of representatives, which is to meet in the state capital. It also provides the people a right of referendum, but exempts several types of legislation.

The legislature has plenary legislative authority which is limited only by the state and federal constitutions (*Daniels v. Watson*, 1966). Court decisions may be modified by legislative enactments in any manner and to any degree, so long as the legislation conforms to constitutional standards (*Ferguson v. New Mexico State Highway Commission*, 1982).

The categories of legislation not subject to referendum, and the omission by the framers of the constitution of the words "necessary" and "immediate" in the language of the exception clause, result in a much narrower right of referendum than is allowed to people in the other states in which the right is reserved (*Otto v. Buck*, 1956). Furthermore, the authority of the legislature to initiate constitutional amendments is not subject to referendum (*Hutcheson v. Gonzales*, 1937), and neither can a joint resolution ratifying a proposed amendment to the U.S. Constitution be submitted to the people (*Opinion of the Attorney General* No. 50, 1919–20).

SECTION 2

Powers generally; disaster emergency procedure. In addition to the powers herein enumerated, the legislature shall have all powers necessary to the legislature of a free state, including the power to enact reasonable and appropriate laws to guarantee the continuity and effective operation of state and local government by providing emergency procedure for use only during periods of disaster emergency. A disaster emergency is defined as a period when damage or injury to persons or property in this state, caused by enemy attack, is of such magnitude that a state of martial law is declared to exist in the state, and a disaster emergency is declared by the chief executive officer to the United States and the chief executive officer of this state, and the legislature has not declared by joint resolution that the disaster emergency is ended. Upon the declaration of a disaster emergency the chief executive of the state shall within seven days call a special session of the legislature, which shall remain in continuous session during the disaster emergency, and may recess from time to time for [not] more than three days.

This section delegates to the legislature the general legislative powers needed in a democratic state. In 1960, this section was amended to empower the legislature to enact reasonable and appropriate measures to allow the continuance of government in the state during periods of disaster and emergency, and to define what constitutes such disaster and emergency.

The legislature may not, under the guise of the police powers, impose unnecessary and unreasonable restrictions upon the use of private property or the pursuit of useful activities. The statute (40A-17-5, 1953 Comp., now repealed) that defined arson to include any "intentional" burning of property, was an unreasonable exercise of police power, for it could be used to punish innocent and beneficial destruction of property (*State v. Dennis*, 1969).

SECTION 3

Number and qualifications of members; single-member districts; reapportionment. A. Senators shall not be less than twenty-five years of age and representatives not less than twenty-one years of age at the time of their election. If any senator or representative permanently removes his residence from or maintains no residence in the district from which he was elected, then he shall be deemed to have resigned and his successor shall be selected as provided in Section 4 of this article. No person shall be eligible to serve in the legislature who, at the time of qualifying, holds any office of trust or profit with the state, county or national governments, except notaries public and officers of the militia who receive no salary.

B. The senate shall be composed of no more than forty-two members elected from single-member districts.

C. The house of representatives shall be composed of not more than seventy members elected from single-member districts.

D. Once following publication of the official report of each federal decennial census hereafter conducted, the legislature may by statute reapportion its membership.

The number and qualifications of senators and representatives are set out by this section. It was amended in 1976 to require that both senators and representatives be elected from single-member districts and provide that the legislature reapportion these districts following the federal decennial census. The former Subsection B of this section that required at least one senator be elected from each county is invalid under the Fourteenth Amendment (*Beauchamp v. Campbell*, 1966).

SECTION 4

Terms of office of members; time of election; filling of vacancies. Members of the legislature shall be elected as follows: those senators from Bernalillo, Chaves, Curry, DeBaca, Grant, Lea, Lincoln, Luna, Sanoval, San Juan, San Miguel, Socorro, Taos, Torrance, Union and Valencia counties for a term of six years starting January 1, 1961, and after serving such terms shall be elected for a term of four years thereafter, those senators from all other counties for the terms of four years, and members of the house of representatives for a term of two years. They shall be elected on the day provided by law for holding the general election of state officers or representatives in congress. If a vacancy occurs in the office of senator or member of the house of representatives, for any reason, the county commissioners of the county wherein the vacancy occurs shall fill such vacancy by appointment.

Such legislative appointments as provided in this section shall be for a term ending on December 31, subsequent to the next succeeding general election.

This section provides that senators shall be elected for four-year terms with some terms starting every second year, and that representatives will be elected for two-year terms. Legislative elections will be held on the day the legislature designates for the election of members of Congress. It also provides for the filling of vacancies in the legislature, until the next general election. A 1953 amendment changed the method of filling vacancies occurring in either house (vacancies were formerly filled by election held as designated by the governor), and added the last paragraph providing the term of such appointments. An amendment ratified in 1960 modified the description of how county commissioners are to fill vacant legislative seats. The first paragraph is unconstitutional insofar as it refers to the senate or senators, because it violates the equal protection clause of the Fourteenth Amendment (*Beauchamp v. Campbell*, 1966).

SECTION 5

Time and length of sessions; items considered in even-numbered years. A. Each regular session of the legislature shall begin annually at 12:00 noon on the third Tuesday of January. Every regular session of the legislature convening during an odd-numbered year shall remain in session not to exceed sixty days, and every regular session of the legislature convening during an even-numbered year shall remain in session not to exceed thirty days. No special session of the legislature shall exceed thirty days.

B. Every regular session of the legislature convening during an even-numbered year shall consider only the following:

(1) budgets, appropriations and revenue bills;

(2) bills drawn pursuant to special messages of the governor; and

(3) bills of the last previous regular session vetoed by the governor.

The constitution establishes a part-time citizen's legislature and limits the length of the sessions of the legislature and further limits sessions held in even-numbered years to tax and spending matters, to matters included in the governor's special message, and to overriding vetoes of bills of the last regular session of the legislature. The legislature, however, pursuant to Article XIX, may propose constitutional amendments during the session held in even-numbered years (*State ex rel Chavez v. Vigil-Giron*, 1988). This section was amended in 1940; that amendment provided that the legislature only meet in regular session every two years, for a 60-day session, divided into two 30-day sessions with a 30-day recess between them, and provided that no special session could last more than 30 days. A 1946 amendment returned the length of regular session to 60 days without the recess. A 1964 amendment established the present wording of this section.

SECTION 6

Special session; extraordinary session. Special sessions of the legislature may be called by the governor, but no business shall be transacted except such as relates to the objects specified in this proclamation. Provided, however, that when three-fifths of the members elected to the house of representatives and three-fifths of the members elected to the senate shall have certified to the governor of the state of New Mexico that in their opinion an emergency exists in the affairs of the state of New Mexico, it shall thereupon be the duty of said governor and mandatory upon him, within five days from the receipt of such certificate or certificates, to convene said legislature in extraordinary session for all purposes; and in the event said governor shall, within said time, Sundays excluded, fail or refuse to convene said legislature as aforesaid, then and in that event said legislature may convene itself in extraordinary session, as if convened in regular session, for all purposes, provided that such extraordinary self-convened session shall be limited to a period of thirty days, unless at the expiration of said period, there shall be pending an impeachment trial of some officer of the state government, in which event the legislature shall be authorized to remain in session until such trial shall have been completed.

This section provides that the governor may call special sessions of the legislature to consider only matters included in his call. The mechanism for convening special sessions was expanded by a 1948 amendment that provided that a super-majority of each house may mandate the governor to call a special session and, if that is not done, it may convene itself in extraordinary session. It was the intent of the framers of the constitution to limit the introduction of amendments to regular sessions of the legislature, as opposed to special sessions, not to limit the enactment of amendments to odd-numbered rather than even-numbered years or to unrestricted rather than restricted regular sessions (*State ex rel Chavez v. Vigil-Giron*, 1988), see requirements for amendments Article XIX § 1.

SECTION 7

Judge of election and qualifications of members; quorum. Each house shall be the judge of the election and qualifications of its own members. A majority of either house shall constitute a quorum to do business, but a less number may effect a temporary organization, adjourn from day to day and compel the attendance of absent members.

This section provides that once candidates are elected, the legislature is the sole judge as to qualification for seating members. It also requires that a majority of either house must be present to do business, and allows the legislature to compel the attendance of absent members. This section has not been the subject of judicial interpretation.

SECTION 8

Call to order; presiding officers. The senate shall be called to order by the lieutenant governor. The senate shall elect a president pro tempore who shall preside in the absence of the lieutenant governor and shall be called to order in the hall of said house by the secretary of state. He shall preside until the election of a speaker, who shall be the member receiving the highest number of votes for that office.

The provision for calling the legislature to order at the beginning of a session and the presiding officers of each house are designated by this section. This section has not been judicially interpreted.

SECTION 9

Selection and compensation of officers and employees. The legislature shall select its own officers and employees and fix their compensation. Each house shall have one chaplain, one chief clerk and one sergeant at arms; and there shall be one assistant chief clerk and one assistant sergeant at arms for each house; and each house may employ such enrolling clerks, reading clerks, stenographers, janitors and such subordinate employees in addition to those enumerated, as they may reasonably require and their compensation shall be fixed by the said legislature at the beginning of each

This section provides for the selection of officers and employees of the legislature, designates several of the major positions, and empowers the legislature to set the compensation of its employees. A 1948 amendment of this section deleted provisions that set the maximum compensation for legislative employees.

SECTION 10

Compensation of members. Each member of the legislature shall receive:
A. as per diem expense the sum of not more than seventy-five dollars ($75.00) for each day's attendance during each session, as provided by law, and twenty-five cents ($.25) for each mile traveled in going to and returning from the seat of government by the usual traveled route, once each session as defined by Article 4, Section 5 of this constitution;
B. per diem expense and mileage at the same rates as provided in subsection A of this section for service at meetings required by legislative committees established by the legislature to meet in the interim between sessions; and
C. no other compensation, perquisite or allowance.

The members of the New Mexico legislature serve without a salary or other compensation except for specific per diem expenses and travel allowances, which are specified by amount in this section. This section reflects the reluctance of New Mexicans to provide more than minimal expense money to legislators. This section was amended four times (in 1944, 1953, 1971, and 1982) to increase the amount of per diem expenses and travel allowances; similar amendments failed ratification in 1965, 1980, and 1990. An amendment, proposed in 1974, to create a legislative compensation commission to set the salaries and expense allowances of legislators failed ratification. A similar amendment proposed in 1994 also failed.

SECTION 11

Rules of procedure; contempt or disorderly conduct; expulsion of members. Each house may determine the rules of procedure, punish its members or others for contempt or disorderly behavior in its presence and protect its members against violence; and may, with the concurrence of two-thirds of its members, expel a member, but not a second time for the same act. Punishment for contempt or disorderly behavior or by expulsion shall not be a bar to criminal prosecution.

This section allows the members of each house to set its own rules of procedure and conduct. It also requires a two-thirds vote of the chamber's membership to expel one of its members, and allows for the criminal prosecution of expelled members.

SECTION 12

Public sessions; journals. All sessions of each house shall be public. Each house shall keep a journal of its proceedings and the yeas and nays on any questions shall, at the request of one-fifth of the members present, be entered thereon. The original thereof shall be filed with the secretary of state at the close of the session, and shall be printed and published under his authority.

This section requires that meetings of the legislature be held in public, and for the maintenance and publication of a journal of each house. The supreme court will at times take notice of the journals as indicators of legislative intent (*Clary v. Denman Drilling Co.*, 1954).

SECTION 13

Privileges and immunities. Members of the legislature shall, in all cases except treason, felony and breach of the peace, be privileged from arrest during their attendance at the sessions of their respective houses, and on going to and returning from the same. And they shall not be questioned in any other place for any speech or debate or for any vote cast in either house.

This section reflects the long-standing principle of English law that protects legislators from harassment by other branches of the government. It mirrors similar provisions in Article I § 6 of the U.S. Constitution.

SECTION 14

Adjournment. Neither house shall, without the consent of the other, adjourn for more than three days, Sundays excepted; nor to any other place than that where the two houses are sitting; and on the day of the final adjournment they shall adjourn at twelve o'clock, noon.

The conditions for adjournment of the houses are provided in this section. The limit on the length of time for which adjournment can be called is intended to maintain the session within a relatively short period of the year as provided in Article IV § 5.

SECTION 15

Laws to be passed by bill; alteration of bill; enacting clause; printing and reading of bill. No law shall be passed except by bill, and no bill shall be so altered or amended on its passage through either house as to change its original purpose. The enacting clause of all bills shall be: "Be it enacted by the legislature of the state of New Mexico." Any bill may originate in either house. No bill, except bills to provide for the public peace, health and safety, and the codification or revision of the laws, shall become a law unless it has been printed, and read three different times in each house, not more than two of which readings shall be on the same day, and the third of which shall be in full.

This provision insures the public nature of the legislative process by requiring that measures considered for enactment are clear, and it prohibits amendments not germane to subject of legislation expressed in the title of the act to be amended. This section is not violated merely by broadening a bill and making it more comprehensive as to its details (*Black Hawk Consolidated Mines Co. v. Gallegos*, 1948).

SECTION 16

Subject of bill in title; appropriation bills. The subject of every bill shall be clearly expressed in its title, and no bill embracing more than one subject shall be passed except general appropriation bills and bills for the codification or revision of the laws; but if any subject is embraced in any act which is not expressed in its title, only so much of the act as is not so expressed shall be void. General appropriation bills shall embrace nothing but appropriations for the expense of the executive, legislative and judiciary departments, interest, sinking fund payments on the public debt, public schools and other expenses required by existing laws; but if any such bill contain any other matter, only so much thereof as is hereby forbidden to be placed therein shall be void. All other appropriations shall be made by separate bills.

This section is intended to prevent fraud, logrolling legislation, and surprise by means of concealed provisions or acts with hidden provisions which the title fails to express. It provides a mechanism to apprise the people of the subjects of legislation. It does not require that the title be an index of everything in the act itself, but only that it give notice of the subject matter of the legislation (*In re Estate of Welch*, 1969). If the subject matter of the bill is reasonably germane to its title, it is sufficient to be valid under this section (*United States Brewers Association v. Director N. M. Dept. of ABC*, 1983; *Bureau of Revenue v. Dale J. Bellamah Corp.*, 1970). Constitutional questions raised under this section or any other section of the constitution will be decided only when necessary to a disposition of the case at hand (*Ratliff v. Wingfield*, 1951).

SECTION 17

Passage of bills. No bill shall be passed except by a vote of a majority of the members present in each house, nor unless on its final passage a vote be taken by yeas and nays, and entered on the journal.

This section sets a requirement for majority vote in both houses to pass all legislation. It also requires accountability of the legislators by requiring that their vote be recorded on the final passage of all bills.

SECTION 18

Amendment of statutes. No law shall be revised or amended, or the provisions thereof extended by reference to its title only; but each section thereof as revised, amended or extended shall be set out in full.

Notwithstanding the foregoing or any other provision of this constitution, the legislature, in any law imposing a tax or taxes, may define the amount on, in respect to or by which such tax or taxes are imposed or measured, by reference to any provision of the laws of the United States as the same may be or become effective at any time or from time to time, and may prescribe exceptions or modifications to any such provision.

This provision is intended to eradicate the harm of so-called "blind legislation," that is, legislation that undertakes to amend, revise, or extend existing legislation in a way that the effect of the resulting statute cannot be determined without examining the previous legislation as well. For example, a 1927 act which made other laws apply to underground water, without designating such laws, was void because it violated this section, since it was blind legislation (*Yeo v. Tweedy*, 1929). A 1964 amendment added the second paragraph to this section.

SECTION 19

Introduction of bills. Time limitation on the introduction of bills at any session of the legislature shall be established by law.

This section's intent is to prevent fraud; and surprise caused by introducing and logrolling a bill through the legislature in the closing days of the session. Before this section was amended in 1960, it was concerned only with appropriation bills and set the deadline for the introduction of bills in a session; it now calls on the legislature to set such deadlines, which it has done in 2-6-1 NMSA 1978.

SECTION 20

Enrollment, engrossment and signing of bills. Immediately after the passage of any bill or resolution, it shall be enrolled and engrossed, and read publicly in full in each house, and thereupon shall be signed by the presiding officers of each house in open session, and the fact of such reading and signing shall be entered on the journal. No interlineation or erasure in a signed bill, shall be effective, unless certified thereon in express terms by the presiding officer of each house quoting the words interlined or erased, not unless the fact of the making of such interlineation or erasure be publicly announced in each house and entered on the journal.

This section provides the procedure for formalizing the passage of bills and resolutions, with protections to insure that only the bill as it was actually passed is recorded as an act of the legislature. When a law in the form enacted by the legislature is enrolled and engrossed and read publicly in full in each house, and deposited with the secretary of state, constitutional requirements are met (*State v. Armstrong*, 1924); therefore, an enrolled and engrossed bill, properly signed and authenticated, approved by the governor, and deposited with the secretary of state is conclusive as to the regularity of its enactment, and the courts cannot look behind it to the journals to determine if constitutional requirements have been met (*Thompson v. Saunders*, 1947; *Dillon v. King*, 1974).

SECTION 21

Alteration or theft of bill. Any person who shall, without lawful authority, materially change or alter, or make away with, any bill pending in or passed by the legislature, shall be deemed guilty of a felony and upon conviction thereof shall be punished by imprisonment in the penitentiary for not less than one year nor more than five years.

This section protects the integrity of the legislative process by defining the unauthorized alteration or theft of a bill, before or after its passage, as a felony and sets the criminal punishment for such acts.

SECTION 22

Governor's approval or veto of bills. Every bill passed by the legislature shall, before it becomes a law, be presented to the governor for approval. If he approves, he shall sign it, and deposit it with the secretary of state; otherwise, he shall return it to the house in which it originated, with his objections, which shall be entered at large upon the journal; and such bill shall not become a law unless thereafter approved by two-thirds of the members present and voting in each house by yea and nay vote entered upon its journal. Any bill not returned by the governor within three days, Sundays excepted, after being presented to him, shall become a law, whether signed by him or not, unless the legislature by adjournment prevent such return. Every bill presented to the governor during the last three days or the session shall be approved by him within twenty days after the adjournment and shall be by him immediately deposited with the secretary of state. Unless so approved and signed by him such bill shall not become a law. The governor may in like manner approve or disapprove any part or parts, item or items, of any bill appropriating money, and such parts or items approved shall become a law, and such as are disapproved shall be void unless passed over his veto, as herein provided.

This section sets out the legislative role of the governor in approving or vetoing bills passed by the legislature. It provides that the governor must approve or veto within certain time limits or the bill will become law without his signature, and it provides the procedure for the legislature to override a veto. It also allows the governor to veto line items in "any bill appropriating money"; this includes appropriations other than those made in general appropriation bills. In exercising a line item veto, the governor may only delete appropriated amounts, not alter, enlarge, or decrease the items (*State ex rel Dickson v. Saiz,* 1957). An amendment adopted in 1953 substituted "approved by him within twenty days after the adjournment" for "approved or disapproved by him within six day after adjournment" in the fourth sentence of this section.

SECTION 23

Effective date of law; emergency acts. Laws shall go into effect ninety days after the adjournment of the legislature enacting them, except general appropriation laws, which shall go into effect immediately upon their passage and approval. Any act necessary for the preservation of the public peace, health or safety, shall take effect immediately upon its passage and approval, provided it be passed by two-thirds vote of each house and such necessity be stated in a separate section.

This section provides that acts passed by legislature become effective 90 days after the adjournment of the legislature, but provides that general appropriation laws take effect immediately upon their passage, and provides that with a two-thirds vote of each house the emergency acts can go into effect sooner than 90 days. This section does not preclude the legislature from fixing a longer period for laws to become effective (*State ex rel New Mexico State Bank v. Montoya,* 1916).

SECTION 24

Local or special laws. The legislature shall not pass local or special laws in any of the following cases: regulating county, precinct or district affairs; the jurisdiction and duties of justices of the peace, police magistrates and constables; the practice in courts of justice; the rate of interest on money; the punishment for crimes and misdemeanors; the assessment or collection of taxes or extending the time of collection thereof; the summoning and impaneling of jurors; the management of public schools;

the sale or mortgaging of real estate of minors or others under disability; the change of venue in civil or criminal cases. Nor in the following cases: granting divorces; laying out, opening, altering or working roads or highways, except as to state roads extending into more than one county, and military roads; vacating roads, town plats, streets, alleys or public grounds; locating or changing county seats, or changing county lines, exchanging or amending the charter of any city, town or village; the opening or conducting of any election or designating the place of voting; declaring any person of age; chartering or licensing ferries, toll bridges, toll roads, banks, insurance companies or loan and trust companies; remitting fines, penalties, forfeitures or taxes; or refunding money paid into the state treasury, or relinquishing, extending or extinguishing, in whole or in part, any indebtedness or liability of any person or corporation, to the state or any municipality therein; creating, increasing or decreasing fees, percentages or allowances of public officers; changing the laws of descent; granting to any corporation, association or individual the right to lay down railroad tracks or any special or exclusive privilege, immunity or franchise, or amending existing charters for such purpose; changing the rules of evidence in any trail or inquiry; the limitation of actions; giving effect to any informal or invalid deed, will or other instrument; exempting property from taxation; restoring to citizenship any person convicted of an infamous crime; the adoption or legitimizing of children; changing the name of persons or places; and the creation, extension or impairment of liens. In every other case where a general law can be made applicable, no special law shall be enacted.

This section forbids the legislature from enacting laws treating any political subdivision of the state or class of persons differently from any other. In short, "where a general law can be made applicable, no special law shall be enacted." A general law relates to a subject of a general nature, or it affects all the people of the state, or of a particular class (*State v. Atchison, T. & S. F. Railroad*, 1915; *City of Raton v. Sproule*, 1967); and it is only necessary that it be framed in general terms and operate on all objects of legislation distinguished by a reasonable classification (*Davy v. McNiell*, 1925). A special law is legislation written in terms which make it applicable only to named individuals, classes, or determinative situations (*Keiderling v. Sanchez*, 1977). Legislating against particular crimes (*State v. Foster*, 1922), or repeat offenses (*State v. Bejar*, Ct. App. 1985), or appropriations for projects in a particular county (*State ex rel Apodaca v. New Mexico Bd. of Education*, 1971) do not violate the special law prohibition.

SECTION 25

Validating unauthorized official acts; fines against officers, etc. No law shall be enacted legalizing the unauthorized or invalid act of any officer, remitting any fine, penalty or judgment against any office or validating any illegal use of public funds.

The legislature is forbidden to set aside the judgment against any public officials for crimes committed when in office. The power of pardon and reprieve is assigned to the governor by Article V § 6 of the constitution.

SECTION 26

Grant of franchise or privilege. The legislature shall not grant to any corporation or person, any rights, franchises, privileges, immunities or exemptions, which shall not, upon the same terms and under like conditions, inure equally to all persons or corporations; no exclusive right, franchise, privilege or immunity shall be granted by the legislature or any municipality in the state.

The purpose of this provision is similar to that of Section 24 of this article; it is to prevent unequal and partial legislation or action that favors certain groups or individuals (*State ex rel Interstate Stream Commission v. Reynolds*, 1963). Legislation which results in granting exclusive franchise or license by municipalities or executive agencies of the state (such as, public utility franchises, state park concessions, and motor carrier licenses) are generally upheld as not violating this section, when they are granted on the basis that the public interest is served by the regulation of the industry, and that all citizens are afforded an equal opportunity to receive a franchise; see for example *Gomez v. City of Las Vegas*, 1956.

SECTION 27

Extra or increased compensation for officers, contractors, etc. No law shall be enacted giving any extra compensation to any public officer, servant, agent or contractor after services are rendered or contract made; nor shall the compensation of any officer be increased or diminished during his term of office, except as otherwise provided in this constitution.

This section is intended to limit graft and undue influence on officers. The provision forbidding the change in compensation of officials during their term in office is designed to secure independence for these officials so that they can act without fear of losing compensation (*Dorman v. Sargent*, 1915).

SECTION 28

Appointment of present and former legislators to office; interest of legislators in contracts. No member of the legislature shall, during the term for which he was elected, be appointed to any civil office created, or the emoluments of which were increased during such term; nor shall any member of the legislature during the term for which he was elected not within one year thereafter, be interested directly or indirectly in any contract with the state or any municipality thereof, which was authorized by any law passed during such term.

This provision is concerned about the conflict of interest involved in serving in the legislature while receiving other compensation from the state, and is intended to prevent legislators, as a result of an act of the legislature of which they are members, from benefiting at the expense of the general welfare. A legislator who resigns from office is not removed from this ban. A civil office is one that was vested with the authority to operate by the legislature. These provisions are intended to take away, as far as possible, any improper bias in the vote of the representative, and secure for the constituents an assurance of his disinterestedness (*State ex rel. Anaya v. McBride*, 1975).

SECTION 29

Laws creating debts. No law authorizing indebtedness shall be enacted which does not provide for levying a tax sufficient to pay the interest, and for the payment at maturity of the principal.

The section is intended to prevent the legislature from issuing bonds for which the state cannot meet the obligation.

SECTION 30

Payments from treasury to be upon appropriations and warrant. Except interest or other payments on the public debt, money shall be paid out of the treasury only upon appropriations made by the legislature. No money shall be paid therefrom except upon warrant drawn by the proper officer. Every law making an appropriation shall distinctly specify the sum appropriated and the object to which it is to be applied.

The constitution gives the legislature the authority to lay taxes and appropriate the revenues of the state; this section establishes the mechanism for using state money to pay for those things appropriated for by the legislature and insures legislative control of the public treasury (*Gamble v. Velarde*, 1932; *State ex rel Constitutional Convention v. Evans*, 1969).

SECTION 31

Appropriations for charitable, educational, etc., purposes. No appropriation shall be made for charitable, educational or other benevolent purposes to any person, corporation, association, institution or community, not under the absolute control of the state, but the legislature may, in its discretion, make appropriations for the charitable institutions and hospitals, for the maintenance of which annual appropriations were made by the legislative assembly of nineteen hundred and nine.

This section allows the legislature to appropriate funds only to state agencies, and forbids all appropriations, even for benevolent purposes, to private persons, corporations, or associations. This limitation was modified somewhat by a 1995 amendment to Article 9 § 14.

SECTION 32

Remission of debts due state or municipalities. No obligation or liability of any person, association or corporation held or owned by or owing to the state, or any municipal corporation therein, shall ever be exchanged, transferred, remitted, released, postponed or in any way diminished by the legislature, nor shall any such obligation or liability be extinguished except by the payment thereof into the proper treasury, or by proper proceeding in court. Provided that the obligations created by Special Session Laws 1955, Chapter 5, running to the state or any of its agencies, remaining unpaid on the effective date of this amendment are void.

This provision is intended to prevent public officials from releasing debts justly owed to the state or its political subdivisions and to discourage collusion between public officials and private citizens. A 1958 amendment added the second sentence; it voided a 1955 act of the legislature (Laws 1955 [Special Session] chap. 5) which allowed the recovery of public assistance payments by claims against recipients' estates and liens against their real property.

SECTION 33

Prosecutions under repealed laws. No person shall be exempt from prosecution and punishment for any crime of offenses against any law of this state by reason of the subsequent repeal of such law.

Persons who violate a criminal statute, which is later repealed, are, nevertheless still answerable for their acts. The fact that a statute under which a defendant was charged was repealed after he was arrested, but before filing information, did not bar or abate the proceedings against the defendants (*State v. McAdams*, 1972). This section makes general application of the principle that underlies Section 25.

SECTION 34

Change of rights or procedure in pending cases. No act of the legislature shall affect the right or remedy of either party, or change the rules of evidence or procedure, in any pending case.

This provision insures the basic fairness required by due process of law. Persons cannot prepare a defense or pursue reasonable course in a suit at law if they must do so under changing rules. The supreme court has held that this section applies to rules of courts as well as statutes (*Marquez v. Wylie*, 1967), and to rules made by regulatory agencies created by the legislature (*Pineda v. Grande Drilling Corp.*, 1991). Where a case is pending when an amended statute is enacted, the old statute applies in the case (*US Life Title Ins. Co. v. Romero*, 1982).

SECTION 35

Power and procedure for impeachment and trial. The sole power of impeachment shall be vested in the house of representatives, and concurrence of a majority of all the members elected shall be necessary to the proper exercise thereof. All impeachments shall be tried by the senate. When sitting for that purpose the senators shall be under oath or affirmation to do justice according to the law and the evidence. When the governor or lieutenant governor is on trial, the chief justice of the supreme court shall preside. No person shall be convicted without the concurrence of two-thirds of the senators elected.

This section provides that public officials can be removed from office by the voting of a bill of impeachment by a majority of the members of the House of Representatives, and a trial in the Senate with conviction by a vote of a majority of the senators. Officers of the state appointed by the governor with the advice and consent of the Senate can be removed by the governor under the provisions of Article V § 5 regardless of whether he is subject to impeachment (*Ulrick v. Sanchez*, 1926).

SECTION 36

Officers subject to impeachment. All state officers and judges of the district court shall be liable to impeachment for crimes, misdemeanors and malfeasance in office and disqualification to hold any office of honor, trust or profit, or to vote under the laws of this state; but such officer or judge, whether convicted or acquitted shall, nevertheless, be liable to prosecution, trial, judgment, punishment or civil action, according to law. No officer shall exercise any powers or duties of his office after notice of his impeachment is served upon him until he is acquitted.

This section identifies the public officials who are liable to impeachment. It also sets limits on the effects of conviction by the Senate, and provides that whether convicted or not, the officials are still liable to prosecution or to civil action under the law. Finally, it forbids officers to exercise any power of their office after they are served with a notice of impeachment. Officers appointed by the governor are subject to removal by him, whether or not they may be impeached (*Ulrick v. Sanchez*, 1926).

SECTION 37

Railroad passes. It shall be unlawful for a member of the legislature to purchase or receive transportation over any railroad upon terms not open to the general public; and the violation of this section shall work a forfeiture of the office.

This provision reflects the power of the railroads in the western United States in the nineteenth century. Its primary purpose was to eliminate graft upon the part of legislators and relieve them of any feeling of obligation toward a railroad company because they possessed free passes. Prohibition of the use of railroad passes by other public officers is established in Article XX § 14.

SECTION 38

Monopolies. The legislature shall enact laws to prevent trusts, monopolies and combinations in restraint of trade.

The constitutional prohibition contained in this section is aimed at preventing such monopolies and combinations as would in effect do away with a free market, by practically destroying competition. A detailed explanation of purpose of this section is given in *Skaggs Drug Center v. General Electric Co.* (1957).

SECTION 39

"Bribery" and "solicitation" defined. Any member of the legislature who shall vote or use his influence for or against any matter pending in either house in consideration of any money, thing of value or promise thereof, shall be deemed guilty of bribery; and any member of the legislature or other person who shall directly or indirectly offer, give or promise any money, thing of value, privilege or personal advantage, to any member of the legislature to influence him to vote or work for or against any matter pending in either house; or any member of the legislature who shall solicit from any person or corporation any money, thing of value or personal advantage for his vote or influence as such member shall be deemed guilty of solicitation of bribery.

This section defines three activities involving legislators which are crimes: (1) a legislator voting for or influencing the outcome of pending legislation in consideration of money, a thing of value, or the promise thereof is guilty of bribery; (2) a legislator or any other person who offers, gives, or promises anything of value to a member of the legislature to vote or work for or against pending legislation is guilty of solicitation of bribery; and (3) any legislator who asks for anything of value for his vote or influence is guilty of solicitation of bribery. An indictment under this section need not allege that the matter at hand was pending before the legislature (*State v. Lucero*, 1915).

SECTION 40

Penalty for bribery. Any person convicted of any of the offenses mentioned in Sections thirty-seven and thirty-nine hereof, shall be deemed guilty of a felony and upon conviction shall be punished by fine of not more than one thousand dollars [($1,000)] or by imprisonment in the penitentiary for not less than one nor more than five years.

This section declares violations of Article XX §§37 and 39 to be a felony and sets the criminal punishment for such acts.

SECTION 41

Compelling testimony in bribery cases. Any person may be compelled to testify in any lawful investigation or judicial proceeding against another charged with bribery or solicitation of bribery as defined herein, and shall not be permitted to withhold his testimony on the ground that it might incriminate or subject him to public infamy; but such testimony shall not be used against him in any judicial proceeding against him except for perjury in giving such testimony.

This section provides that persons may be compelled to give testimony in investigations and proceedings against someone charged with bribery or solicitation of bribery and provides limited immunity for them, in that such testimony cannot be used as evidence to convict them of these crimes. The constitutional guarantee against compulsory self-incrimination is provided in Article II § 15.

SECTION 42

Hearings on confirmation of gubernatorial appointments. The senate, in exercising its advice and consent responsibilities over gubernatorial appointments, may by resolution designate the members of an appropriate standing committee to operate as an interim committee during the interim between legislative sessions for the purpose of conducting hearings and taking testimony on the confirmation or rejection of gubernatorial appointments. Recommendations of the committee shall be submitted to the senate for action at the next succeeding legislative session. Members of such committee shall be paid per diem and mileage for attendance at such hearings at the same rates as legislators are paid for attendance at joint legislative interim committee meetings. The governor shall submit all appointments requiring senate confirmation to such committee within thirty days after the date of appointment.

This section makes provisions for interim committee hearings to consider the confirmation of gubernatorial appointments, made outside of the legislative session. A 1986 amendment added this section to the constitution.

The conclusion of Article IV, entitled "Apportionment" and relating to the apportionment of legislative districts, was repealed by a 1949 amendment, which set a new standard for apportionment in Article IV § 3.

Failed Proposed Amendments to This Article

A 1965 amendment, that would have added a section to this article providing for the appointment of a legislative auditor, was rejected by the people. A second 1965 amendment, that would have added a section to this article providing for the weighing of legislative votes in order to secure equal protection of the laws for the people of New Mexico, was also rejected by the people.

Article V

Executive Department

SECTION 1

Composition of department; terms of office of members; residing and maintaining records at seat of government. The executive department shall consist of a governor, lieutenant governor, secretary of state, state auditor, state treasurer, attorney general and commissioner of public lands, who shall, unless otherwise provided in the constitution of New Mexico, be elected for terms of four years beginning on the first day of January next after their election. The governor and lieutenant governor shall be elected jointly by the casting by each single voter of a single vote applicable to both offices.

Such officers shall, after having served two terms in a state office be ineligible to hold that state office until one full term has intervened.

The officers of the executive department, except the lieutenant governor, shall during their terms of office, reside and keep the public records, books, papers and seals of office at the seat of government.

Upon the adoption of this amendment by the people, the terms provided for in this section shall apply to those officers elected at the general election in 1990 and all state executive officers elected thereafter.

The constitution provides for a plural executive, with the executive authority of the state divided among six officials (the lieutenant governor exercises no separate executive authority, but rather exercises the authority of the governor as provided in Section 7 of this article). This section enumerates the executive offices that constitute the executive department, requires that the governor and lieutenant governor be elected as a team, establishes the terms of office for each, and requires these officers, except the lieutenant governor, to reside and maintain offices in the state capital.

Throughout the constitution, the secretary of state is assigned several functions, Article IV §§ 1, 8, 22; Article V §§ 2, 7, 10. The secretary of state has no inherent powers, but only those assigned by the constitution or statute (*Weldon v. Sanders*, 1982). In order to avail themselves of the federal land grant provided by the Enabling Act, the constitutional framers created the office of the commissioner of public lands (*State ex rel Evans v. Field*, 1921). The duties of the office are described in Article XIII, § 2.

No common law powers reside in the office of attorney general (*State ex rel Attorney General v. Reese*, 1967). The only constitutionally defined duty of the attorney general is to be the attorney for the state corporations commission, Article XI § 4.

The constitution does not define the duties of the state auditor or state treasurer. The supreme court, however, has determined that the state auditor is a completely independent representative of the people, accountable to no one else, with the power, duty, and authority to examine and pass upon the activities of state officers and agencies receiving and expending public funds (*Thompson v. Legislative Audit Commission*, 1968).

This section was amended in 1914, 1958, 1962, 1970, and 1986. These amendments changed the officers named in this section and the lengths of their terms, and provided for the joint election of the governor and lieutenant governor.

SECTION 2

Canvass of elections; tie votes. The returns of every election for state officers shall be sealed up and transmitted to the secretary of state, who, with the governor and chief justice, shall constitute the state canvassing board which shall canvass and declare the result of the election. The joint candidates having the highest number of votes cast for governor and lieutenant governor and the persons having the highest number of votes for any other office, as shown by said returns, shall be declared duly elected. If two or more have an equal, and the highest, number of votes for the same office or offices, one of them, or any two for whom joint votes were cast for governor and lieutenant governor respectively, shall be chosen therefor by the legislature on joint ballot.

This section provides for canvassing and certifying the result of elections of officers elected statewide. The canvassers have the power only to pass on the genuineness of the returns they receive, not to determine if illegal or fraudulent votes have been cast. This presents a judicial question to be resolved by the courts (*Chavez v. Hockenhull,* 1934). The section also provides that ties in elections for state officers shall be resolved by a vote of the legislature.

SECTION 3

Qualifications of executive officers. No person shall be eligible to any office specified in Section One, hereof, unless he be a citizen of the United States, at least thirty years of age, not unless he shall have resided continuously in New Mexico for five years next preceding his election; nor to the office of attorney general, unless he be a licensed attorney of the supreme court of New Mexico in good standing; not to the office of superintendent of public instruction unless he be a trained and experienced educator.

This section establishes the qualifications for the offices specified in Section 1 of this article. It does not reflect the change in Section 1 made by a 1958 amendment that removed the office of superintendent of public instruction as an elected officer. The courts have interpreted this section to be read together with Article VII § 2, which also sets out qualifications for holding elective office and requires that candidates be a qualified elector in New Mexico (*State ex rel. Chavez v. Evens,* 1968).

SECTION 4

Governor's executive power; commander of militia. The supreme executive power of the state shall be vested in the governor, who shall take care that the laws be faithfully executed. He shall be commander in chief of the military forces of the state, except when they are called into the service of the United States. He shall have power to call out the militia to preserve the public peace, execute the laws, suppress insurrection and repel invasion.

This section initiates the enumeration of the executive powers of the governor by vesting the supreme executive power in the governor, with the responsibility to see that the laws are administered and followed. It also makes the governor commander of the state militia, and provides the authority to use the militia in the situations listed. The governor is the sole judge of the facts as to what conditions call for the use of the militia (*State ex rel. Charlton v. French,* 1940). When the governor calls out the militia to quell insurrection, those military forces have power that supersedes that of civil authorities (*State ex rel. Roberts v. Swope,* 1933).

SECTION 5

Governor's appointive and removal power; interim appointees. The governor shall nominate and, by and with the consent of the senate, appoint all officers whose appointment or election is not otherwise provided for and may remove any officer appointed by him unless otherwise provided by law. Should a vacancy occur in any state office, except lieutenant governor and member of the legislature, the governor shall fill such office by appointment, and such appointee shall hold office until the next general election, when his successor shall be chosen for the unexpired term.

The governor has authority to remove those officers he appoints, including those appointed by and with the consent of the senate (*State ex rel. Ulrick v. Sanchez*, 1926; *State ex rel Duran v. Anaya*, 1985). The governor may remove policy-making appointees for political reasons, without hearing or notice; however, a contrary rule may apply to non-policy-making officers (*Mitchell v. King*, 1976; this decision was made before the 1988 amendment that added the phrase "unless otherwise provided by law" and "for incompetency, neglect of duty or malfeasance in office" to the first sentence).

SECTION 6

Governor's power to pardon and reprieve. Subject to such regulations as may be prescribed by law, the governor shall have power to grant reprieves and pardons, after conviction for all offenses except treason and in cases of impeachment.

This provision is self-executing and requires no enabling legislation, and in exercising it the governor is unrestrained by any considerations beyond his conscience, wisdom, and sense of public duty (*Ex parte Bustillos*, 1920). But a statute authorizing district courts to suspend sentences does not violate this section (*Ex parte Bates*, 1915). The governor's power of pardon extends to convictions for contempt of court (*Ex parte Magee*, 1925; and *State v. Magee Publishing Co.*, 1924). A gubernatorial pardon of a life sentence under the habitual criminal act does not deny the courts authority to impose the same sentence if subsequent to the pardon the prisoner commits another felony (*Shankle v. Woodruff*, 1958).

SECTION 7

Succession to governorship. If at the time fixed for the beginning of the term of governor, the governor-elect shall have died, the lieutenant governor-elect shall become governor. If a governor shall not have been chosen before the time fixed for the beginning of his term, or if the governor-elect shall have failed to qualify, the lieutenant governor-elect shall act as governor until a governor shall have qualified; and the legislature may by law provide for the case wherein neither a governor-elect nor a lieutenant governor-elect shall have qualified, declaring who shall then act as governor, or the manner in which one who is to act shall be selected, and such person shall act accordingly until a governor or lieutenant governor shall have qualified.

If after the governor-elect has qualified a vacancy occurs in the office of governor, the lieutenant governor shall succeed to that office, and to all the powers, duties and emoluments thereof, provided he has by that time qualified for the office of lieutenant governor. In case the governor is absent from the state, or in case he is for any reason unable to perform the duties of governor, and, in case there is no secretary of state, then the president pro tempore of the senate, or in case there is no president pro tempore of the senate, or he is for any reason unable to perform the duties of governor, then the speaker of the house shall succeed to the office of governor, or act as governor as hereinbefore provided.

The various detailed provisions for succession to the governorship have never been needed. Lieutenant governors have, however, made extensive use of the provision that when the governor is absent from the state, "the lieutenant governor shall act as governor, with all the powers, duties and emoluments of that office." A 1948 amendment rewrote this section, adding the first paragraph, and made numerous changes in the second paragraph.

SECTION 8

Lieutenant governor to be president of senate. The lieutenant governor shall be president of the senate, but shall vote only when the senate is equally divided.

The only constitutional duty of the lieutenant governor beyond succession responsibilities is to serve as president of the Senate. The lieutenant governor executes delegated duties assigned by the governor; the constitutionality of that practice has not been challenged in court, but has been upheld as constitutional by the Attorney General (*Opinion of Attorney General* No. 71-15, 1971).

SECTION 9

Public accounts and reports. Each officer of the executive department and of the public institutions of the state shall keep an account of all moneys received by him and make reports thereof to the governor under oath, annually, and at such other times as the governor may require, and shall, at least thirty days preceding each regular session of the legislature, make a full and complete report to the governor, who shall transmit the same to the legislature.

This provision seeks to insure accountability in the expenditure of public funds. State higher education institutions that receive federal funds must make a full report on these funds to the governor, who must make the reports available to the legislature. The legislature, however, may not limit or control the use of these funds; that power rests with the board of regents, subject to applicable law (*State ex rel Sego v. Kirkpatrick*, 1974).

SECTION 10

State seal. There shall be a state seal which shall be called the "Great Seal of the State of New Mexico," and shall be kept by the secretary of state.

This seal is imprinted on acts of the legislature signed into law, gubernatorial proclamations, and other official documents of state. Removal of the seal from the state is considered to be a violation of law (*Opinion of Attorney General* No. 71-15, 1955-56).

SECTION 11

Commissions. All commissions shall issue in the name of the state, be signed by the governor and attested by the secretary of state, who shall affix the state seal thereto.

An appointment to office is complete upon delivery of a signed and sealed commission; that commission is prima facie evidence that the person holding it is lawfully entitled to the office (*Conklin v. Cunningham*, 1894).

SECTION 12

Compensation of executive officers. The annual compensation to be paid to the officers mentioned in Section One of this article shall be as follows: governor, five thousand dollars; secretary of state, three thousand dollars; state auditor, three thousand dollars; state treasurer, three thousand dollars; attorney general, four thousand dollars; superintendent of public instruction, three thousand dollars; and commissioner of public lands, three thousand dollars; which compensation shall be paid to the respective officers in equal quarterly payments.

The lieutenant governor shall receive ten dollars per diem while acting as presiding officer of the senate, and mileage at the same rate as a state senator.

The salaries of the executive officers are set by this provision with provision for the legislature to increase or decrease them (see 8-1-1 NMSA 1978 for the current salary schedule). The legislature has provided a salary for the lieutenant governor. An amendment proposed in 1961 that would have removed the specific dollar amounts for salaries listed in this section was rejected by the people.

SECTION 13

Residence of public officers. All district and municipal officers, county, county commissioners, school board members and municipal governing body members shall be residents of the political subdivision or district from which they are elected or for which they are appointed.

Counties, school districts and municipalities may be divided by their governing bodies into districts composed of populations as nearly equal as practicable for the purpose of electing the members of the respective governing bodies.

The reason for restricting candidates to residents of the district from which they seek election is to insure that elected representatives have a knowledge of the problems and needs of the district (*State ex rel. Rudolph v. Lujan*, 1973). Doubt concerning residence is to be resolved in favor of permanency of residence in the precinct wherein the candidate casts his vote (*State ex rel. Magee v. Williams*, 1953). This section was amended in 1960 to provide for dividing counties into commission districts. A 1986 amendment repealed this section and adopted the present wording.

SECTION 14

State highway commission. There is created a "state highway commission." The members of the state highway commission shall be appointed, shall have power and shall perform such duties as may be provided by law. Notwithstanding the provisions of Article 5, Section 5, of the constitution of New Mexico, state highway commissioners shall only be removed as provided by law.

This section was rewritten by amendments in 1949, 1955, and 1967; proposed amendments failed in 1959, 1961, 1963, and 1994. The 1955 amendment gave the state highway commission extensive powers to determine all matters relating to highway and bridge policy and the expenditure of state money for the construction and maintenance of public roads and bridges (*State ex rel State Highway Commission v. City of Albuquerque*, 1960). The 1967 amendment limits the commission's duties to those provided by law. Individual members of the commission, while participating in commission meetings, enjoy all the privileges and immunities of the body as a whole (*Adams v. Tatsch*, 1961).

Article VI

Judicial Department

SECTION 1

Judicial power vested. The judicial power of the state shall be vested in the senate when sitting as a court of impeachment, a supreme court, a court of appeals, district courts, probate courts, magistrate courts and such other courts inferior to the district courts as may be established by law from time to time in any district, county or municipality of the state.

The legislature is limited to creating only those courts provided by this section (*State ex rel Hovey Concrete Products Co. v. Mechem,* 1957). Only the legislature, not political subdivisions, may establish the inferior courts allowed by this section (*Stout v. City of Clovis,* 1932). The legislature may not provide for direct appeal to the supreme court from courts inferior to the district court (*State v. Eychanter,* 1937).

The power to determine the rights and liabilities between individuals rests in the courts alone; however, the legislature may confer quasi-judicial powers on administrative boards for the protection of the rights of the public (*State ex rel Hovey Concrete Products Co. v. Mechem,* 1957). The courts are limited to the exercise of judicial power and may not review or interfere with the acts of the legislative or executive departments, except when those acts plainly violate the constitution (*State ex rel Gomez v. Campbell,* 1965), nor is the duty of the courts to consider the wisdom of legislation, but only to ascertain and declare the intentions of the legislature and give effect to that intent as expressed in the laws (*Raton Public Service Commission v. Hobbes*, 1966).

An Indian may, as any other person may, invoke the jurisdiction of the state courts to protect his legal rights in matters not related to federal law or tribal relations (*Paiz v. Hughes*, 1966).

A 1965 amendment added the words "a court of appeals" after "a supreme court." In 1966, an amendment substituted "magistrate courts" for "justice of the peace" after "probate courts," inserted "district," preceding "county or municipality," and deleted "including juvenile courts" at the end of the section.

SECTION 2

Supreme court; appellate jurisdiction. Appeals from a judgment of the district court imposing a sentence of death or life imprisonment shall be taken directly to the supreme court. In all other cases, criminal and civil, the supreme court shall exercise appellate jurisdiction as may be provided by law; provided that an aggrieved party shall have an absolute right to one appeal.

This section provides a constitutional right of one appeal to the aggrieved party in a lawsuit. An aggrieved party is the one whose interests are adversely affected by an order of the court (*State v. Castillo*, 1980). The state may be the aggrieved party when it makes a claim that a trial court made a disposition in a criminal case contrary to law (*State v. Santillanes*, 1980), and where the trial court refuses to enforce a state sentencing statute on the basis it is unconstitutional; however, the state does not have an absolute right to appeal in every case where it may feel aggrieved (*State v. Aguilar*, 1981).

Under this section, as amended in 1965, courts can no longer deny appeals of convictions of criminal contempt committed in the presence of the court (*State v. Watson*, 1971).

A 1965 amendment added the provision for direct appeal to the supreme court in certain criminal cases, and for other appeals to the supreme court as provided by law, and the guarantee of an absolute right to one appeal.

SECTION 3

Supreme court; original jurisdiction; supervisory control; extraordinary writs. The supreme court shall have original jurisdiction in quo warranto and mandamus against all state officers, boards and commissions, and shall have a superintending control over all inferior courts; it shall also have power to issue writs of mandamus, error, prohibition, habeas corpus, certiorari, injunction and all other writs necessary or proper for the complete exercise of its jurisdiction and to hear and determine the same. Such writs may be issued by direction of the court or by any justice thereof.

> Each justice shall have power to issue writs of habeas corpus upon petition by or on behalf of a person held in actual custody, and make such writs returnable before himself or before the supreme court, or before any of the district courts or any judge thereof.

The supreme court's power of superintending control is the power to control the ordinary litigation in inferior courts, as exercised at common law by the Court of the King's Bench and by use of the writs specifically mentioned in the constitution (*State v. Roy,* 1936); that power is distinct from appellate and original jurisdiction and will be exercised if the remedy by appeal is wholly or substantially inadequate, or its exercise will prevent irreparable mischief, extraordinary hardships, or costly delays (*State ex rel DuBois v. Ryan,* 1973). Therefore, superintending control will not be invoked merely to perform the office of appeal (*State Game Commission v. Tackett,* 1962).

The grant of superintending control gives the supreme court ultimate authority over the administrative matters of the state's courts (*Russillo v. Scarborough,* 1989). Furthermore, it provides the supreme court with the inherent power to regulate all pleadings, practice, and procedure affecting the judicial branch of government; therefore, the legislature lacks the power to prescribe by statute rules of evidence and procedure, nor can it provide for *de novo* hearing for appeal from the district court (*Ammerman v. Hubbard Broadcasting, Inc.,* 1976).

The purpose of the supreme courts quo warranto power is to ascertain whether a public officer is constitutionally and legally authorized to perform any act in or exercise any function of the office to which he lays claim (*State ex rel Anaya v. McBride,* 1975). The court can use writs of mandamus to compel the performance of statutory duties by all state officers, boards, and commissions (*State ex rel. Sego v. Kirkpatrick,* 1974). Both the supreme court and district courts have original jurisdiction in mandamus and quo warranto petitions against all public officials in all cases; therefore, the supreme court will decline jurisdiction unless it is necessary, and in all cases brought at the instance of a private suitor (*State ex rel. Owen v. Van Stone,* 1912).

This section gives the supreme court original jurisdiction in habeas corpus proceedings (*Payton v. Nord,* 1968), but in the absence of controlling necessity, this power will be exercised by the district courts, which have concurrent jurisdiction (*Ex Parte Nabors,* 1928).

SECTION 4

> **Supreme court; number, term and election of justices; chief justice.** The supreme court of the state shall consist of at least five justices who shall be chosen as provided in this constitution. One of the justices shall be selected as chief justice as provided by law.

For the power of the legislature to increase the number of justices to five see Article VI § 10; as to vacancy in the supreme court see Article XX § 4. This section and Article VI § 10 made clear the intent for staggered terms of office for the office of supreme court judge (*State ex rel Swope v. Mechem*, 1954). This section was amended by a 1988 amendment that rewrote the former section addressing the same matters. An amendment proposed in 1982 that would have provided the legislature with the authority to increase the size of the court to more than five justices was rejected by the voters.

SECTION 5

Supreme court; quorum; majority concurring in judgments. A majority of the justices of the supreme court shall be necessary to constitute a quorum for the transaction of business, and a majority of the justices must concur in any judgment of the court.

This provision allows the supreme court to decide cases sitting in panels of three; however, if the three justices on the panel do not concur in the decision, it must be reconsidered by the whole court in order to have a majority agree with the opinion of the court.

SECTION 6

Supreme court; absent or disqualified justice. When a justice of the supreme court shall be interested in any case, or be absent, or incapacitated, the remaining justices of the court may, in their discretion, call in any district judge of the state to act as a justice of the court.

Article VI § 18 provides authority to the chief justice to designate a judge of the court of appeals to act as a supreme court justice.

SECTION 7

Supreme court; terms, sessions and recesses. The supreme court shall hold one term each year, commencing on the second Wednesday in January, and shall be at all times in session at the seat of government; provided, that the court may, from time to time, take such recess as in its judgment may be proper.

The supreme court has the authority to set aside an order of dismissal two days after it was issued, because both actions were in the same term, and the court has full control of judgments entered during a single term (*Henderson v. Dreyfus*, 1920).

SECTION 8

Supreme court; qualifications of justices. No person shall be qualified to hold office of justice of the supreme court unless that person is at least thirty-five years old and has been in the actual practice of law for at least ten years preceding that person's assumption of office and has resided in this state for at least three years immediately preceding that person's assumption of office. The actual practice of law shall include a lawyer's service upon the bench in any court of the state. The increased qualifications provided by this 1988 amendment shall not apply to justices and judges serving at the time this amendment passes or elected at the general election in 1988.

This section that sets the qualification of those the people can elect to the supreme court was changed significantly by a 1988 amendment. Article VI § 19 provides that supreme court justices are ineligible for nomination and election to nonjudicial office.

SECTION 9

Supreme court; officers. The supreme court may appoint and remove at pleasure its reporter, bailiff, clerk and such other officers and assistants as may be prescribed by law.

The legislature made provision for the employment of a law clerk by each justice (34-2-7 NMSA 1978).

SECTION 10

Supreme court; additional justices. After the publication of the census of the United States in the year nineteen hundred and twenty; the legislature shall have power to increase the number of justices of the supreme court to five; provided, however, that no more than two of said justices shall be elected at one time, except to fill vacancy.

In 1929, the legislature increased the number of justices of the supreme court from three to five (34-2-1 NMSA 1978).

SECTION 11

Supreme court; salary of justices. The justices of the supreme court shall each receive such salary as may hereafter be fixed by law.

This section originally set the salary of the justices at $6,000. A 1953 amendment provided for setting the salary by law, which is done by 34-2-2 NMSA 1978.

The salary of judges of constitutional courts is not subject to the constitutional prohibition against the increase in compensation for public officials during the term for which they were elected (*Opinion of the Attorney General* No. 79-27, 1979).

SECTION 12

Judicial districts; election and terms of district judges. The state shall be divided into judicial districts as may be provided by law. One or more judges shall be chosen for each district as provided in this constitution.

A 1988 amendment replaced constitutional enumeration of judicial districts with provision for legislative designation of the districts and number of judges in a district. Article VI §§ 16 and 25 also address this issue. There are currently thirteen districts (see 34-6-1 NMSA 1978). An amendment proposed in 1982 that would have changed the constitutionally designated number of judicial districts from eight to thirteen was rejected by the people.

SECTION 13

District courts; jurisdiction and terms. The district court shall have original jurisdiction in all matters and causes not excepted in this constitution, and such jurisdiction of special cases and proceedings as may be conferred by law, and appellate jurisdiction of all cases originating in inferior courts and tribunals in their respective districts, and supervisory control over the same. The district courts, on any judge thereof, shall have power to issue writs of habeas corpus, mandamus, injunction, quo warranto, certiorari, prohibition and all other writs, remedial or otherwise in the exercise of their jurisdiction; provided that no such writs shall issue directed to judges of equal or superior jurisdiction. The district courts shall have the power of naturalization in accordance with the laws of the United States. Until otherwise provided by law, at least two terms of the district court shall be held annually in each county, at the county seat.

The district courts are the state's courts of general jurisdiction (*Sanchez v. Attorney General*, 1979); and are courts of original jurisdiction for equity cases (*Durham v. Rasco*, 1924).

The district courts have sole and exclusive jurisdiction for the trial of felony charges (*State v. Garcia*, 1979); the legislature may not assign authority to accept felony guilty pleas to trial courts inferior to the district courts (*State v. Klantcheck*, 1955). Formerly called justice of the peace courts, the state's limited jurisdiction trial courts are now reorganized as magistrate courts. Misdemeanor charges linked to felony charges must be tried in district court (*State v. Muise*, 1985).

The district courts have de novo appellate jurisdiction over decisions of inferior trial courts (*Lea County State Bank v. McCaskey Register Co.*, 1935). In de novo appeals to district court, the court is limited to the amount of damages it can award by the maximum award allowed in the limited jurisdiction court (*Sanchez v. Reilly*, 1950).

The legislative creation of administrative hearing and licensing boards does not contravene this section (*Fischer v. Rakagis*, 1955). The statutory requirement that parties exhaust administrative remedies before resorting to the courts does not violate the general original jurisdiction of the district courts (*Southwest Public Service Co. v. Artesia Alfalfa Growers' Association*, 1960). The question of jurisdiction between the courts and administrative agencies is settled by the legal doctrine of comity, and depends on whether the questions presented are exclusively factual issues within the peculiar expertise of the commission or if statutory interpretation or issues of law are significant, and specific legislative declarations that common-law remedies are unimpaired are uniformly respected when primary jurisdiction questions arise (*O'Hare v. Valley Utility, Inc.*, 1976). The supreme court and district court have concurrent jurisdiction in habeas corpus cases (*Ex parte Nabors*, 1928).

SECTION 14

District court; qualifications and residence requirement of judges. The qualifications of the district judges shall be the same as those of justices of the supreme court except that district judges shall have been in the actual practice of law for at least six years preceding assumption of office. Each district judge shall reside in the district for which the judge was elected or appointed. The increased qualifications provided by this 1988 amendment shall not apply to district judges serving at the time this amendment passes or elected in the general election in 1988.

The requirement that a qualified judge must have practiced law and resided in New Mexico for a specific number of years refers to the years immediately preceding election or appointment (*Hannett v. Jones*, 1986). A 1988 amendment rewrote this section to provide these qualifications for district judges; the requirements were formerly the same as for supreme court justices. A 1982 amendment proposing the appointment, rather than the election, of district judges was rejected by the people.

SECTION 15

District court; judges pro tempore. A. Any district judge may hold district court in any county at the request of the judge of such district.

B. Whenever the public business may require, the chief justice of the supreme court shall designate any district judge of the state, or any justice of the supreme court when no district judge may be available within a reasonable time, to hold court in any district, and two or more judges may sit in any district or county separately at the same time.
C. If any district judge is disqualified from hearing any cause or is unable to expeditiously dispose of any cause in the district, the chief justice of the supreme court may designate any retired New Mexico district judge, court of appeals judge or supreme court justice, with said designees' consent, to hear and determine the cause and to act as judge pro tempore therein.
D. If any judge shall be disqualified from hearing any cause in the district, the parties to such cause, or their attorneys of record, may select some member of the bar to hear and determine said cause and act as judge protempore therein.

A district judge may hold court in a district other than his own at the request of a judge of that district (*Massengill v. City of Clovis*, 1928). A judge lawfully sitting in a district other than his has jurisdiction in all matters requiring action during the period of his designation, whether or not they were pending in court at the time the judge's assistance was requested (*State v. Reed*, 1951); therefore, a visiting judge may render default judgment (*Hoffman v. White*, 1932), and sign a bill of exception (*State Bank v. McNew*, 1927).

Whenever public good demands, it becomes the mandatory duty of the chief justice to designate a district judge to hold court in any district of the state which requires another judge, and if no judge is available in a reasonable length of time, he may designate a supreme court justice (*State ex rel Sedillo v. Anderson*, 1949; *State ex rel Vigil v. Reese*, 1981). Designation by the chief justice of a district judge to hold court in another district vests the designated judge with the same power possessed by the regular judge of the district (*Ravany v. Equitable Life Assurance Society of United States*, 1920).

A 1938 amendment of this section made provision for a supreme court justice to hold court in a district where no district judge would be available within a reasonable length of time. A 1978 amendment added the subsection designations to this section.

SECTION 16

District court; additional judges; redistricting. The legislature may increase the number of district judges in any judicial district, and they shall be elected or appointed as other district judges for that district. At any session after the publication of the census of the United States in the year nineteen hundred and twenty; the legislature may rearrange the districts of the state, increase the number thereof, and make provisions for a district judge for any additional district.

This section should be read in conjunction with Article VI § 12. A 1988 amendment added "or appointed as other district judges for the district."

SECTION 17

District court; judges' compensation. The legislature shall provide by law for the compensation of the judges of the district courts.

This section was amended in 1953 to provide for the compensation of district judges by statute, and replaced a section that designated a specific amount for an annual salary. Compensation for district judges is provided for in 34-6-3 NMSA 1978.

SECTION 18

Disqualification of judges or magistrates. No justice or magistrate of any court shall, except by consent of all parties, sit in any cause in which either of the parties are related to him by affinity or consanguinity within the degree of first cousin, or in which he was counsel, or in the trial of which he presided in any inferior court, or in which he has an interest.

This section is to protect litigants' rights to a fair and impartial trial by an impartial and unbiased tribunal (*State ex rel. Bardacke v. Welsh*, 1985).

The New Mexico Code of Judicial Conduct establishes an objective standard for guiding judges in disqualifying themselves, beyond the standards set in the constitution (*State ex rel. Bardacke v. Walsh*, 1985). The interest necessary to disqualify a judge must be a present pecuniary interest in the result, or actual bias or prejudice, and not some indirect, remote, speculative, theoretical, or possible interest (*State ex rel. Anaya v. Scarborough*, 1966). The state as a party in a criminal case is entitled to file an affidavit of disqualification of a district judge (*State ex rel Tittmann v. Hay*, 1936).

A 1966 amendment substituted "justice, judge or magistrate of any court" for "judge of any court nor justice of the peace."

SECTION 19

Ineligibility of justices or judges for nonjudicial offices. No justice of the supreme court, judge of the court of appeals, judge of the district court or judge of a metropolitan court, while serving, shall be nominated, appointed or elected to any other office in this state except a judicial office.

This section intends to set judges apart from the "political branches" of government by disallowing them from campaigning for offices in those branches.

A 1988 amendment substituted the present provision for the former provision which read, "No judge of the supreme court or district court shall be nominated or elected to any other than a judicial office in this state."

SECTION 20

Style of writs and processes. All writs and process shall issue, and all prosecution shall be conducted in the name of "The State of New Mexico."

This section indicates that in legal proceedings and papers the state shall be known as "The State of New Mexico." This is in contrast with some other states, which use the designations "The Commonwealth of . . ." or "The People of . . ."

SECTION 21

Judges as conservators of the peace; preliminary examinations in criminal cases. Justices of the supreme court in the state, and district judges and magistrates, in their respective jurisdictions, shall be conservators of the peace. District judges and other judges or magistrates designated by law may hold preliminary examinations in criminal cases.

This section provides that judges of the state's limited jurisdiction courts can preside over such preliminary matters as initial pleas, providing for autopsies, setting bail, and the disposition of arrests for driving while intoxicated (*State v. Rue*, 1963). Nonresident judges who sit at the request of a resident judge are vested with all of the latter's powers, including that of holding preliminary hearings (*State v. Encinias*, 1949). A 1966 amendment changed the wording of this section to take into account the abolition of justice of the peace courts and the creation of magistrate courts.

SECTION 22

County clerk as district and probate court clerk. Unless otherwise provided by law, a county clerk shall be elected in each county who shall, in the county for which he is elected perform all the duties not performed by the clerks of the district courts and clerks of the probate courts.

A transcript of judgment may properly be certified by a county clerk unless a statutory change of designation has been made (*Cannon v. First National Bank*, 1930). Statutes now provide for the appointment of a clerk for each county of a judicial district and deputy clerks (see 34-6-19 NMSA 1978).

SECTION 23

Probate court. A probate court is hereby established for each county, which shall be a court of record, and, until otherwise provided by law, shall have the same jurisdiction as heretofore exercised by the probate courts of New Mexico and shall also have jurisdiction to determine heirship with respect to real property in all proceedings for the administration of decedents' estates. The legislature shall have power from time to time to confer upon the probate court in any county in this state jurisdiction to determine heirship in all probate proceedings, and shall have power also from time to time to confer upon the probate court in any county in this state general civil jurisdiction coextensive with the county; provided, however, that such court shall not have jurisdiction in civil causes in which the matter in controversy shall exceed in value three thousand dollars ($3,000.00) exclusive of interest and cost; nor in any action for malicious prosecution, slander and libel; nor in any action against officers for misconduct in office; nor in any action for the specific performance of contracts for the sale of real estate; nor in any action for the possession of land; nor in any matter wherein the title or boundaries of land may be in dispute or drawn in question, except as title to real property may be affected by the determination of heirship; nor to grant writs of injunction, habeas corpus or extraordinary writs. Jurisdiction may be conferred upon the judges of said court to act as examining and committing magistrates in criminal cases, and upon said courts for the trial of misdemeanors in which the punishment cannot be imprisonment in the penitentiary, or in which the fine cannot be in excess of one thousand dollars ($1,000). A jury for the trial of such cases shall consist of six men. The legislature shall prescribe the qualifications and fix the compensation of probate judges.

The phrase "until otherwise provided by law" means that the legislature has power to modify or alter jurisdiction of probate courts; included within this grant is the power to confer concurrent probate jurisdiction upon district courts (*In re Will of Hickok*, 1956). Probate courts have no jurisdiction to try or determine title to either real or personal property as between an estate or heirs and devises on one hand and strangers to the state on the other, the district court retains jurisdiction in such matters (*Conley v. Quinn*, 1954).

The general authority of the probate courts is defined in the Probate Code, Chapter 45 NMSA 1978. A 1949 amendment revised this section to provide the probate courts with jurisdiction to determine the heirship of real property in the administration of estates, assign the legislature with the authority to prescribe the qualifications and fix the compensation of probate judges, and to delete a provision relating to transfer of cases in which the probate judge was disqualified.

SECTION 24

District attorneys. There shall be a district attorney for each judicial district, who shall be learned in the law, and who shall have been a resident of New Mexico for three years next prior to his election, shall be elected for a term of four years and shall perform such duties and receive such salary as may be prescribed by law.

The legislature shall have the power to provide for the election of additional district attorneys in any judicial district and to designate the counties therein for which the district attorneys shall serve; but no district attorney shall be elected for any district of which he is not a resident.

The phrase "learned in the law" is synonymous for "licensed attorney" (*State ex rel Chavez v. Evans*, 1968). The district attorney is a judicial officer in the sense in which those words are used in law relating to bribery of officers (*State v. Collins*, 1922). The attorney general and district attorneys may appear as relators on the state's behalf (*State ex rel McCulloh v. Polhemur*, 1947), and file suits on the state's behalf to recover salary improperly paid (*State ex rel Attorney General v. Reese*, 1967). District Attorneys may not exact extra compensation for any legal service rendered to the county commissioners (*Hanagan v. Board of County Commissioners*, 1958).

SECTION 25

Judicial districts designated; new counties to be allocated to districts.

The state shall be divided into eight judicial districts, as follows:

First District. The counties of Santa Fe, Rio Arriba and San Juan.

Second District. The counties of Bernalillo, McKinley and Sandoval.

Third District. The counties of Doña Ana, Otero, Lincoln and Torrance.

Fourth District. The counties of San Miguel, Mora and Guadalupe.

Fifth District. The counties of Eddy, Chaves, Roosevelt and Curry.

Sixth District. The counties of Grant and Luna.

Seventh District. The counties of Socorro, Valencia and Sierra.

Eighth District. The counties of Taos, Colfax, Union and Quay.

In case of the creation of new counties the legislature shall have power to attach them to any contiguous district for judicial purposes.

This section is made obsolete by amendments to Article VI §§ 12 and 16.

SECTION 26

Magistrate court. The legislature shall establish a magistrate court to exercise limited original jurisdiction as may be provided by law. The magistrate court shall be composed of such districts and elective magistrates as may be provided by law. Magistrates shall be qualified electors of, and reside in, their respective districts, and the legislature shall prescribe other qualifications. Magistrates shall receive compensation as may be provided by law, which compensation shall not be diminished during their term of office. Metropolitan court judges shall be chosen as provided in this constitution.

This section was amended in 1966 to reflect the state's efforts to modernize and unify its court system. The amendment replaced justice of the peace courts with a system of magistrate courts. Limited jurisdiction courts may only consider those kinds of cases for which they are affirmatively granted authority (*State v. Vega*, 1977). Limited jurisdiction courts are not vested with equitable jurisdiction (*Durham v. Rasco*, 1924). Magistrate courts have no jurisdiction to set aside a jury verdict (*Jaramillo v. O'Toole*, 1982).

SECTION 27

Appeals from probate courts and other inferior courts. Appeals shall be allowed in all cases from the final judgments and decisions of the probate courts and other inferior courts to the district courts, and in all such appeals, trial shall be had de novo unless otherwise provided by law.

District courts have appellate jurisdiction over all cases originating in justice of the peace [now magistrate courts] (*Lea County State Bank v. McCaskey Register Co.*, 1935). The state is permitted to appeal to the district court from a final judgment or decision of a magistrate court (*State v. Barber*, 1989). A defendant who properly enters a plea of guilty or nolo contendere in metropolitan court is not an "aggrieved" party entitled to appeal to district court for a de novo trial (*State v. Ball*, 1986). A 1966 amendment changed the wording of this section to reflect the replacement of the justice of the peace courts with the magistrate system.

SECTION 28

Court of appeals; number, qualifications, compensation, terms and election of judges; quorum; majority concurring in judgment. The court of appeals shall consist of not less than seven judges who shall be chosen as provided in this constitution, whose qualifications shall be the same as those of justices of the supreme court and whose compensation shall be as provided by law. The increased qualifications provided by this 1988 amendment shall not apply to court of appeals judges serving at the time this amendment passes or elected at the general election in 1988.

Three judges of the court of appeals shall constitute a quorum for the transaction of business, and a majority of those participating must concur in any judgment of the court.

When necessary, the chief justice of the supreme court may designate any justice of the supreme court, or any district judge of the state, to act as a judge of the court of appeals, and the chief justice may designate any judge of the court of appeals to hold court in any district, or to act as a justice of the supreme court.

This section was added to the constitution by an amendment in 1965 to reflect the state's efforts to modernize and unify its court system. The amendment established an intermediate court of appeals. It was amended again in 1988 to reflect the changes in the judicial selection process provided in Article VI §§ 33 and 35. A proposed amendment intended to clarify the beginning and end of terms of office for judges of the court of appeals was rejected by the people in 1982.

The section provides that the court will sit in three-judge panels with a majority on the panel being sufficient for a judgment of the court. When the majority of the judges agree only in result, the opinion is not binding precedent (*Chadwick v. Public Service Commission,* 1986). The court may assign cases to an advisory committee of experienced attorneys without delegating their constitutional power, if the judges review the records and briefs and decide the cases (*Thompson v. Ruidoso-Sunland, Inc.,* 1987).

SECTION 29

Court of appeals; jurisdiction; issuance of writs. The court of appeals shall have no original jurisdiction. It may be authorized by law to review directly decisions of administrative agencies of the state, and it may be authorized by rules of the supreme court to issue all writs necessary or appropriate in aid of its appellate jurisdiction. In all other cases, it shall exercise appellate jurisdiction as may be provided by law.

The court of appeals was created to assist the supreme court with the appellate caseload; its jurisdiction is limited to appeals from final judgments, interlocutory orders which practically dispose of the merits of an action, and final orders after the entry of a judgment which affect substantial rights (*Thornton v. Gamble,* 1984; and *Mitchell v. Mitchell,* 1986). The appellate review of the court of appeals extends to regulations made by state agencies pursuant to statutory requirements (*Wylie Brothers Contracting Co. v. Albuquerque-Bernalillo County Air Quality Board,* 1969), and decisions of regulatory-administrative commissions (*Union County Feedlot, Inc. v. Vigil,* 1968).

The court of appeals is not bound by the trial court's interpretation of statutes and rules; rather it reviews them to determine whether they are legally correct (*State v. Herrera,* Ct. App. 1978). The court of appeals must follow the precedents of the supreme court; it is not free to abolish instructions approved by the supreme court, although in appropriate situations it may consider whether the supreme court precedent is applicable (*State v. Scott,* 1982). This section was added to the constitution by the 1965 amendment that created the court of appeals.

SECTION 30

Fees collected by judiciary paid to state treasury. All fees collected by the judicial department shall be paid into the state treasury as may be provided by law and no justice, judge or magistrate of any court shall retain any fees as compensation or otherwise.

This provision insures that the judges will not benefit personally from fees collected by the court system. This section was added to the constitution by a 1966 amendment.

SECTION 31

Justices of the peace abolished. Justices of the peace shall be abolished not later than five years from the effective date of this amendment and may, within this period, be abolished by law, and magistrate courts vested with appropriate jurisdiction. Until so abolished, justices of the peace shall be continued under existing laws.

This section was added by a 1966 amendment as part of the state's efforts to modernize and unify its court system. The amendment provided for the abolition of the justice of the peace courts, as they were replaced by the magistrate courts created by Article VI § 26.

SECTION 32

Judicial standards commission. There is created the "judicial standards commission," consisting of two justices or judges and two lawyers selected as may be provided by law to serve for terms of four years, and five citizens, none of whom is a justice, judge or magistrate of any court or licensed to practice law in this state, who shall be appointed by the governor for five-year staggered terms as may be provided by law. If a position on the commission becomes vacant for any reason, the successor shall be selected by the original appointing authority in the same manner as the original appointment was made and shall serve for the remainder of the term vacated. No act of the commission is valid unless concurred in by a majority of its members. The commission shall select one of the members appointed by the governor to serve as chairman.

In accordance with this section, any justice, judge or magistrate of any court may be disciplined or removed for willful misconduct in office, persistent failure or inability to perform a judge's duties, or habitual intemperance, or he may be retired for disability seriously interfering with the performance of his duties which is, or is likely to become, of a permanent character. The commission may, after investigation it deems necessary, order a hearing to be held before it concerning the discipline, removal or retirement of a justice, judge or magistrate, or the commission may appoint three masters who are justices or judges of courts of record to hear and take evidence in the matter and to report their findings to the commission. After hearing or after considering the record and the findings and report of the masters, if the commission finds good cause, it shall recommend to the supreme court the discipline, removal or retirement of the justice, judge or magistrate.

The supreme court shall review the record of the proceedings on the law and facts and may permit the introduction of additional evidence, and it shall order the discipline, removal or retirement as it finds just and proper or wholly reject the recommendation. Upon an order for his retirement, any justice, judge or magistrate participating in a statutory retirement program shall be retired with the same rights as if he had retired pursuant to the retirement program. Upon an order for removal, the justice, judge or magistrate shall thereby be removed from office, and his salary shall cease from the date of the order.

All papers filed with the commission or its masters, and proceedings before the commission or its masters, are confidential. The filing of papers and giving of testimony before the commission or its masters is privileged in any action for defamation, except that the record filed by the commission in the supreme court continues privileged but, upon its filing, loses it confidential character, and a writing which was privileged prior to its filing with the commission or its masters does not lose its privilege by the filing. The commission shall promulgate regulations establishing procedures for hearings under this section. No justice or judge who is a member of the commission or supreme court shall participate in any proceeding involving his own discipline, removal or retirement.

This section was added to the constitution by a 1967 amendment to create a judicial standards commission; a 1978 amendment added the present wording of the first sentence of the second paragraph. The section explicitly provides grounds for the general procedures to be followed in removing judges from office; the legislature may not create alternative means of removing judges (*Cooper v. Albuquerque City Commissioners*, 1974). In reviewing the finding of the commission, the supreme court makes its own independent decision as to the removal of a judge (*In re Martinez*, 1982).

Acts of misconduct on the part of a judge of any court in the state, committed in his official capacity during a prior term of judicial office, follow the judge to any subsequent judicial office. Those acts may be the subject of disciplinary proceeding before the judicial standards commission during a different term of judicial office (*In re Romero*, 1983).

Mistakes made by attorneys in making applications for temporary restraining orders which are not noticed or corrected by judges do not automatically constitute unjudicial conduct (*In re Martinez*, 1982).

SECTION 33

Retention or rejection at general election. A. Each justice of the supreme court, judge of the court of appeals, district judge or metropolitan court judge shall have been elected to that position in a partisan election prior to being eligible for a nonpartisan retention election. Thereafter, each such justice or judge shall be subject to retention or rejection on a nonpartisan ballot. Retention of the judicial office shall require at least fifty-seven percent of the vote cast on the question of retention or rejection.

B. Each justice of the supreme court or judge of the court of appeals shall be subject to retention or rejection in like manner at the general election every eighth year.

C. Each district judge shall be subject to retention or rejection in like manner at the general election every sixth year.

D. Each metropolitan court judge shall be subject to retention or rejection in like manner at the general election every fourth year.

E. Every justice of the supreme court, judge of the court of appeals, district judge or metropolitan court judge holding office on January 1 next following the date of the election at which this amendment is adopted shall be deemed to have fulfilled the requirements of Subsection A of this section and the justice or judge shall be eligible for retention or rejection by the electorate at the general election next preceding the end of the term of which the justice or judge was last elected prior to the adoption of this amendment.

This section is the product of a 1988 amendment that adopted a composite system for selecting judges that combines merit appointment, partisan elections, and nonpartisan retention elections. This section provides for the nonpartisan retention election and was added to the constitution by a 1988 amendment. A 1994 amendment added the requirement that in order to retain his office an incumbent must receive at least 57 percent of the votes cast in the nonpartisan retention election.

SECTION 34

Vacancies in office; date for filing declaration of candidacy. The office of any justice or judge subject to the provisions of Section 33 of Article 6 of this constitution becomes vacant on January 1 immediately following the general election at which the justice or judge is rejected by more than forty-three percent of those voting on the question of this retention or rejection or January 1 immediately following the date he fails to file a declaration of candidacy for the retention election of his office in the general election at which the justice or judge would be subject to retention or rejection by the electorate. Otherwise, the office becomes vacant upon the date of the death, resignation or removal by impeachment of the justice or judge. The date for filing a declaration of candidacy for retention of office shall be the same as that for filing a declaration of candidacy in a primary election.

This section was added to the constitution by a 1988 amendment; it defines vacancies in judicial office and sets the time for filing for election to those offices. A district judge may not file for retention in office and, in the same election, file as a candidate in a primary election for statewide judicial office (*Opinion of the Attorney General* No. 90-04, 1990). A 1994 amendment to Section 33 requires that to remain in office, an incumbent must receive at least 57 percent of the votes cast in the nonpartisan retention election.

SECTION 35

Appellate judges nominating commission. There is created the "appellate judges nominating commission," consisting of: the chief justice of the supreme court or the chief justice's designee from the supreme court; two judges of the court of appeals appointed by the chief judge of the court of appeals; the governor, the speaker of the house of representatives and the president pro tempore of the senate shall each appoint two persons, one of whom shall be an attorney licensed to practice law in this state and the other who shall be a citizen who is not licensed to practice law in any state; the dean of the university of New Mexico school of law, who shall serve as chairman of the commission and shall vote only in the event of a tie vote; four members of the state bar of New Mexico, representing civil and criminal prosecution and defense, appointed by the president of the state bar and the judges on this committee. The appointments shall be made in such manner that each of the two largest major political parties, as defined by the Election Code, shall be equally represented on the commission. If necessary, the president of the state bar and the judges on this committee shall make the minimum number of additional appointments of members of the state bar as is necessary to make each of the two largest major political parties be equally represented on the commission. These additional members of the state bar shall be appointed such that the diverse interests of the state bar are represented. The dean of the university of New Mexico school of law shall be the final arbiter of whether such diverse interests are represented. Members of the commission shall be appointed for terms as may be provided by law. It shall be selected by the original appointing authority in the same manner as the original appointment was made and shall serve for the remainder of the term vacated.

The commission shall actively solicit, accept and evaluate applications from qualified lawyers for the position of justice of the supreme court or judge of the court of appeals and may require an applicant to submit any information it deems relevant to the consideration of his application.

Upon the occurrence of an actual vacancy in the office of justice of the supreme court or judge of the court of appeals, the commission shall meet within thirty days and within the period submit to the governor the names of persons qualified for the judicial office and recommended for appointment to that office by a majority of the commission.

Immediately after receiving the commission nominations, the governor may make one request of the commission for submission of additional names, and the commission shall promptly submit such additional names if a majority of the commission finds that additional persons would be qualified and recommends those persons for appointment to the judicial office. The governor shall fill a vacancy or appoint a successor to fill an impending vacancy in the office of justice of the supreme court or judge of the court of appeals within thirty days after receiving final nominations from the commission by appointing one of the persons nominated by the commission for appointment to that office. If the governor fails to make the appointment within that period or from those nominations, the appointment shall be made from those nominations by the chief justice or the acting chief justice of the supreme court. Any person appointed shall serve until the next general election. That person's successor shall be chosen at such election and shall hold the office until the expiration of the original term.

This section provides for a commission to recommend to the governor persons qualified to fill vacancies on appellate courts, and that the governor shall appoint one of these persons; and provides that should the governor fail to fill the seat, the chief justice of the supreme court shall appoint one of the nominees. The appointee shall serve until the seat is filled at the next general election. This section was added to the constitution by a 1988 amendment.

SECTION 36

District court judges nominating committee. There is created the "district court judges nominating committee" for each judicial district. Each and every provision of Section 35 of Article 6 of this constitution shall apply to the "district judges nominating committee" except that: the chief judge of the district court of that judicial district or the chief judge's designee from that district court shall sit on the committee; there shall be only one appointment from the court of appeals; and the citizen members and state bar members shall be persons who reside in that judicial district.

This section makes provision for the nomination of candidates to fill vacancies on district courts, similar to those provided for appellate courts by Article VI § 35. This section was added to the constitution by a 1988 amendment.

SECTION 37

Metropolitan court judges nominating committee. There is created the "metropolitan court judges nominating committee" for each metropolitan court. Each and every provision of Section 35 of Article 6 of this constitution shall apply to the "metropolitan court nominating committee" except that: no judge of the court of appeals shall sit on the committee; the chief judge of the district court of the judicial district in which the metropolitan court is located or the chief judge's designee from that district court shall sit on the committee; the chief judge of that metropolitan court or the chief judge's designee from that metropolitan court; and the citizen members and state bar members shall be persons who reside in the judicial district in which that metropolitan court is located.

This section makes provision for the nomination of candidates to fill vacancies on metropolitan courts, similar to those provided for appellate courts by Article VI § 35. This section was added to the constitution by a 1988 amendment.

SECTION 38

Chief judge of district and metropolitan court districts. Each judicial district and metropolitan court district shall have a chief judge who shall have the administrative responsibility for that judicial district or metropolitan court district. Each chief judge shall be selected by a majority of the district judges or, in the case of the metropolitan court, by a majority of the metropolitan court judges in that judicial district or metropolitan court district. In the event of a tie, the senior judge shall be the chief judge.

This section provides for the selection of a chief judge for each judicial district and metropolitan court district who will have the administrative responsibility for the court. This section was added to the constitution by a 1988 amendment.

Article VII

Elective Franchise

SECTION 1

Qualifications of voters; absentee voting; school elections; registration. Every citizen of the United States, who is over the age of twenty-one years, and has resided in New Mexico twelve months, in the county ninety days, and in the precinct where he offers to vote thirty days, next preceding the election, except idiots, insane persons and persons convicted of felonious or infamous crime unless restored to political rights, shall be qualified to vote at all elections for public officers. The legislature may enact laws providing for absentee voting by qualified electors. All school elections shall be held at different times from other elections.

The legislature shall have the power to require the registration of the qualified electors as a requisite for voting, and shall regulate the manner, time and places of voting. The legislature shall enact such laws as will secure the secrecy of the ballot, the purity of elections and guard against the abuse of elective franchise. Not more than two members of the board of registration, and not more than two judges of elections shall belong to the same political party at the time of their appointment.

This section has been the subject of eighteen proposed amendments. The only one to pass was a 1967 amendment which removed "male" before "citizen" and "Indians not taxed" before "shall be qualified to vote," and added the sentence, "The legislature may enact laws providing for absentee voting by qualified electors." Amendments that proposed removing the voting restrictions on women and Indians failed to be ratified in 1955, 1958, 1961, and 1964. Amendments providing for absentee voting failed to be ratified in elections in 1919, 1937, 1939, 1949, 1951, 1955, 1957, 1961, and 1963. A proposed amendment in 1970 that would have repealed Article VII and adopted a new Article VII failed ratification. Amendments to extend the franchise to eighteen-year-olds failed in 1969, 1971, and 1973; a right now granted by the Twenty-Sixth Amendment of the U.S. Constitution. Proposals to change the residency requirements failed in 1969 and 1973. The voters rejected a 1994 proposed amendment to lower the voting age to eighteen, remove specific residency requirements, and to change the reference to "idiots and insane persons" to "persons found by a court to be incapacitated."

The authority granted to the legislature in this section is limited to the regulation of the mechanics and method of voting, the legislature cannot enlarge the right to vote beyond that delineated in the first paragraph (*Chase v. Lujan*, 1944). Casting a secret ballot is the personal privilege of voters and can only be compromised in cases of paramount public importance to insure the purity of elections, and a person who votes illegally has no privilege against testifying as to the persons he voted for (*Kiehne v. Atwood*, 1979).

Residency requirements for qualification for voting in this section were substantially changed by amendments to the federal Voting Rights Act of 1970 (42 U.S.C. §§ 1973aa to 1973bb), which required a residency period of only 30 days in elections for president.

Residence on an Indian reservation lying within the boundaries of the state is a part of the state, and a residence for voting purposes, under the meaning of this constitution (*Montoya v. Bolack*, 1962).

SECTION 2

Qualifications for holding office. A. Every citizen of the United States who is a legal resident of the state and is a qualified elector therein, shall be qualified to hold any elective public office except as otherwise provided in this constitution.

B. The legislature may provide by law for such qualifications and standards as may be necessary for holding an appointive position by any public officer or employee.

C. The right to hold public office in New Mexico shall not be denied or abridged on account of sex, and wherever the masculine gender is used in this constitution, in defining the qualifications for specific offices, it shall be construed to include the feminine gender. The payment of public road poll tax, school poll tax or service on juries shall not be made a prerequisite to the right of a person to vote or hold office.

This section provides the general qualifications for holding elective public office, more specific requirements for particular offices are found at Article IV § 3 (legislators), Article V § 3 (executive officers), and § 13 (local officials),

Article VI §§ 8, 14, and 28 (Oudges), Article VI § 24 (district attorneys), and Article X § 6 (municipal officials). These sections must be construed as a whole to determine the qualifications to hold a particular office (*State ex rel Chavez v. Evans*, 1968).

A public office is one created by the constitution or the legislature or municipality or other body as authorized through the legislature. It possesses a portion of the sovereign power of government, those powers are defined by the legislature, the duties arising from those powers are performed independently, and it has some continuity and permanence (*Opinion of Attorney General* No. 58-10, 1957–58).

This section was amended in 1921 to remove language that disallowed women from holding any public office except county school superintendent, school director, or member of board of education. A 1961 amendment divided the section into subsections and a 1973 amendment extended the exemption for nonpayment of poll taxes to all persons; formerly it applied only to women.

The constitution does not provide that all qualified voters may hold public office without additional burdens or conditions (*Board of Commissioners v. District Court*, 1924); the legislature may prohibit certain state employees from simultaneously holding public office as a condition of employment by the state (*State ex rel Gonzales v. Manzagol*, 1975).

The only general restriction against any citizen of the United States who is a resident of and qualified voter in the state to hold public office is that all must reside within the political subdivision for which they are elected or appointed (*Gibbany v. Ford*, 1924).

SECTION 3

Religious and racial equality protected; restrictions on amendments. The rights of any citizen of the state to vote, hold office or sit upon juries, shall never be restricted, abridged or impaired on account of religion, race, language or color, or inability to speak, read or write the English or Spanish languages except as may be otherwise provided in this constitution; and the provisions of this section and of Section One of this article shall never be amended except upon a vote of the people of this state in an election at which at least three-fourths of the electors voting in the whole state, and at least two-thirds of those voting in each county of the state, shall vote for such amendments.

The phrase "at least three-fourths of the electors voting in the whole state" is construed to mean three-fourths of all those voting on that particular proposition, even though they might constitute less than three-fourths of all those voting at that election. The requirement in this section of a two-thirds majority in each county to amend its provision violates the federal constitutional standard of "one person one vote" (*State ex rel. Witt v. State Canvassing Board,* 1968). Provisions concerning restrictions on the amendment of this section are given at Article VII § 1, and Article XIX § 1.

SECTION 4

Residence. No person shall be deemed to have acquired or lost residence by reason of his presence or absence while employed in the service of the United States or of the state, nor while a student at any school.

This section does not mean that a soldier stationed in the state may not acquire residence, but he may not do so from the mere fact that he was stationed therein for whatever period of time. A new domicile may be acquired by a soldier just as by any civilian provided both the fact and the intent concur (*Allen v. Allen,* 1948). This section deals only with residence for voting or holding office and, therefore, the legislature can, for the purpose of divorce jurisdiction, confer resident status on military personnel stationed within the state (*Wilson v. Wilson,* 1954; *Crownover v. Crownover,* 1954). In 1953 the voters rejected an amendment to this section that would have provided for absentee voting.

SECTION 5

Election by ballot; plurality elects candidate. All elections shall be by ballot, and the person who receives the highest number of votes for any office, except in the cases of the office of governor and lieutenant governor, shall be declared elected thereto. The joint candidates receiving the highest number of votes for the offices of governor and lieutenant governor shall be declared elected to those offices.

A complaint claiming that a candidate received a majority of the votes cast, and that improper conduct of election officials deprived him of the majority, is sufficient to support an election contest (*Steele v. Smith,* 1947; *Weldon v. Sanders,* 1982).

The statutory requirement that a list of signatures of qualified voters, declaring party affiliation or endorsement of party's principles, be submitted by minority parties that make nominations other than with a party convention in order to place nominees on the ballot, are consistent with the legislature's authority and duty to secure the purity of elections and does not violate this section (*People's Constitutional Party v. Evans,* 1971). A 1962 amendment inserted "except in the cases of the governor and lieutenant governor" following "office" in the first sentence and added the second sentence.

Article VIII

Taxation and Revenue

SECTION 1

Levy to be proportionate to value; uniform and equal taxes; percentage of value taxed. Taxes levied upon tangible property shall be in proportion to the value thereof, and taxes shall be equal and uniform upon subjects of taxation of the same class. Different methods may be provided by law to determine value of different kinds of property, but the percentage of value against which tax rates are assessed shall not exceed thirty-three and one-third percent.

The 1971 amendment to this section added the second sentence; the 1914 amendment rewrote the first sentence, which formerly read: "The rates of taxation shall be equal and uniform upon all subjects of taxation." Amendments proposed to rewrite this section failed to be ratified in 1969 and 1970.

The enumeration of subjects of taxation in this article merely confirms the legislature's inherent power to tax, and is not a limitation thereon (*State ex rel. Capitol Addition Building Commission v. Connelly*, 1935). The term "taxes" in this section applies only to taxes, in the proper sense of the word, levied to raise revenue for general purposes (*State v. Ingalls*, 1913). "Tangible property" means real or personal property (*Hamilton v. Arch Hurley Conservancy District*, 1938).

All tangible property in the state is subject to taxation in proportion to its value and should be taxed, unless specifically exempted by the constitution (*Sims v. Vosburg*, 1939). An annual auto license fee is not an unconstitutional property tax fixed without regard to the value of the property (*State v. Ingalls*, 1913). A tax on oil and gas extracted from the earth is not a property tax, but an excise tax (*Flynn, Welch & Yates, Inc. v. State Tax Commission*, 1934). The requirement that taxes be equal and uniform requires that tax classifications are reasonable and that all subjects within a class are taxed equally and uniformly (*Anaconda Co. v. Property Tax Department*, 1979), but application of the tax does not require mathematical exactitude (*Ernest W. Hahn, Inc. v. County Assessor*, 1978).

SECTION 2

Property tax limits; exception. Taxes levied upon real or personal property for state revenue shall not exceed four mills annually on each dollar of the assessed valuation thereof except for the support of the educational, penal and charitable institutions of the state, payment of the state debt and interest thereon; and the total annual tax levy upon such property for all state purposes exclusive of necessary levies for state debts shall not exceed ten mills; provided, however that taxes levied upon real or personal tangible property for all purposes, except special levies on specific classes of property and except necessary levies for public debt, shall not exceed twenty mills annually on each dollar of the assessed valuation thereof, but laws may be passed authorizing additional taxes to be levied outside of such limitations when approved by at least a majority of the qualified electors of the taxing district who paid a property tax therein during the preceding year voting on such propositions.

This section sets limits and exceptions on the state's power to tax property. To arrive at uniformity in the assessment of property for taxation, the taxing authority and the taxpayer can introduce evidence regarding the ratios of assessed values to market values in the taxing district (*Peterson Properties v. Valencia County Valuation Protest Board*, 1976). This section does not limit the legislature's power to levy excise tax on gasoline (*Lujan v. Triangle Oil Co.*, 1934).

A 1914 amendment to this section replaced an earlier section which described broader taxing authority for the legislature. A 1933 amendment added the proviso beginning with "except." In 1967, an amendment added "qualified" preceding "electors" and "who paid a property tax therein during the preceding year," preceding "voting on" in the proviso.

SECTION 3

Tax-exempt property. The property of the United States and all counties, towns, cities and school districts and other municipal corporations, public libraries, community ditches and all laterals thereof, all church property not used for commercial purposes, all property used for educational or charitable purposes, all cemeteries not used or held for private or corporate profit and all bonds of the state of

New Mexico, and of the counties, municipalities and districts thereof shall be exempt from taxation.

Provided, however, that any property acquired by public libraries, community ditches and all laterals thereof, property acquired by churches, property acquired for educational or charitable purposes, and property acquired by cemeteries not used or held for private or corporate profit and property acquired by Indian service and property acquired by the United states government or by the state of New Mexico by outright purchase or trade, where such property was, prior to such transfer, subject to the lien of any tax or assessment for the principle or interest of any bonded indebtedness shall not be exempt from such lien, nor from the payment of such taxes or assessments.

Exemptions of personal property from ad valorem taxation may be provided by law if approved by a three-fourths majority vote of all the members elected to each house of the legislature.

The purpose of tax exemption is to encourage religious, charitable, scientific, literary, and educational activities of associations not operating for the profit of any private shareholder or individual (*NRA Special Contribution Fund v. Board of County Commissioners*, 1978; and *Sisters of Charity v. Bernalillo County*, 1979). The constitution places tangible property into one of three classes: that which is exempt from taxation, that which may be exempted, and that which must be taxed (*State ex rel. Attorney General v. State Tax Commission*, 1936).

This section was amended in 1914 to bring it into agreement with a companion amendment to Section 2, which narrowed the scope of the legislature's taxing power. The proviso beginning with "provided" was added by a 1946 amendment, and "not for commercial purposes" following "church property" was added by a 1972 amendment.

SECTION 4

Misuse and deposit of public money. Any public officer making any profit out of public money or using the same for any purpose not authorized by law, shall be deemed guilty of a felony and shall be punished as provided by law and shall be disqualified to hold public office. All public money not invested in interest-bearing securities shall be deposited in national banks in this state, in banks or trust companies incorporated under the laws of the state, in federal savings and loan associations in this state, in savings and loan associations incorporated under the laws of this state whose deposits are insured by an agency of the United States and in credit unions incorporated under the laws of this state or the United States to the extent that such deposits of public money in credit unions are insured by an agency of the United States, and the interest derived therefrom shall be applied in the manner prescribed by law. The conditions of such deposits shall be provided by law.

This section requires that public funds, not immediately needed, shall be deposited for safekeeping in the named institutions; but when the funds are required to meet public obligation they may be expended according to business practices (*Davy v. Day*, 1926). This section does not require that a public official be convicted of a felony before he can be disqualified, but merely requires a judicial finding that the officer has knowingly misused public funds (*State ex rel. Martinez v. Padilla*, 1980). The state treasurer is not required to exact interest from banks in which public money is deposited; but where money does earn interest, the interest income is the property of the state and cannot be awarded to any person (*Catron v. Marron*, 1914). A 1914 amendment inserted this language to replace the former language, which provided for tax exemptions similar to those now found in Section 3e. A 1967 amendment inserted the provisions authorizing deposits in federal or insured domestic savings and loan associations and added the last sentence. In 1989 an amendment added the provisions relating to credit unions in the second sentence.

SECTION 5

Head of family and veteran exemptions. The legislature shall exempt from taxation the property of each head of the family to the amount of two thousand dollars ($2,000) as follows: in 1989, the legislature shall exempt from taxation eight hundred dollars ($800), in 1991, one thousand four hundred dollars ($1,400) and beginning in 1993, two thousand dollars ($2,000). The legislature shall also exempt from taxation the property, including the community or joint property of husband and wife, of every honorably discharged member of the armed forces of the United States who served in such armed forces during the period in which they were or are engaged in armed conflict under orders of the president of the United States, and the widow or widower of every such honorably discharged member of the armed forces of the United States in the sum of two thousand dollars ($2,000). Provided, that in every case where exemption is claimed on the grounds of the claimant's having served with the armed forces of the United States as aforesaid, the burden of proving actual and bone fide ownership of such property upon which exemption is claimed, shall be upon the claimant.

The legislature may require listing of all persons to whom property tax exemptions may be allowed, and the claimant of an exemption has the burden of establishing the right to a tax exemption (*Dillard v. New Mexico State Tax Commissioner*, 1948). The provisions for tax exemptions have been extensively amended; a 1914 amendment inserted the present first clause, and deleted a provision for a state board of equalization. In 1921, an amendment added an exemption for honorably discharged military personnel. In 1949, an amendment inserted "including the community or joint property of husband and wife." A 1953 amendment reworded the clause concerning the widows of military personnel, to make it clear the exemption applied both to the personnel and their widows, and a 1973 amendment inserted "or widower." A 1988 amendment substituted "shall" for "may" in the first sentence and added the scheme for increasing the exemptions which completes the sentence. A proposed 1969 amendment to allow the legislature to set the exemptions from property taxation was rejected by the voters.

SECTION 6

Assessment of lands. Lands held in large tracts shall not be assessed for taxation at any lower value per acre then [than] lands of the same character or quality and similarly situated, held in smaller tracts. The plowing of land shall not be considered as adding value thereto for the purpose of taxation.

The bracketed word "than" was inserted by the compiler of the constitution although the word "then" appears in the 1914 amendment as enrolled. The word "than" conforms to the wording as it appeared in the original constitution. The present section was substituted, by a 1914 amendment, to replace the former wording that provided the legislature could not release any political subdivision from its proportionate share of taxes levied for any purpose. To have uniform and equal taxes, the valuations must be established by some standard, and after valuations are fixed, the taxes based on those valuations must be levied by a standard method; in this way, each taxpayer bears a fair share of the burden of government (*Gerner v. State Tax Commission*, 1963).

SECTION 7

Judgments against local officials. No execution shall issue upon judgment rendered against the board of county commissioners of any county, or against any incorporated city, town or village, school district or board of education; or against any officer of any county, incorporated city, town or village, school district or board of education, upon any judgment recovered against him in his official capacity and for which the county, incorporated city, town or village, school district or board of education, is liable, but the same shall be paid out of the proceeds of a tax levy as other liabilities of counties, incorporated cities, towns or villages, school districts or boards of education, and when so collected shall be paid by the county treasurer to the judgment of the creditor.

This section cannot be relied on to enforce an unauthorized judgment, nor is it self-executing. Only the school district benefiting from the funds used shall be called upon to pay for the benefits, and mandamus will not compel a levy against property in the whole county to pay judgment against a county school board (*McAfee v. Gutierrez*, 1944).

A 1914 amendment to Article VIII substituted the present section, which was formerly Section 13 of Article VIII, and former Section 7 of this article was incorporated as the first paragraph of Section 3.

SECTION 8

Exemption of certain personalty in transit through the state. Personal property which is moving in interstate commerce through or over the state of New Mexico, or which was consigned to a warehouse, public or private, or factory within New Mexico from outside the state for storage in transit to a final destination outside the state of New Mexico, manufacturing processing or fabricating while in transit to a final destination, whether specified when transportation begins or afterwards, which destination is also outside the state, shall be deemed not to have acquired a situs in New Mexico for purposes of taxation and shall be exempt from taxation. Such property shall not be deprived of such exemption because while in the warehouse the property is assembled, bound, joined, processed, disassembled, divided, cut, broken in bulk, relabeled or repackaged.

This section provides that property merely in transit through the state or consigned to a warehouse in the state during transit shall not be taxed. But, property that is altered or repackaged or relabeled during transit through the state shall be taxed. In 1914, Article VIII §§ 8 to 13 were deleted, some of their provisions being moved to other places in the article. The present Section 8 was added by a 1973 Amendment.

SECTION 9

Elected governing authority prerequisite to levy of tax. No tax or assessment of any kind shall be levied by any political subdivision whose enabling legislation does not provide for an elected governing authority. This section does not prohibit the levying or collection of a tax or special assessment by an initial appointed governing authority where the appointed governing authority will be replaced by an elected one within six years of the date the appointed authority takes office. The provisions of this section shall not be effective until July 1, 1976.

This provision provides that any political subdivision that levies taxes must have a governing authority answerable to the people through elections. This section was added by a 1974 amendment.

SECTION 10

Severance tax permanent fund. There shall be deposited in a permanent trust fund known as the "severance tax permanent fund" that part of state revenue derived from excise taxes which have been or shall be designated severance taxes imposed upon the severance of natural resources within the state, in excess of that amount which has been or shall be reserved by statute for the payment of principal and interest on outstanding bonds to which severance tax revenue has been or shall be pledged. Money in the severance tax permanent fund shall not be expended but shall be invested as provided by law. The income from investments shall be appropriated by the legislature as other general operating revenue is appropriated for the benefit of the people of the state.

Money credited to the severance tax permanent fund at the time of the adoption of this amendment shall be credited to and become a part of the permanent trust fund known as the "severance tax permanent fund" hereby created.

This section provides that revenue from mineral and oil severance taxes shall be invested in a fund to provide a supplemental revenue for the state's general operating revenue. The provisions for severance tax permanent fund are found at 7-27-3 NMSA 1978. This section was added by a 1976 amendment. It was revised by a 1982 amendment which deleted what was then the third sentence of the first paragraph. A proposed 1994 amendment to change the method for distributing money from the severance tax permanent fund was rejected by the voters.

SECTION 11

[The people rejected an amendment proposed in 1982 that would have added a Section 11 providing an income tax exemption for members of the national guard.]

SECTION 12, 13

[These sections are repealed, see commentary for Section 8.]

SECTION 14

[In 1978 the voters rejected a proposed amendment to Article VIII that would have provided for the accrual of real property taxes during the lifetime of certain elderly taxpayers, and their payment held in abeyance until death or transfer of the property.]

Article IX

State, County, and Municipal Indebtedness

SECTION 1

Debts of territory and its counties assumed. The state hereby assumes the debts and liabilities of the territory of New Mexico, and the debts of the counties thereof, which were valid and subsisting on June twentieth, nineteen hundred and ten, and pledges its faith and credit for the payment thereof. The legislature shall, at its first session, provide for the payment of refunding thereof by the issue and sale of bonds, or otherwise.

This section made the state liable for the debts of the territory; it and Sections 2, 3, and 4 are now obsolete, because the debts and liabilities of the territory have been met. Meeting these debts by issuing certificates of indebtedness and borrowing money was not a violation of this section (*State ex rel Lucero v. Marron*, 1912).

SECTION 2

Payment of county debts by another county. No county shall be required to pay any portion of the debt of any other county so assumed by the state, and the bonds of Grant and Santa Fe counties which were validated, approved and confirmed by act of congress of January sixteenth, eighteen hundred and ninety-seven, shall be paid as hereinafter provided.

For a discussion of the constitutionality of refinancing debts of political subdivisions, by states, see 72 *Am. Jur.*ld "States, Territories and Dependencies" §§ 14, 15.

SECTION 3

State refunding bonds for assumed debts. The bonds authorized by law to provide for the payment of such indebtedness shall be issued in three series, as follows:
Series A. To provide for the payment of such debts and liabilities of the territory of New Mexico.
Series B. To provide for the payment of such debts of said counties.
Series C. To provide for the payment of the bonds and accrued interest thereon of Grant and Santa Fe counties which were validated, approved and confirmed by act of congress, January sixteenth, eighteen hundred and ninety-seven.

For a discussion of the payment of debts incurred when a state was a territory, see 72 *Am. Jur.*ld "States, Territories and Dependencies" § 85.

SECTION 4

Sale of lands for certain bond payments. The proper officers of the state shall, as soon as practicable, select and locate the one million acres of land granted to the state by congress for the payment of the said bonds of Grant and Santa Fe counties, and sell the same or sufficient thereof to pay the interest and principal of the bond of Series C issued as provided in Section Three hereof. The proceeds of rentals and sales of said land shall be kept in a separate fund and applied to the payment of the interest and principal of the bonds of Series C. Whenever there is not sufficient money in said fund to meet the interest and sinking fund requirements therefor, the deficiency shall be paid out of any funds of the state not otherwise appropriated, and shall be repaid to the state or to the several counties which have furnished any portion thereof under a general levy, out of the proceeds subsequently received of rentals and sales from said lands.

Any money received by the state from rentals and sales of said lands in excess of the amounts required for the purpose above-mentioned shall be paid into the current and permanent school funds of the state respectively.

This section made provision for payment of the debts listed in Article IX § 3.

SECTION 5

Remission of county debts to state prohibited. The legislature shall never enact any law releasing any county, or any of the taxable property therein, from its obligation to pay to the state any moneys expended by the state by reason of assumption or payment of the debt of such county.

This section denies the legislature the authority to forgive debts counties may owe to the state.

SECTION 6

Militia warrants. No law shall ever be passed by the legislature validating or legalizing, directly or indirectly, the militia warrants alleged to be outstanding against the territory of New Mexico, or any portion thereof, and no such warrant shall be prima facie or conclusive evidence of the validity of the debt purporting to be evidenced thereby or by any other militia warrant. This provision shall not be construed as authorizing any suit against the state.

During the territorial period the militia incurred considerable expenses fighting Apache and Navajo Indians; these costs were paid by warrants issued by the territorial government. This section forbids the legislature from paying claims of debt outstanding against the militia warrants. It also explicitly forbids suits against the state concerning such claims. The political controversy concerning the repayment of the warrants is discussed in the constitutional history section of this book.

SECTION 7

State indebtedness; purposes. The state may borrow money not exceeding the sum of two hundred thousand dollars [($200,000)] in the aggregate to meet casual deficits or failure in revenue, or for necessary expenses. The state may also contract debts to suppress insurrection and to provide for the public defense.

This section authorizes the legislature to borrow money to meet the state's debts. The legislature is the sole judge of "necessary expenses" (*State ex rel Lucero v. Marron,* 1912). The legislature may allow the issuance of debentures to provide for public need (*Catron v. Marron,* 1914), and in anticipation of tax revenues (*State v. Graham,* 1914). The phrase "to provide for the public defense" is construed to mean to provide for a militia of the kind required by Article XVIII § 2 (*State ex rel Charlton v. French,* 1940).

SECTION 8

State indebtedness; restrictions. No debt other than those specified in the preceding section shall be contracted by or on behalf of this state, unless authorized by law for some specified work or object; which law shall provide for an annual tax levy sufficient to pay the interest and to provide a sinking fund to pay the principal of such debt within fifty years from the time of the contracting thereof. No such law shall take effect until it shall have been submitted to the qualified electors of the state and have received a majority of all the votes cast thereon at a general election; such law shall be published in full in at least one newspaper in each county of the state, if one be published therein, once each week, for four successive weeks next preceding such election. No debt shall be so created if the total indebtedness of the state, exclusive of the debts of the territory, and the several counties thereof, assumed by the state, would thereby be made to exceed one percent of the assessed valuation of all property subject to taxation in the state as shown by the preceding general assessment.

"Debt" is used as comprehending a debt and pledging for its repayment the general faith and credit of the state or municipality, and contemplating the levy of general property tax as the source of funds with which to retire the debt (*State ex rel Capitol Addition Building Commission v. Connelly*, 1935). The state may not assume a debt to build a state office building, even when the debt will be repaid from rentals, unless the debt is approved by the voters (*Bryant v. State Office Building Commission*, 1941; *State Office Building Commission v. Trujillo*, 1941). Bond issues as provided by this section were passed by the legislature and approved by the people in elections in 1960, 1964, 1966, 1972, and 1976.

SECTION 9

Use of borrowed funds. Any money borrowed by the state, or any county, district or municipality thereof, shall be applied to the purpose for which it was obtained, or to repay such loan, and to no other purpose whatever.

This section restricts the use of proceeds from general obligation bonds to the purpose for which they were obtained or to repay the loan (*State ex rel Board of County Commissioners v. Montoya*, 1978). Revenues derived from municipally owned utilities, purchased or improved by the issuance of bonds, may not be spent for other corporate purposes until the obligations to bondholders are met (*Scott v. City of Truth or Consequences*, 1953).

SECTION 10

County indebtedness; restrictions. No county shall borrow money except for the following purposes:

A. erecting, remodeling and making additions to necessary public buildings;

B. constructing or repairing public roads and bridges;

C. constructing or acquiring a system for supplying water, including the acquisition of water and water rights, necessary real estate or right-of-ways and easements;

D. constructing or acquiring a sewer system, including the necessary real estate or right-of-ways and easements;
E. constructing an airport or sanitary landfill, including the necessary real estate; or
F. the purchase of books and other library resources for libraries in the county.

In such cases, indebtedness shall be incurred only after the proposition to create such debt has been submitted to the registered voters of the county and approved by a majority of those voting thereon. No bonds issued for such purpose shall run for more than fifty years. Provided, however, that no money derived from general obligation bonds issued and sold hereunder shall be used for maintaining existing buildings and, if so, such bonds shall be invalid.

This section was amended in 1964 by inserting "remodeling and making additions to" following "erecting" near the beginning of the first sentence, and substituting "has" for "shall have" preceding "been submitted" near the middle of the first sentence, and adding the proviso contained in the last sentence. A 1982 amendment restructured the section into paragraphs and designated the subsections, and eliminated a requirement that electors in bond levies must have paid a property tax in the preceding year. An amendment passed in 1988 added Subsection F, and substituted "registered voters" for "qualified voters" in the first sentence of the last paragraph. A 1994 proposal to amend this section to authorize counties to borrow money to repair building and purchase land for open space was rejected by the people.

This section relates to the debt-contracting powers of the counties and provides that none can be contracted except after the voters of the county approve of a bond issue. Counties must observe the statutory provisions for such bond issues (*State ex reL Hass v. Board of County Commissioners*, 1927). The use of the term "necessary" in this section is construed not to mean "indispensable," but as synonymous with "needful" (*Hutcheson v. Atherton*, 1940). For the meaning of "debt" see commentary on Section 8 above.

SECTION 11

School district indebtedness; restrictions. No school district shall borrow money except for the purpose of erecting, remodeling, making additions to and furnishing school buildings or purchasing and improving school grounds or any combination of these purposes, and in such cases only when the proposition to create the debt has been submitted to a vote of such qualified elector of the district as are owners of real estate within the school district and a majority of those voting on the question have voted in favor of creating such debt. No school district shall ever become indebted in an amount exceeding six percent on the assessed valuation of the taxable property within the school district as shown by the preceding general assessment.

The United States Supreme Court decision in *City of Phoenix v. Kolodziejsky* (1970) renders unconstitutional this section's requirement that only real property owners be permitted to vote in a school bond election (*Board of Education v. Moloney*, 1970). Issuing bonds to obtain funds to erect public buildings requires that notice must be given to the interested electorate of the purpose for the funds; that purpose must be authorized by law and not violate the constitution, and the electorate must be given opportunity to approve or disapprove the bond issue in an election (*Board of Education v. Robinson*, 1953). For the meaning of "debt" see commentary on Section 8 above.

A 1933 amendment expanded the purposes for which school districts could borrow money to include remodeling, making additions to, and finishing school buildings, and to enlarge school grounds. A 1965 amendment substituted "six percent" for the words "six per centum."

SECTION 12

Municipal indebtedness; restrictions. No city, town or village shall contract any debt except by an ordinance, which shall be irrepealable until the indebtedness therein provided for shall have been fully paid or discharged, and which shall specify the purposes to which the funds to be raised shall be applied, and which shall provide for the levy of a tax, not exceeding twelve mills on the dollar upon all taxable property within such city, town or village, sufficient to pay the interest on, and to extinguish the principal of, such debt within fifty years. The proceeds of such tax shall be applied only to the payment of such interest and principal. No such debt shall be created unless the question of incurring the same shall, at a regular election for councilmen, aldermen or other officers of such city, town or village, or at any special election called for such purpose, have been submitted to a vote of such qualified electors thereof as have paid a property tax therein during the preceding year, and a majority of those voting on the question by ballot deposited in a separate ballot box when voting in a regular election, shall have voted in favor of creating such debt. A proposal which does not receive the required number of votes for adoption at any special election called for that purpose, shall not be submitted in any special election within a period of one year. For the purpose, only, of voting on the creation of the debt, any person owning property within the corporate limits of the city, town or village is situated shall be a qualified elector.

This section prohibits cities, towns, and villages from entering into contracts which would, or might, depend on future contingencies, the amount of which is not fixed and certain at the time the contract is made (*Henning v. Town of Hot Springs*, 1940). The intent and object of the constitution is to safeguard municipalities and their citizens from ruinous taxation, therefore, even though excessive debt might be owed to a state agency rather than an individual does not alter the effect (*State ex rel State Highway Commission v. City of Aztec*, 1967). The requirement of the tax levy limitation provided by this section is to prevent municipalities from assuming unmanageable debt (*Lanigan v. Town of Gallup*, 1913).

Revenue bonds repayable from a special fund created for their retirement, payable solely from money derived from sources other than general taxation, do not constitute a general obligation on the part of municipalities (*Village of Deming v. Hosdreg Co.*, 1956). For the meaning of "debt" see commentary on Section 8 above.

The provisions for special elections in the third sentence, and the last two sentences were added to this section by a 1964 amendment.

SECTION 13

County and municipal debt limit; exceptions. No county, city, town or village shall ever become indebted to an amount in the aggregate, including existing indebtedness, exceeding four per centum on the value of the taxable property within such county, city, town or village, as shown by the last preceding assessment for state or county taxes; and all bonds of obligations issued in excess of such amount shall be void; provided, that any such limitation for the construction or purchase of a system for supplying water, or a sewer system, for such city, town or village.

This section aims at protecting municipalities from overoptimistic assessment of their future ability to generate revenue, which might encourage them to adopt an improvement program in excess of their ability to pay for it (*Gutierrez v. Middle Rio Grande Conservancy District*, 1929). The intent of the proviso concerning water and sewer systems is that no constraints should be laid on municipalities in their efforts to procure a water supply (*City of Truth or Consequences v. Robinson*, 1954).

SECTION 14

Aid to private enterprise; veterans' scholarship program; student loans. Neither the state, nor any county, school district or municipality, except as otherwise provided in this constitution, shall directly or indirectly lend or pledge its credit or make any donation or in aid of any person, association or public or private corporation or in aid of any private enterprise for the construction of any railroad: provided

A. nothing in this section shall be construed to prohibit the state or any county or municipality from making provision for the care and maintenance of sick and indigent persons;

B. nothing in this section shall prohibit the state from establishing a veterans' scholarship program for Vietnam conflict veterans who are post-secondary students at educational institutions under the exclusive control of the state by exempting such veterans from the payment of tuition. For the purpose of this subsection, a "Vietnam conflict veteran" is any person who has been honorably discharged from the armed forces of the United States, who was a resident of New Mexico at the original time of entry into the armed forces from New Mexico and who has been awarded a Vietnam campaign medal for service in the armed forces of this country in Vietnam during the period from August 5, 1964 to the official termination date of the Vietnam conflict as designated by executive order of the president of the United States;

C. the state may also establish by law a program of loans to students of the healing arts, as defined by law, for residents of the state who, in return for the payment of educational expenses, contract with the state to practice their profession for a period of years after graduation within areas of the state designated by law; and

D. nothing in this section shall be construed to prohibit the state or a county or municipality from creating new job opportunities by providing land, buildings or infrastructure for facilities to support new or expanding businesses if this assistance is granted pursuant to general implementing legislation that is approved by a majority vote of those elected to each house of the legislature. The implementing legislation shall include adequate safeguards to protect public money or other resources used for the purposes authorized in this subsection. The implementing legislation shall further provide that:

(1) each specific county or municipal project providing assistance pursuant to this subsection need not be approved by the legislature but shall be approved by the county or municipality pursuant to procedures provided in the implementing legislation; and

(2) each specific state project providing assistance pursuant to this subsection shall be approved by law.

This section is intended to prevent the giving of outright grants or the use of a municipality's credit to those who would not be entitled to receive credit in the first instance, and to act as a curb on speculative ventures prevalent at the time of its adoption (*Opinion of Attorney General* No. 6550, 1955–56). That a private enterprise serves a commendable public purpose does not alone warrant a grant or credit from the state or political subdivision (*State ex rel Mechem v. Hannah*, 1957).

The provision for a veterans' scholarship program was added to this section by a 1971 amendment. The last sentence of this section was added by a 1974 amendment. A 1994 amendment added an exemption to the "anti-donation clause," to allow the state and its political subdivisions to provide land, buildings, or infrastructure for facilities to support the development or the expansion of businesses. An amendment to provide for economic development was rejected by the people in 1967, and a proposed amendment to create a state-controlled student loan program was rejected by the voters in 1970.

SECTION 15

State and local refunding bonds. Nothing in this article shall be construed to prohibit the issue of bonds for the purpose of paying or refunding any valid state, county, district or municipal bonds and it shall not be necessary to submit the question of the issue of such bonds to vote as herein provided.

Placing the proceeds of municipal bonds in escrow and investing them in United States bonds for the purpose of paying off indebtedness on existing bonds does not violate this section (*City of Albuquerque v. Gott*, 1964).

SECTION 16

State highway bonds. Laws enacted by the fifth legislature authorizing the issue and sale of state highway bonds for the purpose of providing funds for the construction and improvement of state highways and to enable the state to meet and secure allotments of federal funds to aid in construction and improvement of roads, and laws so enacted authorizing the issue and sale of state highway debentures to anticipate the collection of revenues from motor vehicle licenses and other revenues provided by law for the state road fund, shall take effect without submitting them to the electors of the state, and notwithstanding that the total indebtedness of the state may thereby temporarily exceed one per centum of the assessed valuation of all property subject to taxation in the state. Provided, that the total amount of such state highway bonds payable from proceeds of taxes levied on property outstanding at any one time shall not exceed two million dollars [($2,000,000)]. The legislature shall not enact any law which will decrease the amount of the annual revenues pledged for the payment debentures or which will divert any of such revenues to any other purpose so long as any of the said debentures issued to anticipate the collection thereof remain unpaid.

This section permits debentures in anticipation of gasoline excise tax to be undertaken without referendum (*Lopez v. State Highway Commission*, 1921), and highway debentures are exempted from referendum by Article IV § 1 (*State ex rel. Linn v. Romaro*, 1949). This section was added by a 1921 amendment.

Article X

County and Municipal Corporations

SECTION 1

Classification of counties; salaries and fees of county officers. The legislature shall at its first session classify the counties and fix salaries for all county officers, which shall also apply to those elected at the first election under this constitution. And no county officer shall receive to his own any fees or emoluments other than the annual salary provided by law, and all fees earned by any officer shall be by him collected and paid into the treasury of the county.

Prior to the adoption of the constitution, the officers of the counties of the territory were compensated for their services on a fee basis. This section intended to replace the fee system with salary compensation, with the provision that compensation should neither increase nor diminish during the term of office (*State ex rel Peck v. Velarde*, 1935). All county officers must receive a salary and may not receive any other compensation (*James v. Board of Commissioners*, 1918).

SECTION 2

Terms of county officers. A. In every county all elected officials shall serve four-year terms, subject to the provisions of Subsection B of this section.

B. In those counties that prior to 1992 have not had four-year terms for elected officials, the assessor, sheriff and probate judge shall be elected to four-year terms and the treasurer and clerk shall be elected to two-year terms in the first election following the adoption of this amendment. In subsequent elections, the treasurer and clerk shall be elected to four-year terms.

C. To provide for staggered county commission terms, in counties with three county commissioners, the terms of no more than two commissioners shall expire in the same year; and in counties with five county commissioners, the terms of no more than three commissioners shall expire in the same year.

D. All county officers, after having served two consecutive four-year terms, shall be ineligible to hold any public office for two years thereafter.

This section of the constitution originally limited county officers to two consecutive two-year terms after which they would be ineligible to hold any office for two years. It was the focus of many proposed amendments, each of which sought by some design to extend either the term of office or the number of terms county officials could serve. Such amendments were rejected by the people in 1958, 1961, 1969, 1973, 1976, 1982, and 1986. This provision was adopted in 1992. A county official who resigns before the end of a second consecutive term does not change his ineligibility for a third term (*Stephens v. Myers*, 1984).

SECTION 3

Removal of county seats. No county seats, where are county buildings, shall be removed unless three-fifths of the votes cast by qualified electors on the question of removal at an election called and held as now or hereafter provided by law, be in favor of such removal. The proposition of removal shall not be submitted in the same county oftener than once in eight years.

This section provides for a continuity in the location of the seat of county government.

SECTION 4

Combined city and county corporations. A. The legislature shall, by general law, provide for the formation of combined city and county municipal corporations, and for the manner of determining the territorial limits thereof, each of which shall be known as a "city and country," and, when organized, shall contain a population of at least fifty thousand (50,000) inhabitants. No such city and county shall be formed except by a majority vote of the qualified electors of the area proposed to be included therein, and if the proposed area includes any area not within the existing limits of a city, a majority of those electors living outside the city, voting separately shall be required. Any such city and county shall be permitted to frame a charter for its own government, and amend the same, in manner provided by the legislature by general law for the formation and organization of such corporations.

B. Every such charter shall designate the respective officers of such city and county who shall perform the duties imposed by law upon county officers and shall make provisions for the payment of existing city and county indebtedness as hereinafter required. The officers of a city and county, their compensation, qualifications, term of office and manner of election or appointment, shall be as provided for in its charter, subject to general laws and applicable constitutional provisions. The salary of any elective or appointive officer of a city and county shall not be changed after his election or appointment or during his term of office; nor shall the term of any such officer be extended beyond the period for which he is elected or appointed. Every such city and county shall have and enjoy all rights, powers and privileges asserted in its charter not inconsistent with its general laws, and, in addition thereto, such rights, powers and privileges as may be granted to it, or possessed and enjoyed by cities and counties of like population separately organized.

C. No city or county government existing outside the territorial limits of such city and county shall exercise any police, taxation or other powers within the territorial limits of such city and county, but all such powers shall be exercised by the city and county and the officers thereof, subject to such constitutional provisions and general laws as apply to either cities or counties.

D. In case an existing county is divided in the formation of city and county government, such city and county shall be liable for a just proportion of the existing debts or liabilities of the former county and shall account for and pay the county remaining a just proportion of the value of any real estate or other property owned by the former county and taken over by the city and county government, the method of determining such proportion shall be prescribed by general law, but such division shall not affect the rights of creditors.

E. Nothing herein contained shall be construed to alter or amend the existing constitutional provisions regarding apportionment of representation in the legislature or in the boundaries of legislative districts or judicial districts, nor the jurisdiction or organization of the district or probate courts.

This section makes provisions for the creation of combined city-county governments; the legislature made statutory provision for such governments in 3-16-1 to 18 NMSA 1978. This section was added by a 1949 amendment.

SECTION 5

Incorporated counties. Any county at the time of the adoption of this amendment, which is less than one hundred forty-four square miles in area and has a population of ten thousand or more may become an incorporated county by the following procedure:

A. upon the filing of a petition containing the signatures of at least ten percent of the registered voters in the county, the board of county commissioners shall appoint a charter commission consisting of not less than three persons to draft an incorporated county charter; or

B. the board of county commissioners may, upon its own initiative, appoint a charter commission consisting of not less than three persons to draft an incorporated county charter; and

C. the proposed charter drafted by the charter commission shall be submitted to the qualified voters of the county within one year after the appointment of the commission and if adopted by a majority of the qualified voters voting in the election the county shall become an incorporated county.

The charter of an incorporated county shall provide for the form and organization of the incorporated county government and shall designate those officers which shall be elected, and those officers and employees which shall perform the duties assigned by law to county officers.

An incorporated county may exercise all powers and shall be subject to all limitations granted to municipalities by Article 9, Section 12 of the constitution of New Mexico and all powers granted to municipalities by statute.

A charter of an incorporated county shall be amended in accordance with the provisions of the charter.

Nothing herein contained shall be construed to alter or amend the existing constitutional provisions regarding apportionment or representation in the legislature or in the boundaries of legislative districts or judicial districts, not the jurisdiction or organization of the district or probate courts.

The provisions of this amendment shall be self-executing.

This section provides for counties to incorporate and thereby have more latitude in the form the government will take. This section was added by a 1964 amendment. It has not been the subject of judicial interpretation.

SECTION 6

Municipal home rule. A. For the purpose of electing some or all of the members of the governing body of a municipality:

1. the legislature may authorize a municipality by general law to be districted;
2. if districts have not been established as authorized by law, the governing body of a municipality may, by a resolution, authorize the districting of the municipality. The resolution shall not become effective in the municipality until approved by a majority vote in the municipality; and
3. if districts have not been established as authorized by law or by resolution, the voters of a municipality, by a petition which is signed by not less than five percent of the registered qualified electors of the municipality and which specified the number of members of the governing body to be elected from districts, may require the governing body to submit to the registered qualified electors of the

municipality, at the next regular municipal election held not less than sixty days after the petition is filed, a resolution requiring the districting of the municipality by its governing body. The resolution shall not become effective in the municipality until approved by a majority vote in the municipality. The signatures for a petition shall be collected within a six-months period.

B. Any member of the governing body of a municipality representing a district shall be a resident of, and elected by, the registered qualified electors of that district.

C. The registered qualified electors of a municipality may adopt, amend or repeal a charter in the manner provided by law. In the absence of law, the governing body of a municipality may appoint a charter commission upon its own initiative or shall appoint a charter commission upon the filing of a petition containing the signatures of at least five percent of the registered qualified electors of the municipality. The charter commission shall consist of not less than seven members who shall draft a proposed charter. The proposed charter shall be submitted to the registered qualified electors of the municipality within one year after the appointment of the charter commission. If the charter is approved by a majority vote in the municipality, it shall become effective at the time and in the manner provided in the charter.

D. A municipality which adopts a charter may exercise all legislative powers and perform all functions not expressly denied by general law or charter. This grant of powers shall not include the power to enact private or civil laws governing civil relationships except as incident to the exercise of an independent municipal power, nor shall it include the power to provide for a penalty greater than the penalty provided for a petty misdemeanor. No tax imposed by the governing body of a charter municipality, except a tax authorized by general law, shall become effective until approved by a majority vote in the charter municipality.

E. The purpose of this section is to provide for maximum local self-government. A liberal construction shall be given to the powers of municipalities. (Adopted by the people November 3, 1970.)

This section allows and provides the restrictions on home rule for municipalities. All home-rule municipalities with a population of more than 10,000 must elect city council members from single-member districts (*Casuse v. City of Gallup*, 1987). "General law" means a law that applies generally throughout the state or is of statewide concern as contrasted to "local" or "municipal" law (*Apodaca v. Wilson*, 1974). This section was added by a 1970 amendment.

SECTION 7

Five-member boards of county commissioners. The board of county commissioners by unanimous vote may adopt an ordinance to increase the size of the boards of county commissioners to five members. Upon creation of a five-member board, the county shall be divided by the incumbent board of county commissioners into five county commission districts that shall be compact, contiguous and as nearly equal in population as practicable. One county commissioner shall reside within and be elected from each county commission district. Change of residence to a place outside the district from which a county commissioner was elected shall automatically terminate the service of that commissioner and the office shall be declared vacant.

A county commissioner who served a two-year term under Article X § 2 [amended in 1992], and a four-year term under Article X § 7, may serve an additional four-year term under this section (*Morris v. Gonzales*, 1978). This section was added by a 1973 amendment, and the first and second paragraphs were designated as Subsections A and B by a 1980 amendment. Subsections C and D were added by a 1988 amendment.

SECTION 8

New activity or service mandated by state rule or regulation. A state rule or regulation mandating any county or city to engage in any new activity, to provide any new service or to increase any current level of activity or to provide any service beyond that required by existing law, shall not have the force of law, unless, or until, the state provides sufficient new funding or a means of new funding to the county or city to pay the cost of performing the mandated activity or service for the period of time during which the activity or service is required to be performed. (Adopted by the people November 6, 1984).

B. Every such charter shall designate the respective offices of such city and county who shall perform the duties imposed by law upon county officers and shall make provisions for the payment of existing city and county indebtedness as hereinafter required. The officers of a city and county, their compensation, qualifications, term of office and manner of election or appointment, shall be as provided for in its charter, subject to general laws and applicable constitutional provisions.

This section requires the legislature to provide political subdivisions with funds or the means to execute the mandates it gives them. This section was added by a 1984 amendment.

Article XI

Corporations Other than Municipal

SECTION 1

Creation and composition of state corporation commission. A permanent commission to consist of three members is hereby created, which shall be known as the state corporation commission.

The functions of the corporation commission are not confined to any of the three departments of government, but its duties pervade all three departments (*In re Atchison, T. & S. F. Railroad,* 1933).

SECTION 2

Election and terms of corporation commissioners. The members of the commission shall be elected for the term of six years; provided, that those chosen at the first election for state officers shall immediately qualify and classify themselves by lot, so that one of them shall hold office until two years, one until four years and one until six years from and after January first, nineteen hundred and thirteen; and thereafter one commissioner shall be elected at each general election.

The election and term of office of the members of the corporation commission are established in this section. The meaning of this section has not been the subject of judicial interpretation.

SECTION 3

Disqualifications for corporation commissioners. No officer, agent or employee of any railway, express, telegraph, telephone, sleeping-car or other transportation or transmission company, while representing such company, nor any person financially interested therein, shall hold office as a member of the commission, or perform any of the duties thereof, and no commissioner shall be qualified to act upon any matter pending before the commission, in which he is interested, either as principal, agent or attorney.

A commissioner's comments that constitute prejudgment may constitutionally taint any subsequent hearing and invalidate the ensuing commission order. Should this occur, the company would be free to put its proposed rates into effect as if the commission had not acted (*Mountain States Telephone & Telegraph Co. v. Corporation Commission*, 1982).

SECTION 4

Officers, assistants, procedure and attorney of corporation commission. The commission shall annually elect one of its members chairman and shall have one clerk, and such other officers, assistants and subordinates as may be prescribed by law, all of who shall be appointed and subject to removal by the commission. The commission shall prescribe its own rules of order and a procedure, except so far as specified in this constitution. The attorney general of the state, or his legally authorized representative, shall be the attorney for the commission.

The constitution does not assign the legislature the authority to make rules of procedure for the commission; therefore this section grants that power exclusively to the commission (*In re Atchison, T & S. F. Railroad*, 1933); however, rules allowing suspension of rates is a substantive matter and therefore not assigned to the commission by this section (*Mountain States Telephone & Telegraph Co. v. Corporation Commission*, 1982).

SECTION 5

Quarters, expenses and salaries of corporation commission. The legislature shall provide suitable quarters for the commission, and funds for its lawful expenses, including necessary traveling expenses, witness fees and mileage and cost of executing process issued by the commission, or the supreme court, or the district courts. The salary of each commissioner shall be prescribed by the legislature.

This section requires the legislature to provide the commission with the resources to operate and to set the commissioners' salaries. This section was amended in 1964 by substituting "cost" for "costs," and inserted commas before "and cost of," "or the Supreme Court," and "or the district courts" in the first sentence, and substituted "prescribed by the legislature" for "three thousand dollars per annum, payable quarterly" at the end of the section.

SECTION 6

General duties of corporation commission. Subject to the provisions of this constitution, and of such requirements, rules and regulations as may be prescribed by law, the state corporation commission shall be the department of government through which shall be issued all charters for domestic corporations and amendments or extensions thereof, and all licenses to foreign corporations to do business in this state; and through which shall be carried out all the provisions of this constitution relating to corporations and the laws made in pursuance thereof. The commission shall prescribe the form of all reports which may be required of corporations by this constitution or by law, and shall collect, receive and preserve such reports, and annually tabulate and publish them. All fees required by law to be paid for the filing of articles of incorporation, reports and other documents, shall be collected by the commission and paid into the state treasury. All charters, papers and documents relating to corporations on file in the office of the secretary of the territory, the commissioner of insurance and all other territorial offices, shall be transferred to the office of the commission.

This section does not grant authority to the commission to make determinations preliminary to issuing charters to state banks (*First Thrift & Loan Association v. State ex rel. Robinson*, 1956). The commission does not have the authority to charter drainage districts (*In re Dexter-Greenfield Drainage District*, 1956), or oil pipelines (*Murchinson & Co. v. State Corporation Commission*, 1947). The office of the superintendent was not abolished by this section since all of the functions of that office were not transferred to the corporation commission (*State ex rel. Chavez v. Sargent*, 1914).

SECTION 7

Powers of corporation commission over carriers; duties of supreme court. The commission shall have power and be charged with the duty of fixing, determining, supervising, regulating and controlling all charges and rates of railway, express, telegraph, telephone, sleeping car and other transportation and transmission companies and common carriers within the state and of determining any matters of public convenience and necessity relating to such facilities as expressed herein in the manner which has been or shall be provided by law; to require railway companies to provide and maintain adequate depots, stockpens, station buildings, agents and facilities for the accommodation of passengers and for receiving and delivering freight and express; to provide and maintain necessary crossings, culverts and sidings upon and alongside their roadbeds, whenever in the judgment of the commission the public interests demand, and as may be reasonable and just. The commission shall also have power and be charged with the duty to make and enforce reasonable and just rules requiring the supplying of cars and equipment for the use of shippers and passengers, and to require all intrastate railways, transportation companies or common carriers, to provide such reasonable safety appliances in connection with all equipment, as may be necessary and proper for the safety of its employees and the public, and as are now or may be required by the federal laws, rules and regulations governing interstate commerce. The commission shall have power to change or alter such rates, to change, alter or amend its orders, rules, regulations or determinations, and to enforce the same in the manner prescribed herein; provided, that in the matter of fixing rates of telephone and telegraph companies, due consideration shall be given to the earnings, investment and expenditure as a whole within the state. The commission shall include in that consideration the earnings, investment and expenditures derived from or related to the sale of directory advertising and other directory listing services. No general change in a rate, fare or charge shall be collected by any telephone or telegraph company or common carrier until such proposed increase is approved by the supreme court except as otherwise provided in this constitution. The commission shall have power to subpoena witnesses and enforce their attendance before the commission, through any district court or the supreme court of the state, and through such court to punish for contempt; and it shall have power, upon a hearing, to determine and decide any question given to it here, and in case of failure or refusal of any person, company or corporation to comply with any order within the time limit therein, unless an order of removal shall have been taken from such order by the company or corporation to the supreme court of this state, it shall immediately become the duty of the commission to remove such order, with the evidence adduced upon the hearing, with the documents in the case to the supreme court of this state. Any company, corporation or common carrier which does not comply with the order of the commission within the time limited therefor, may file with the commission a petition to remove such cause to the supreme court, and in the event of such removal by the company, corporation or common carrier, or other party to such hearing, the supreme court may, upon application, in its discretion or of its own motion, require or authorize additional evidence to be taken in such cause; but in the event of removal by the commission, upon failure of the company, corporation or common carrier, no additional evidence shall be allowed. The supreme court, for the consideration of such causes arising hereunder, shall be in session at all times, and shall give precedence to such causes. Any party to such hearing before the commission, shall have the same right to remove the order entered therein to the supreme court of the state, as given under the provisions hereof to the company or corporation against which such order is directed.

In addition to the other powers vested in the supreme court by this constitution and the laws of the state, the said court shall have the power and it shall be its duty to decide such cases on their merits, and carry into effect its judgments, orders and decrees made in such cases, by fine, forfeiture, mandamus, injunction and contempt or other appropriate proceedings.

The rate-regulating power of the commission is plenary, and beyond the control of the legislature; it is limited only by the principles of constitutional law and supreme court review as provided in this article. This involves a balancing of investor and consumer interests, and neither is paramount; however, a properly regulated utility should be allowed to recover only its true costs (*Mountain States Telephone & Telegraph Co. v. Corporation Commission*, 1982).

The provision for supreme court review of orders of the corporation commission is self-executing and the legislature has no authority to regulate the review process (*In re Southern Pacific Co.*, 1932).

A 1964 amendment inserted the phrase regarding public convenience and necessity, and inserted the fourth sentence.

SECTION 8

Hearings before corporation commission. The commission shall determine no question nor issue any order in relation to the matters specified in the preceding section, until after a public hearing held upon ten days' notice to the parties concerned, except in case of default after such notice. At any hearing before the commission involving a general change in a rate, fare or charge, the burden of proof to show that the proposed rate, fare or charge is just and reasonable, shall be upon the telephone or telegraph company or common carrier proposing to establish and collect the rate, fare or charge. The commission shall hear and decide application for a general change in a rate, fare or charge with reasonable promptness. If within six months after having filed such an application the commission has not entered an order disposing of the matter, the company or common carrier may put the proposed change into effect. In the event an aggrieved company or common carrier removes to the supreme court a commission order deciding an application for a general change in rate, fare or charge the supreme court may allow the proposed change to be placed into effect under bond in an amount and subject to terms and conditions as it may prescribe.

"Public hearing" means a completed public hearing, as distinguished from an adjourned hearing, and an order against a company which has not been given a hearing as provided in this section is unenforceable (*In re Atchison, T & S. F. Railroads Protest of Rates*, 1940). Regulated corporations are entitled to notice in advance of hearings, stating definitely the proposed order and the reasons for it, so that the corporation will be able to present evidence showing unreasonableness of the order (*Woody v. Denver & R.G.R.R.*, 1913); however, a corporation that makes a general appearance before the commission waives all irregularities preceding such hearing (*Stewart v. Denver & R.G.R.R.*, 1913). The burden of proof is on the commission to show the reasonableness of its orders (*In re Atchison, T. & S. F. Railroads Protest of Rates*, 1940). The second and succeeding sentences were added by a 1964 amendment.

SECTION 9

Interstate carrier rates. It is hereby made the duty of the commissioners to exercise constant diligence in informing themselves of the rates and charges of transportation and transmission companies and common carriers engaged in the transportation of passengers and property from points in this state; and whenever, it shall come to the knowledge of the commission, by complaint or in any other manner, that rate charged by any transportation or transmission company or common carrier, on interstate business is unjust, excessive or unreasonable, or that such rates discriminate against the citizens of the state, and in the judgment of the commission such complaint is well founded and the public welfare involved, the commission shall institute and prosecute to a final determination before the interstate commerce commission or commerce court, or any lawful authority having jurisdiction in the premises, such proceedings as it may deem expedient to obtain such relief as conditions may require.

The federal Constitution does not allow states to regulate interstate commerce; however, this section of the New Mexico Constitution assigns to the corporation commission the authority to file and pursue complaints with the Interstate Commerce Commission if companies doing interstate business charge rates that are unreasonable or discriminate against citizens of New Mexico.

The term "transmission company" is construed to mean telegraph and telephone companies and does not include gas and electric companies (*La Fallette v. Albuquerque Gas & Electric Company's Rates*, 1932).

SECTION 10

Basis for transportation and transmission rates. No transportation or transmission company or common carrier shall charge or receive any greater compensation, in the aggregate, for the transportation as interstate commerce of passengers, or like kind of property, or for the transmission of the same kind of message, between points in this state, for a shorter than a longer distance over the same line or route in the same direction, the shorter being included within the longer distance; but this section shall not be construed as authorizing any such company or common carrier to charge or receive as great compensation for shorter as for longer distance; provided, that telegraph and telephone companies may, in certain cases, with the approval of the commission, base their charges upon the airline distances instead of the distances actually traveled by the messages. The commission may from time to time authorize any such company or common carrier to disregard the foregoing provisions of this section, by charging such rates as the commission may prescribe as just and equitable between such company or common carrier and the public, to or from any junction or competitive points, or localities, or where the competition of points locate without or within this state may necessitate the prescribing of special rates for the protection of commerce of this state, or in cases of general epidemics, pestilence, calamitous visitations and other exigencies. This section shall not apply to mileage tickets or to any special excursions or commutation rates; nor to special rates for services rendered in the interest of any public or charitable object, when such tickets or rates shall have been prescribed or authorized by the commission, not shall it apply to special rates for services rendered to the United States or this state.

This section establishes the standards for the commission to use in setting intrastate transportation and transmission rates in New Mexico. If the framers of the constitution intended to confer jurisdiction over local gas and electric light companies in the commission, they would have said so in apt words (*La Fallette v. Albuquerque Gas & Electric Company's Rates*, 1932.)

SECTION 11

Records and reports of carriers. The commission shall have the right at all times to inspect the books, papers and records of all such companies and common carriers doing business in this state, and to require from such companies and common carriers from time to time special reports and statements, under oath, concerning their business. The commissioners shall have the power to administer oaths and to certify to their official acts.

The corporation commission is given the powers to obtain the information to set and regulate transportation and transmission rates. This section has not been interpreted by the courts.

SECTION 12

Acceptance of constitution by corporations. No corporation in existence at the time of the adoption of this constitution shall have the benefit of any future legislation, nor shall any amendment or extension to its charter be granted, until such corporation shall have filed in the office of the commission an acceptance of the provisions of this constitution; provided, however, that whether or not they file such acceptance, such corporations shall be subject to the provisions of this constitution and the laws of this state.

This section makes Article XI applicable to all corporations doing business in New Mexico and subject to state regulation (*Stewart v. Denver & R.G.R.R.*, 1913). In practice this is done by requiring foreign corporations to obtain a certificate of registration from the commission, see 53-17-1 NMSA 1978. Corporate businesses were recognized in New Mexico before the adoption of the constitution (*Shillinglaw v. Owen Shillinglaw Fuel Co.*, 1962).

SECTION 13

General corporation laws. The legislature shall provide for the organization of corporations by general law. All laws relating to corporations may be altered, amended or repealed by the legislature, at any time, when necessary for the public good and general welfare, and all corporations, doing business in this state, may, as to such business, be regulated, limited or restrained by laws not in conflict with the constitution of the United States or of this constitution.

The constitution reserves for the state the police powers to make reasonable regulations of corporations, including alteration or amendment of corporate charters (*Westland Development Co. v. Saavedra*, 1969).

SECTION 14

Corporations subject to police power. The police power of this state is supreme over all corporations as well as individuals.

This section provides that corporations have no special standing over individuals and are equally subject to the state's police power. All property rights are subject to fair exercise of police power, and reasonable regulations protecting public health, convenience, safety, or general welfare is not an unconstitutional taking of property in violation of either the national or state constitutions (*Mitchell v. City of Roswell*, 1941).

SECTION 15

Cooperation between carriers. Every railroad, car or express company, shall respectively receive and transport, without delay or discrimination, each other's cars, tonnage or passengers, under such rules and regulations as may be prescribed by the commission.

This section allows the interconnection of railroads operating within the state. This section's provision for railroads to have use of each other's tracks, requiring them to carry each other's passengers and freight is evidently to protect against railroad monopolies. This section has not been subject to judicial interpretation.

SECTION 16

Cooperation between transmission corporations. All telephone and telegraph lines, operated for hire, shall receive and transmit each other's messages without delay or discrimination, and make and maintain connections with each other's lines, under such rules and regulations as may be prescribed by the commission.

With an intent similar to Section 15 this provision requires that telephone and telegraph companies connect with and transmit each other's messages in order that the public will be served. This section has not been interpreted by the courts.

SECTION 17

Construction, intersections and connections of railroads. Any railroad corporation or association organized for the purpose, shall have the right to construct and operate a railroad between any points within this state or elsewhere, and to connect at the state line or elsewhere with the railroads of other states; and, under such terms, order or permission as may be granted in each instance by the commission, shall have the right to cause its road to intersect, connect with or cross any other railroad.

This section secures the right of all railroads operating in the state to make connections with railroads operating in other states.

SECTION 18

Eminent domain of corporate property. The right of eminent domain shall never be so abridged or construed as to prevent the legislature from taking the property and franchises of incorporated companies and subjecting them to the public use, the same as the property of individuals.

This section emphasizes that the legislature has the same right of eminent domain over corporations, just as it applies to individuals. It should be read in conjunction with Article II § 20, which requires the state to provide just compensation when it takes property. Proposed amendments to this section that would have increased the membership of the corporation commission were rejected by the people in 1955 and 1961.

Article XII

Education

SECTION 1

Free public schools. A uniform system of free public schools sufficient for the education of, and open to, all the children of school age in the state shall be established and maintained.

This article and its enabling statutes do not create a contractual relationship for which a person may sue for breach of contract (*Rubio v. Carlsbad Municipal School District,* 1987). Courses required of all students shall be without charge, but reasonable fees may be charged for elective courses, as defined by the New Mexico board of education (*Norton v. Board of Education,* 1976). School districts that are so large that students are unable to travel to and from school in one day deprive students of a free education (*Prince v. Board of Education,* 1975). Both federal and New Mexico law require the state to provide appropriate education to all pre-college-age children. Under federal law, state programs receiving federal assistance are forbidden from discriminating against handicapped children when meeting this obligation (*New Mexico Association for Retarded Children v. New Mexico,* 1982). The statute defining the persons entitled to free public school education can be found at 22-1-4 NMSA 1978.

SECTION 2

Permanent school fund. The permanent school fund of this state shall consist of the proceeds of sales of Section Two, Sixteen, Thirty-Two and Thirty-Six in each township of the state, or the lands selected in lieu thereof; the proceeds of sales of all lands that have been or may hereafter be granted to the state not otherwise appropriated by the terms and conditions of the grant; such portion of the proceeds of sales of land of the United States within the state as has been or may be granted by congress; also all other grants, gifts and devises made to the state, the purpose of which is not otherwise specified.

A permanent fund to support public education was created by Congress in the Ferguson Act of 1889 and confirmed by the 1910 Enabling Act for New Mexico Statehood. Together, these acts transferred approximately 9.2 million surface acres of federal lands and 13.1 million acres of federal mineral interests to New Mexico. This section establishes a permanent fund for the support of public schools. This fund includes the money received from the sale of federal land given the state by Congress, as provided in the statehood enabling act. Rent from national forest lands is also applied to the school fund. In 1994, the voters rejected a proposed amendment to this section to change the methods for making distributions from and many investments of the state's land grant permanent funds. This section has not been the subject of judicial interpretation.

SECTION 3

Control of constitutional educational institutions; use of state land proceeds and other educational funds. The schools, colleges, universities and other educational institutions provided for by this constitution shall forever remain under the exclusive control of the state, and no part of the proceeds arising from the sale or disposal of any lands granted to the state by congress, or any other funds appropriated, levied or collected for educational purposes, shall be used for the support of any sectarian, denominational or private school, college or university.

This section is to insure exclusive state control over the public schools and insure that no state school becomes sectarian. The term "control" has been construed by the courts to mean control over curriculum discipline, finance, administration, and, in general, control over all affairs of the school (*Prince v. Board of Education*, 1975). Salaries to members of religious orders who serve as teachers that are the same as those of other teachers do not comprise aid to religion forbidden by both the state and national constitutions; however, such teachers may not wear religious garb and insignia during the time they teach in public schools. Furthermore, the state may bar members of religious orders from being hired to teach in public schools after they knowingly taught sectarian religion to students during regular school hours (*Zellers v. Huff*, 1951).

SECTION 4

Current school fund. All forefeitures [forfeitures], unless otherwise provided by law, and all fines collected under general laws; the net proceeds of property that may come to the state by escheat; the rentals of all school lands or other lands granted to the state, the disposition of which is not otherwise provided for by the terms of the grant or by act of congress; and the income derived from the permanent school fund, shall constitute the current school fund of the state.

This section expands the permanent school fund by identifying various state revenues that must be added to the fund. County taxes for school maintenance are levied for a public purpose and do not violate this section (*Raynolds v. Swope,* 1922).

This section was amended in 1971 by deleting provisions related to school tax, distribution of the current school fund, and the minimum school year. A 1986 amendment deleted "fines and" before "forfeitures" and added "unless otherwise provided by law and all fines" after "forfeitures." Proposed amendments of this section failed in 1961, 1969, and 1970. In 1994, the voters rejected a proposed amendment to this section to change the methods for making distributions from and investments of the state's land grant permanent funds.

SECTION 5

Compulsory school attendance. Every child of school age and of sufficient physical and mental ability shall be required to attend a public school or other school during such period and for such time as may be prescribed by law.

This compulsory attendance requirement established by this section does not create a contractual right to education, over which the state can be sued (*Rubio v. Carlsbad Municipal School District,* 1987). The legislature's provisions for compulsory school attendance are found at 22-12-1 to 8 NMSA 1978.

SECTION 6

State department of public education; state board of education. A. There is hereby created a "state department of public education; and a "state board of education." The state board of education shall determine public school policy and vocational educational policy and shall have control, management and direction, including financial direction, distribution of school funds and financial accounting for all public schools, pursuant to authority and powers provided by law. The board shall appoint a qualified, experienced educational administrator to be known as the superintendent of public instruction, who shall, subject to the policies established by the board, direct the operation of the state department of public education.

B. Ten members of the state board of education who shall be state officers shall be elected for staggered terms of four years as provided by law. Board members shall be residents of the board of education district from which they are elected. Change of residency of a board member to a place outside the district from which he was elected shall automatically terminate the term of that member.

C. Five members of the state board of education who shall be nominated and by and with the consent of the senate appointed by the governor from five districts substantially equal in population for staggered four-year terms as provided by law. Those appointed by the governor shall be qualified electors of the state of New Mexico, no more than one-half or a simple majority of whom at the time of their appointment shall be members of the same political party. After 1990, the number of appointed members may be changed by law not to exceed five members.

D. The governor shall fill vacancies on the board by appointment of a resident from the district in which the vacancy occurs until the next regular election for membership on the board.

E. Upon adoption of this amendment, all functions related to the distribution of school funds and financial accounting for the public school shall be transferred to the state department of public education to be performed as provided by law.

This section is not self-executing (*Amador v. State Bd. of Education*, 1969); the state board has control, management, and direction of public schools but only as provided by law (*Fort Sumner Municipal School Bd. v. Parsons*, 1971). The judicial powers conferred on the state board of education by the legislature (55-101, 1941, since repealed) fall clearly within the constitutional authority conferred on the board (*McCormick v. Board of Education*, 1954).

School employment procedures provided by the legislature should not be the subject of court review as to their appropriateness as policy (*Wickersham v. State Bd. of Education*, 1970), and deciding whether or not an administrator is fit to perform his duties is a question of policy, and the court will not alter the state board's ruling unless its unreasonableness is supported by substantial evidence (*Board of Education v. Jennings*, 1982). The power to hire and fire teachers and other employees is reposed in local boards, not the state board of education (*Bourne v. Board of Education*, 1942); therefore, the state board only has jurisdiction over teacher employment when the teacher appeals from an adverse ruling by the local board (*Amador v. State Bd. of Education*, 1969).

The state board has statutory authority to set the standard for curriculum in private schools but this does not extend to supervision or management of private schools (*Santa Fe Community School v. State Bd. of Education*, 1974), nor does the state board have exclusive power to remove members of district boards of education (*State ex rel. Hannah v. Armijo*, 1933), and the suspension of a teacher for incompatibility with membership on the state board does not fall within the purpose of insuring high quality education (*Amador v. State Bd. of Education*, 1969).

This section was completely rewritten by a 1958 amendment. Prior to that amendment the board consisted of the governor, state superintendent of public instruction, and five members appointed by the governor. A 1986 amendment completely repealed this section and replaced it with the current wording.

SECTION 7

Investment of permanent school fund. The principal of the permanent school fund, and other permanent funds, shall be invested by a state investment officer in accordance with policy regulations promulgated by a state investment council. The legislature may by a three-fourth vote of the members elected to each house provide that said fund may be invested in interest-bearing or other securities.

In making investments, the state investment officer, under the supervision of the state investment council, shall exercise the judgment and care under the circumstances then prevailing which businessmen of ordinary prudence, discretion and intelligence exercise in the management of their own affairs not in regard to speculation but in regard to the permanent disposition of their funds, considering the probable income as well as the probable safety of their capital; provided, not more than fifty percent of the permanent school fund or other permanent fund, shall be invested at any given time in corporate stocks and bonds nor shall more than ten percent of the voting stock of a corporation be held and provided further, stock eligible for purchase shall be restricted to those stocks of businesses incorporated within the United States prior to the date of purchase and which are listed upon a national stock exchange.

The standards for the prudent investment of the permanent school fund are set out in this section. The purchase by a state investment officer of stock in a corporation formed in, and a legal entity in, a foreign nation violated this section (*State ex rel. Udall v. Colonial Penn Ins. Co.*, 1991).

In its original form this section required that the principal of the fund be invested in bonds of New Mexico, or its political subdivisions, with the proviso that the legislature by a three-fourths vote may provide for investment in other interest-bearing securities; however, all investments had to be approved by the governor, attorney general, and secretary of state; and all losses from such investments had to be reimbursed by the state. A 1958 amendment rewrote the section deleting the reference to state bonds, and the requirement for approval of the listed officials. It also provided for the establishment of a state investment council and set a 25 percent maximum as the proportion of the fund to be invested in corporate stocks and bonds. A 1965 amendment inserted a paragraph relating to the sale of interest-bearing notes at less than their original acquisition costs under certain circumstances, and increased the maximum investment in corporate stocks and bonds to 50 percent. An amendment ratified in 1989 deleted the paragraph inserted in 1965, and deleted the requirement that all losses from such investments had to be reimbursed by the state. An amendment that would have deleted the proviso beginning "and provided further" was rejected by the people in 1990. The state investment council provided for in this section was established by the legislature, see 6-8-1 to 6-8-16 NMSA 1978. In 1994, the voters rejected a proposed amendment to this section to change the methods for making distributions from and investments of the state's land grant permanent funds.

SECTION 8

Teachers to learn English and Spanish. The legislature shall provide for the training of teachers in the normal schools or otherwise so that they may become proficient in both the English and Spanish languages, to qualify them to teach Spanish-speaking pupils and students in the public schools and educational institutions of the state, and shall provide proper means and methods to facilitate the teaching of the English language and other branches of learning to such pupils and students.

This section has never been the subject of judicial interpretation; however, attorney generals' opinions have asserted that its clear intent is to teach English to Spanish-speaking students. The section mandates the legislature to provide teachers proficient in both English and Spanish to teach Spanish-speaking pupils; it does not require all teachers to have this proficiency. For comments on this issue see "Education and the Spanish-Speaking—An Attorney General's Opinion on Article XII, Section 8 of the New Mexico Constitution," 3 *New Mexico Law Review* 364 (1973).

SECTION 9

Religious tests in schools. No religious test shall ever be required as a condition of admission into the public school or any educational institution of this state, either as a teacher or student, and no teacher or student of such school or institution shall ever be required to attend or participate in any religious service whatsoever.

The use or incorporation of religious doctrine or beliefs in the public schools is absolutely prohibited by this section. Nor can any religious test be required of either students or teachers. A law prohibiting paying religious sisters who are qualified and employed to teach in public schools would violate this provision (Opinion of the Attorney General No. 35, 1939-40); however, members of religious orders teaching in public school can teach only secular subjects and must refrain from wearing religious garb or insignia (*Zellers v. Huff*, 1951). The courts may properly enjoin dissemination of sectarian literature in schoolrooms (*Miller v. Cooper*, 1952).

SECTION 10

Educational rights of children of Spanish descent. Children of Spanish descent in the state of New Mexico shall never be denied the right and privilege of admission and attendance in the public schools or other public educational institutions of the state, and they shall never be classed in separate schools, but shall forever enjoy perfect equality with other children in all public schools and educational institutions of the state, and the legislature shall provide penalties for the violation of this section. This section shall never be amended except upon a vote of the people of this state, in an election at which at least three-fourths of the electors voting in the whole state and at least two-thirds of those voting in each county in the state shall vote for such amendment.

This section provides affirmative protection against discrimination by the school system for children who are descendants of Spanish-speaking people. Further discussion of this issue can be found in the note "Bilingual Education: *Serna v. Portales Municipal Schools,*" 5 *New Mexico Law Review* 321 (1975).

The affirmative vote of two-thirds of the voters in each county required for amendment of this section is, no doubt, void. Similar provisions in Article VII § 3 and Article XIX § 1 were held to violate the "one man, one vote" requirement of the U.S. Constitution in *State ex rel Witt v. State Canvassing Board* (1968); in that decision, the court did not rule on this section. For a construction of "electors voting" see Article VII § 3 in this commentary.

SECTION 11

State educational institutions. The university of New Mexico, at Albuquerque; the New Mexico state university, near Las Cruces, formerly known as New Mexico college of agriculture and mechanic arts; the New Mexico highlands university, at Las Vegas, formerly known as New Mexico normal university; the western New Mexico university, at Silver City, formerly known as New Mexico western college and New Mexico normal school; the eastern New Mexico university, at Portales, formerly known as eastern New Mexico normal school; the New Mexico institute of mining and technology, at Socorro, formerly known as New Mexico school of mines; the New Mexico military institute, at Roswell, formerly known as New Mexico military institute; the New Mexico school for the visually handicapped, at Alamogordo, formerly known as New Mexico institute for the blind; the New Mexico school for the deaf, at Santa Fe, formerly known as New Mexico asylum for deaf and dumb; the northern New Mexico state school, at El Rito, formerly known as Spanish-American school; are hereby confirmed as state educational institutions. All lands, together with the natural products, held in trust thereof and the money proceeds of any lands and products, held in trust for the institutions, respectively, under their former names, and all properties heretofore granted to, or owned by, or which, may hereafter be granted or conveyed to, the institutions respectively, under their former names, shall, in like manner as heretofore, be held in trust for, or owned by or be considered granted to, the institutions individually under their name as hereinabove adopted and confirmed. The appropriations made and which may hereinafter be made to the state by the United States for agriculture and mechanical colleges and experiment stations in connection therewith shall be paid to the New Mexico state university, formerly known as New Mexico college of agriculture and mechanic arts.

The state was made the owner of state educational institutions by this section (*State v. Regents of University of New Mexico*, 1927). Governmental immunity from tort suits applies to state educational institutions (*Livingston v. N.M. College of Agriculture & Mechanic Arts*, 1958), nor can such suits be brought in federal court because such action is in effect against the state of New Mexico and the Tenth Amendment bars federal jurisdiction (*Korgich v. Regents of New Mexico School of Mines*, 10th Cir. 1978).

This section has been amended twice. A 1960 amendment changed the names of several institutions and added the present second sentence. A 1964 amendment changed the name of New Mexico Western College to Western New Mexico University.

SECTION 12

Acceptance and use of Enabling Act educational grants. All lands granted under the provisions of the act of congress, entitled, "An act to enable the people of New Mexico to form a constitution and state government and be admitted into the union on an equal footing with the original states; and to enable the people of Arizona to form a constitution and state government and be admitted into the union on an equal footing with the original states," for the purpose of said several institutions are hereby accepted and confirmed to said institutions, and shall be exclusively used for the purpose for which they were granted; provided, that one hundred and seventy thousand acres of the land granted by said act for normal school purposes are hereby equally apportioned between said three normal institutions, and the remaining thirty thousand acres thereof is reserved for a normal school which shall be established by the legislature and located in one of the counties of Union, Quay, Curry, Rossevelt, Chaves, or Eddy.

The reference to "the act of congress" is to the Enabling Act of June 20, 1910. Building and improvement bonds issued under statutory authority to anticipate income from institutional lands, granted by the Enabling Act and accepted by this section for university purposes are not obligations of the state, notwithstanding that the constitution makes the state the owner of state institutions (*State v. Regents of University of New Mexico*, 1927).

SECTION 13

Boards of regents for educational institutions. The legislature shall provide for the control and management of each of said institutions, except the university of New Mexico, by a board of regents for each institution, consisting of five members, four of whom shall be qualified electors of the state of New Mexico, one of whom shall be a member of the student body of the institution and no more than three of whom at the time of their appointment shall be members of the same political party; provided however that the student body member provision in this section shall not apply to the New Mexico school for the deaf, the New Mexico military institute, the northern New Mexico state school or the New Mexico school for the visually handicapped, and for each of those four institutions all five members of the board of regents shall be qualified electors of the state of New Mexico. The governor shall nominate and by and with the consent of the senate shall appoint the members of each board of regents for each of said institutions. The term of said nonstudent members shall be for six years, provided that of the five first appointed the terms of two shall be for two years, the terms of two shall be for four years, and the term of one shall be for six years. Following the approval by the voters of this amendment and upon the first vacancy of a position held by a nonstudent member of each eligible institution's board of regents, the governor shall nominate and by and with the consent of the senate shall appoint a student to serve a two-year term. The governor shall select, with the advice and consent of the senate, a student member from a list provided by the president of the institution. In making the list, the president of the institution shall give due consideration to the recommendations of the student body president of the institution.

The legislature shall provide for the control and management of the university of New Mexico by a board of regents consisting of seven members, six of whom shall be qualified electors of the state of New Mexico, one of whom shall be a member of the student body of the university of New Mexico and no more than four of whom shall be a member of the same political party. The governor shall nominate and by and with the consent of the senate shall appoint the members the board of regents. The present five members shall serve out their present terms. The two additional members shall be appointed in 1987 for terms of six years. Following the approval by the voters of this amendment and upon the first vacancy of a position held by a nonstudent member of the university of New Mexico's board of regents, the governor shall nominate and by the consent of the senate shall appoint a student member to serve a two-year term. The governor shall select, with the advice and consent of the senate, a student member from a list provided by the president of the university of New Mexico. In making the list, the president of the university of New Mexico shall give due consideration to the recommendations of the student body president of the university.

Members of the board shall not be removed except for incompetence, neglect of duty or malfeasance in office.

Provided, however, no removal shall be made without notice of hearing and opportunity to be heard having first been given such member.

The supreme court of the state of New Mexico is hereby given exclusive original jurisdiction of proceeding to remove members of the board under such rules as it may promulgate, and its decisions in connection with such matters shall be final.

Boards of regents are to oversee the administration of the state's educational institutions. Persons serving as regents owe their duties to the state, not to a private person; therefore, a taxpayer has no standing to enforce by mandamus a duty owing to the public (*Womack v. Regents of University of New Mexico*, 1971).

The board of regents is given broad discretion in its power to control the institution. Inherent in this power is requiring students to adhere to generally accepted standards of conduct; it may therefore place limits on visitations by persons of opposite sex in residence halls or dormitory bedrooms (*Futrell v. Ahrens*, 1976). The legislature has expressly recognized the authority of institutions of higher learning to receive revenues from various sources, and to buy, sell, lease, or mortgage real estate and do all things which, in the view of the respective board of regents, will promote the best interests of their institutions; therefore the legislature lacks the authority to appropriate these funds or to control the use of them through appropriations (*State ex rel Sego v. Kirkpatrick*, 1974).

This section has been amended three times. The requirement that the regents be qualified electors, and a change from four- to six-year terms were added by a 1949 amendment. A 1986 amendment added "except the University of New Mexico" and added the present second paragraph. A 1994 amendment added the provisions that a student should be one of the members of each board except at the named institutions, and provided for the selection and terms of the student members. A 1970 attempt to amend this section to revise provisions relating to terms of office and removal from office failed to be ratified.

SECTION 14

Recall of local school board members. Any elected local school board member is subject to recall by the voters of the school district from which elected. A petition for a recall election must cite grounds of malfeasance or misfeasance in office or violation of the oath of office by the member concerned. The recall petition shall be signed by registered voters not less in number than thirty-three and one-third percent of those who voted for the office at the last preceding election at which the office was voted upon. Procedures for filing petitions and for determining validity of signatures shall be provided by law. If at the special election a majority of the votes cast on the question of recall are in favor thereof, the local school board member is recalled from office and the vacancy shall be filled as provided by law.

This section was added by a 1973 amendment, and is the only provision in the constitution providing for the recall of elected officials. It was amended in

1986 to substitute the present fourth sentence for the existing one and to delete the former last sentence. An amendment to this section proposed in 1994 to eliminate the provision authorizing recall elections of school board officials was rejected by the voters. This section has not been interpreted by the courts.

SECTION 15

Local school boards having seven single-member districts. In those local school districts having a population of more than two hundred thousand, as shown by the most recent decennial census, the qualified electors of the districts may choose to have a local school board composed of seven members, residents of and elected from single member districts.

If a majority of the qualified electors voting in such a district vote to have a seven-member board, the school district shall be divided into seven local school board member districts which shall be compact, contiguous and as nearly equal in population as possible. One school board member shall reside within, and be elected from each local school board member district. Change of residence to a place outside of the district from which a school board member was elected shall automatically terminate the service of that school board member and the office shall be declared vacant.

The school board member districts shall be established by resolution of the local school board with the approval of the state legislature, and may be changed once after each federal decennial census by the local school board with the approval of the state legislature.

The elections required under this amendment shall be called and conducted as provided by law for other local school board elections. The state board of education shall, by resolution, establish the terms of the first board elected after the creation of such seven-member board.

This section, added by a 1980 amendment provides that school districts with populations of more than 200,000 may choose to increase the size of the board to seven members, providing that they are elected from single-member districts of which they are residents. This section has not been the subject of judicial interpretation.

Article XIII

Public Lands

SECTION 1

Disposition of state lands. All lands belonging to the territory of New Mexico, and all lands granted, transferred, or confirmed to the state by congress, and all lands hereafter acquired, are declared to be public lands of the state to be held or disposed of as may be provided by law for the purpose for which they have been or may be granted, donated or otherwise acquired; provided, that such of school Sections Two, Thirty-Two, Sixteen and Thirty-Six as are not contiguous to other state lands shall not be sold within the period of ten years next after the admission of New Mexico as a state for less than ten dollars [($10.00)] per acre.

This section governs the disposition of state lands. The term "public lands" in this section is construed to be limited to lands acquired in a proprietary capacity; it does not include lands taken through tax proceedings; these are to be sold and the money promptly remitted to the agencies that assessed the taxes and the lands are to be returned to the tax rolls (*Greene v. Esquibel*, 1954). The United States as a grantor of public lands can impose conditions on their use and has the right to exact performance of such conditions (*Ervien v. United States*, 1919). The title to state lands cannot be gained through the legal doctrine of acquiescence; this rule also applies to municipal lands (*Stone v. Rhodes*, 1988).

SECTION 2

Duties of land commissioner. The commissioner of public lands shall select, locate, classify and have the direction, control, care and disposition of all public lands, under the provisions of the acts of congress relating thereto and such regulations as may be provided by law.

This section assigns the general duties of the office of commissioner of public lands created by Article V § 1. These duties are further defined by statutory law (19-1-1 to 10-1-24 NMSA 1978). The commissioner has only those powers conferred by the constitution and granted by law (*State ex rel. Del Curto v. District Court*, 1947). In selling state lands the commission is merely an agent of the state and has only those powers granted by law (*Zinn v. Hampson*, 1956). Leases of state lands for a longer term than five years are required to be advertised for sale and sold to the highest bidder (*Hart v. Walker*, 1935; and *State ex rel. McElroy v. Vesely*, 1935). Persons and corporations which have trespassed and made improvements on land cannot gain by circumvention that land; the commissioner has no power to cancel the contract to purchase the land (*In re Dasburg*, 1941).

The state may reserve ownership in the mineral rights to public lands it sells. The state must necessarily be a party to a title suit brought by one holding a contract of purchase of state lands against lessees of land from the state to explore for oil and gas, seeking to set aside reservation of minerals in the contract (*American Trust & Savings Bank v. Scobee*, 1924), nor can a writ of mandamus compel the commissioner to issue a deed conveying public lands free from reservation of minerals therein, a reservation that was contained in the contract of sale, because the writ is in effect an action against the state (*State ex rel. Evans v. Field*, 1921).

SECTION 3

Patents for public lands. The provisions of the Enabling Act (36 Stat. 557, 563) which prohibits the granting of a patent for a portion of a tract of public lands under sales contract because the full consideration for the entire tract is not or was not paid, are waived with respect to the following sales:

A. sale of a portion of a tract of public lands under sales contract; if the patent to that portion was issued on or before September 4, 1956;

B. sale of a portion of a tract under sales contract if the right to purchase the portion is derived from an assignment made on or before September 4, 1956; or

C. sale of a portion of a tract under sales contract or under a contract entered into in substitution of such contract, if the right to purchase all other portions of the tract were assigned or relinquished on or before September 4, 1956 by the person holding the contract.

The legislature may enact laws to carry out the purposes of this amendment.

This section was added by an amendment ratified in 1963. In a decision issued prior to that amendment the supreme court held that the commissioner did not have the authority to issue a patent to a portion of a tract sold under contract, when only the part covered by patent had been paid for and the balance due and the contract had not been paid (*Zinn v. Hampson*, 1956).

Article XIV

Public Institutions

SECTION 1

State institutions. The penitentiary at Santa Fe, the miners' hospital at Raton, the New Mexico state hospital at Las Vegas, the New Mexico boys' school at Springer, the girls' welfare home at Albuquerque, the Carrie Tingley crippled children's hospital at Truth or Consequences and the Los Lunas mental hospital at Los Lunas are hereby confirmed as state institutions.

By this section the state takes title to the public institutions of the territory of New Mexico. The section was amended in 1955 to change the terms "insane asylum" to the "state hospital" and the "reform school" to "boys' school." A 1960 amendment added the institutions presently listed after the boys' school. A 1994 proposal to amend this section to change the name of the state hospital in Las Vegas failed to be ratified.

This section expressly accepted conditions imposed on land trusts for the hospital for disabled miners, confirmed the hospital at Raton to be that hospital, and stated that the lands would be used exclusively for the purpose for which they were granted (*U.S. v. New Mexico*, 1976).

The statute found at 41-1-1 NMSA 1953 (now repealed), creating the state penitentiary as a public corporation with power to sue and be sued, did not grant the right to sue in tort because such suit would be a suit against the state (*Vigil v. Penitentiary of New Mexico*, 1948). The present statute governing such suits is the

Tort Claims Act (41-4-1 to 41-4-27 NMSA 1978). The locations of the institutions listed in this section are descriptive and not a mandatory requirement of where the institutions must be located (*Opinion of the Attorney General* No. 5628, 1954).

SECTION 2

Federal land grants and donations. All lands which have been or which may be granted to the state by congress for the purpose of said several institutions are hereby accepted for said several institutions with all other grants, donations or devices for the benefit of the same and shall be exclusively used for the purpose for which they were or may be granted, donated or devised.

This section accepts the lands granted from the United States to support the institutions listed in Section 1, and obligates the state to insure that all income received from the lands will be used only for the purposes specified by the grant. So long as the institutions remain land grant beneficiaries, no amendment to Section 1 is necessary should one of the institutions move to another location (*Opinion of the Attorney General* No. 80-16, 1980).

SECTION 3

Control and management. Each of said institutions shall be under such control and management as may be provided by law.

A 1955 amendment deleted the earlier provisions for a five-member board to control each of the institutions, the appointment of the members, and the length of their terms of office. The present section grants the legislature the authority to determine how the institutions will be controlled.

Article XV

Agriculture and Conservation

SECTION 1

Department of agriculture. There shall be a department of agriculture which shall be under the control of the board of regents of the college of agriculture and mechanic arts; and the legislature shall provide lands and funds necessary for experimental farming and demonstrating by said department.

This section creates a department of agriculture and places it under the control of the board of regents of New Mexico State University (the name of the College of Agriculture and Mechanic Arts was changed by a 1960 amendment to Article XII § 11). This section has not been the subject of judicial interpretation.

SECTION 2

Forest fire prevention. The police power of the state shall extend to such control of private forest lands as shall be necessary for the prevention and suppression of forest fires.

This section explicitly gives the state the authority to exercise police powers over private land to prevent and suppress forest fires. For further comments on this matter see "Forest Fire Protection on Public and Private Lands in New Mexico," 4 *Natural Resources Journal* 374 (1964).

Article XVI

Irrigation and Water Rights

SECTION 1

Existing water rights confirmed. All existing rights to the use of any water in this state for any useful or beneficial purpose are hereby recognized and confirmed.

This article addresses one of the most contentious areas of law in and among western states. The term "water" in this article includes and indicates waters of underground streams, channels, artesian basins, reservoirs, and lakes the boundaries of which may be reasonably ascertained (*State ex rel Reynolds v. Mears*, 1974; and *McBee v. Reynolds*, 1965). Rights to water for irrigation established prior to enactment of the water code enacted under this section (72-9-1 NMSA 1978) are protected (*State ex rel Bliss v. Davis*, 1957).

All parties in disputes over acquisition of water rights, including the United States, are governed by the New Mexico Constitution and statutory law, and case law of federal, territorial, and New Mexico courts (*U.S. v. Ballard*, 1960), except Pueblo Indians in New Mexico, who are not controlled by state water law or prior appropriations (*New Mexico v. Aamodt*, 1976). The more expansive water rights of Pueblo Indians are discussed by O'Brien in "Indian Pueblo Water Rights Not Subject to State Law Prior to Appropriation," *Natural Resources Journal* 17: 341–344 (1977).

The state may use its police power to require a license of any person drilling wells in areas determined by state engineers to be an underground water source, the boundaries of which have been determined to be reasonably ascertainable (*State v. Myers*, 1958). The state may exercise eminent domain to store and convey water, not only for irrigation or domestic purposes alone, but to provide all beneficial uses of water (*Kaiser Steel Corp. v. W. S. Ranch Co.*, 1970).

SECTION 2

Appropriation of water. The unappropriated water of every natural stream, perennial or torrential, within the state of New Mexico, is hereby declared to belong to the public and to be subject to appropriation for beneficial use, in accordance with the laws of the state. Priority of appropriation shall give the better right.

This section claims plenary state control over public water, subject only to governmental uses of the United States, and the section is declaratory of and recognizes prior existing law (*State ex rel. Game Commission v. Red River Valley Co.*, 1945). Therefore, statutes, enacted on the authority of this section, that claim public ownership of underground waters, artesian basins, reservoirs, and lakes, are not subversive of vested rights of owners of land overlying such waters because those statutes are declaratory of existing law (*Yeo v. Tweedy*, 1929). This section cannot deprive a party of the right of title derived from a congressional act of conformation or based on an early Mexican grant (*State ex rel. State Game Commission v. Red River Valley Co.*, 1945).

Artificial waters are not subject to appropriation under the laws of New Mexico. The creator of the artificial flow of water is owner of the water so long as it is confined to his property (*Hagerman Irrigation Co. v. East Grand Plains Drainage Dist.*, 1920). The owner of surface water rights does not have a right to receive a particular silt content that has existed historically (*Ensenada Land & Water Ass'n v. Sleeper*, 1988).

The state controls the use of water because it does not part with ownership; it only allows an immediate use of water (*Jicarilla Apache Tribe v. United States*, 1981). Waters need not be appropriated for public use since they are already reserved for such use, subject to being specifically appropriated for private beneficial use. Thus, a sportsman may fish from public waters so long as he does not trespass on the land of another, and the owner of underlying land cannot complain of fishing from boats upon the public water above. Where two perennial streams were public water prior to building a dam, they remain public after being impounded (*State ex rel. Game Commission v. Red River Valley Co.*, 1945).

New Mexico has adopted the appropriation doctrine of water use (*Hinderlider v. La Plata River & Cherry Creek Ditch Co.*, 1938); the adjudication of rights is essential for the appropriation doctrine to function (*New Mexico v. Aamodt*, 1976). Under this doctrine the appropriator does not acquire any right to specific water flowing in a public stream, though he may take a given quantity of water for a specific purpose (*State ex re I. Game Commission v. Red River Valley Co.,* 1945).

The determination of "beneficial use" of water is a question of fact (*Jicarilla Apache Tribe v. United States,* 1981). "Beneficial use" of public waters is construed as the use of such water as may be necessary for some useful and beneficial purpose in connection with the land from which it is taken (*State ex rel. Erickson v. McLean,* 1957).

Private property can be taken through eminent domain, but only for public use; however, the effect of New Mexico water law is to carve an exception to this constitutional principle in recognition of overriding considerations borne of necessity in an arid land where water is the lifeblood of the community (*W. S. Ranch Co. v. Kaiser Steel Corp,* 1967).

Equitable apportionment is the doctrine of federal common law that governs disputes between states concerning their rights to water use of interstate streams. When both states have adopted the doctrine of prior appropriation, priority becomes the "guiding principle" in an allocation between competing states, but state law is not controlling. While the equities supporting the protection of established, senior users are substantial, it is also appropriate to consider additional factors relevant to a just apportionment, such as the conservation measures available to both states and the balance of harm and benefit that might result from a diversion sought by the senior user (*Colorado v. New Mexico,* 1982). Water is treated like any other natural resource for the purpose of constitutional analysis under the commerce clause of the U.S. Constitution. New Mexico's prohibition of the out-of-state export of ground water, derived from Article XVI §§2 and 3 is unconstitutional, because such an embargo violates the commerce clause (*City of El Paso ex rel. Its Public Service Bd. v. Reynolds,* 1983).

SECTION 3

Beneficial use of water. Beneficial use shall be the basis, the measure and the limit of the right to use of water.

"Beneficial use" of public waters is construed as the use of such water as may be necessary for some useful and beneficial purpose in connection with the land from which it is taken (*State ex rel. Erickson v. McLean,* 1957); it also includes fishing and recreation as well as irrigation and domestic uses (*State ex rel. Game Commission v. Red River Valley Co.,* 1945); moreover, the use of water must not only be beneficial to the lands of the appropriator, but it must also be reasonable in relation thereto, and no matter how early a person's priority of appropriation may be, he is not entitled to use more water than is necessary for his actual use. Excessive, wasteful diversion of water is not diversion to beneficial use (*State ex rel. Erickson v. McLean,* 1957). For the purpose of constitutional analysis under the commerce clause of the U.S. Constitution, water is to be treated the same as other natural resources (*City of El Paso ex rel. Its Public Service Bd. v. Reynolds*, 1983).

The attainment of the state's conservation purposes constitutes a useful or beneficial application of waters (*U.S. v. Ballard*, 1960), and the amount of water consumed in a beneficial use is a measure of the quantity of appropriation (*State ex rel. Erickson v. McLean*, 1957). The appropriator can only take that which he can beneficially use (*Worley v. United States Borax & Chemical Corp.*, 1967). "Beneficial use" takes into account the amount of water necessary for effective use under the particular circumstances of soil conditions, method of conveyance, topography, and climate (*State ex rel. Reynolds v. Mears*, 1974). For a city to store water in amounts greatly in excess of its current needs on the strength of mere speculation as to the demands of possible sales in the future is unreasonable and does not constitute beneficial use (*Jicarilla Apache Tribe v. United States*, 1981). Beneficial use is the basis, measure, and limit of the right to use water in New Mexico, and unused water rights may be forfeited (*United States ex rel. Acoma & Laguna Indian Pueblos v. Bluewater-Toltec Irrigation Dist.*, 1984). When water is wasted willfully and negligently, civil liability attaches to that misuse (*Holloway v. Evans*, 1951).

SECTION 4

Drainage districts and systems. The legislature is authorized to provide by law for the organization and operation of drainage districts and systems.

Although New Mexico rainfall averages around eight inches per year, much of this rain comes in brief, heavy thunderstorms, which can result in extensive local flooding. This section provides for a system of drainage ditches (in Spanish, *arroyos*), to divert waters for beneficial use and to prevent flooding. This section does not require legislative implementation of this section; it designates the authority for such water control as a "drainage district" (*Albuquerque Metropolitan Arroyo Flood Control Authority v. Swinburne*, 1964); nor does this section necessarily contemplate that drainage districts shall be corporations (*In re Dexter-Greenfield Drainage Dist.*, 1915). Extensive provisions for implementing this section are provided in Chapter 73 NMSA 1978.

SECTION 5

Appeals in matters relating to water rights. In any appeal to the district court from decision, act or refusal to act of any state executive officer or body in matters relating to water rights, the proceeding upon appeal shall be de novo as cases originally docketed in the district court unless otherwise provided by law.

A trial de novo in response to an appeal of the state engineer's findings in regard to water rights, that considers evidence adduced at a hearing before the engineer, meets this section's requirements for a de novo trial, so long as all relevant evidence desired by the parties was also considered. The court, however, should present the substance of its judgment rather than merely affirming the finding of the engineer (*Fort Sumner Irrigation Dist. v. Carlsbad Irrigation Dist.*, 1974).

A provision added to the water rights statutes in 1967 that allowed a hearing related to underground waters in district court, prior to a decision by the state engineer, was an unconstitutional violation of the separation of power provisions of Article III. The subsequent adoption of this Article XVI § 5 did not validate that statute, because this section provides for appeals; the statute provided for original proceedings (*Fellows v. Shultz*, 1970).

This section was added by a 1967 amendment; an amendment that proposed a similar provision was rejected by the voters in 1965.

Article XVII

Mines and Mining

SECTION 1

Inspector of mines. There shall be a state mine inspector who shall be appointed by the governor, by and with the advice and consent of the senate, for a term of four years, and whose duties and salary shall be prescribed by law. The legislature may pass laws prescribing reasonable qualifications for the state mine inspector and deputy mine inspectors, and current legislative enactments prescribing such qualifications are declared to be in full force and effect.

This section provides for a state mine inspector; it was amended in 1961, by substituting "a state mine inspector" in place of "an inspector of mines," and by adding the second sentence. For the applicability of the federal Mining Inspection Act of 1891, see Article XXII § 3. Legislation relating to state inspector of mines can be found in Chapter 69, Articles 5 and 8 NMSA 1978.

SECTION 2

Mining regulations; employment of children under fourteen. The legislature shall enact laws requiring the proper ventilation of mines, the construction and maintenance of escapement shafts or slopes, and the adoption and use of appliances necessary to protect the health and secure the safety of employees therein. No children under the age of fourteen shall be employed in mines.

The intent of this section is to provide for the safety of those working in the mines. Laws 1912, ch. 80 (now repealed) was evidently enacted with the intent to comply with this section's requirements (*Melkusch v. Victor American Fuel Co.*, 1916). Current legislation pertaining to this section includes the prohibition of certain mining work by children under eighteen (50-6-5 NMSA 1978), the New Mexico Mine Safety Act (69-8-1 to 69-8-15 NMSA 1978), and safety regulations (69-15-1 to 69-15-16 NMSA 1978).

Article XVIII

Militia

SECTION 1

Composition, name and commander in chief of militia. The militia of this state shall consist of all able-bodied male citizens between the ages of eighteen and forty-five, except such as are exempt by laws of the United States or of this state. The organized militia shall be called the "national guard of New Mexico," of which the governor shall be commander in chief.

The apparent intent of this section is to provide the state with a military force to meet the possibility of civil unrest or natural disaster. This section should be read in conjunction with Article II § 9, which provides that the military will always be subordinate to the civil authority and that soldiers shall not be quartered in homes during peacetime, and with Article V § 4, which also designates the governor as commander in chief of the militia.

SECTION 2

Organization, discipline and equipment of militia. The legislature shall provide for the organization, discipline and equipment of the militia, which shall consist as nearly as practicable to the organization, discipline and equipment of the regular army of the United States, and shall provide for the maintenance thereof.

This section does not mandate the legislature to organize the militia, but requires it to provide for its organization, and the legislature has declared its policy of establishing a militia (*State ex rel Charlton v. French*, 1940). This section does not authorize the legislature to provide for the court-martial of a militiaman accused of a felony when no state of war or public danger exists (*State ex rel. Sage v. Montoya*, 1959).

This section should be read in conjunction with Article IX § 9, which provides for contracting debts to provide for public defense.

Article XIX

Amendments

SECTION 1

Proposing and ratifying amendments. Any amendment or amendments to this constitution may be proposed in either house of the legislature at any regular session thereof; and if a majority of all members elected to each of the two houses voting separately shall vote in favor thereof, such proposed amendment or amendments shall be entered on their respective journals with the yeas and nays thereon.

The secretary of state shall cause any such amendment or amendments to be published in at least one newspaper in every county of the state, where a newspaper is published once each week, for four consecutive weeks, in English and Spanish when newspapers in both of said languages are published in such counties, the last publication to be not more than two weeks prior to the election at which time said amendment or amendments shall be submitted to the electors of the state for their approval or rejection; and the said amendment or amendments shall be voted upon at the next regular election held in said state after the adjournment of the legislature proposing such amendment or amendments, or at such special election to be held not less than six months after the adjournment of said legislature may by law provide. If the same be ratified by a majority of the electors voting thereon such amendment or amendments shall become part of this constitution. If two or more amendments are proposed, they shall be so submitted as to enable the electors to vote on each of them separately: provided that no amendment shall apply to or affect the provisions

> of Sections One and Three of Article VII hereof, on elective franchise, and Sections Eight and Ten of Article XII hereof, on education, unless it be proposed by a vote of three-fourths of the members elected to each house and be ratified by a vote of the people of this state in an election at which at least three-fourths of the electors voting in the whole state and at least two-thirds of those voting in each county in the state shall vote for such amendment.

This article of the constitution was, in effect, rewritten by Congress as requirement of the resolution of August 21, 1911, which provided for admission of New Mexico as a state and stipulated the amendment of this article as a prerequisite to admission. The amendment was ratified on November 7, 1911, at the time the people elected the first officers of the state. The 1911 amendment added the requirement that notice of proposed amendments be published in both English and Spanish, the provision for a special election for amending the constitution, and the requirement for a supermajority to amend Article VII §§1 and 3, Article XII §§ 8 and 10. The amendment also changed to a majority vote the former requirement of a two-thirds majority necessary for the legislature to propose amendments. The amendment also deleted a requirement that amendments be ratified by a vote of 40 percent of all votes cast in an election cast statewide and in half of the counties, and a limitation on the number of amendments to be submitted in each election. A restriction on the amendment of this section is given in Article XIX § 5.

An amendment is a change in the constitution, either by adding to it or deleting material from it. The constitution puts a number of constraints and limits on state government; these constraints can be removed or altered only by amending the constitution. Changes in the purpose of grants of land made by the congressional Enabling Act of 1910, may not be made without a constitutional amendment (*State v. State Bd. of Finance*, 1922). An office created by the constitution may be abolished only by amending the provision creating the office (*In re Thaxton*, 1968).

This section applies where one or more amendments are being considered, but does not apply where an entirely new constitution is being proposed (*State ex rel. Constitutional Convention v. Evans*, 1969). Amendments to different sections of the constitution should be submitted to the people as separate amendments. This section limits introduction of amendments to regular as opposed to special sessions; they may be introduced by both even-numbered and odd-numbered sessions, and by both restricted and unrestricted regular sessions (*State ex rel. Chavez v. Vigil-Giron*, 1988).

When an amendment is proposed to the people and there is a difference between the enrolled and engrossed resolution proposing it and the legislative journal, where the journal tends to show that the resolution did not receive the number of votes required, the enrolled and engrossed resolution, properly authenticated, is to prevail (*Smith v. Lucero*, 1917). The authority of the legislature to initiate constitutional amendments is different from its power to legislate and is not subject to the provision for referendum in Article IV § 1 (*Hutcheson v. Gonzales*, 1934).

The supreme court has original jurisdiction at the petition of an individual voter to mandate the secretary of state to publish proposed amendments to the constitution (*Hutcheson v. Gonzales*, 1934).

The purpose of the requirement that amendments be ratified separately is to avoid "logrolling" or "jockeying"; the danger of logrolling or submitting double or multiple propositions to the voters is the question of whether the propositions could have carried by vote had they been submitted singly; however, the general submission of several subjects is valid if all the changes are germane to one object (*City of Raton v. Sproule*, 1967). The phrase "electors voting in the whole state" is construed to mean all electors voting on a particular amendment. The requirement that amendments must pass by a two-thirds vote in every county violates the "one person, one vote" rule required by the Fourteenth Amendment (*State ex rel. Witt v. State Canvassing Board*, 1968).

SECTION 2

Constitutional conventions. Whenever, during the first twenty-five years after the adoption of this constitution, the legislature, by three-fourths vote of the members elected to each house, or after the expiration of said twenty-five years, by a vote of two-thirds vote of the members elected to each house, shall deem it necessary to call a convention to revise or amend this constitution, they shall submit the question of calling such convention to the electors at the next general election, and if a majority of all the electors voting on such question at said election the state shall vote in favor of calling a convention the legislature shall, at the next session, provide by law for calling the same. Such convention shall consist of at least as many delegates as there are members of the house of representatives. The constitution adopted by such convention shall have no validity until it has been submitted to and ratified by the people.

This section, too, was amended at the behest of Congress as a condition to being admitted to statehood. The 1911 amendment added "on such questions" following "electors voting" near the end of the first sentence and deleted a requirement that the calling of a constitutional convention must be approved by a majority of those voting in at least half of the counties. There has been only one constitutional convention since statehood was achieved; it was called in 1969 and drafted a new constitution which was rejected by the voters.

The question of holding a convention must be submitted to the voters throughout the state (*State v. Perrault*, 1969). In the case of *State ex rel Constitutional Convention v. Evans* (1969), the supreme court was called on to make several applications of this section. Among them were that this section and Article XIX § 1 are of equal dignity. This section is not to be read as if Section 1 does not exist; nor is there reason to read into this section the limitations relating to publication found in Section 1. Interpretation that gives complete effect to both sections is required; therefore, a statutory requirement that the constitution be published when the question of a new constitution is published is reasonable. The convention cannot legislate, and once called cannot exercise powers outside those mentioned in Article XIX § 2.

SECTION 3

Initiative restricted. If this constitution be in any way so amended as to allow laws to be enacted by direct vote of the electors the laws which may be so enacted shall be only such as might be enacted by the legislature under the provision of this constitution.

This section provides that, should a provision for enacting laws by initiative ever be added to the constitution, laws enacted by the people must meet the same constitutional requirements as those enacted by the legislature. As originally adopted, this section was worded as it is in the present text; nevertheless, it was included in the amendment which Congress required as a condition for New Mexico's admission to the Union. That amendment was adopted in 1911. This section has not been the subject of judicial interpretation.

SECTION 4

Amendment of compact with United States. When the United States shall consent thereto, the legislature, by a majority vote of the members in each house, may submit to the people the question of amending any provision of Article XXI of this constitution on compact with the United States to the extent allowed by the act of congress permitting the same, and if a majority of the qualified electors who vote upon any such amendment shall vote in favor thereof the said article shall be thereby amended accordingly.

This section recognizes that the people may amend sections of Article XXI, the compact with the United States, so long as the restrictions of the Enabling Act are observed. In fact, Article XXI § 10 provides that no amendment to the compact with the United States may be made without the approval of Congress. This wording was in the constitution as it was originally adopted; nevertheless, it was included in the amendment which Congress required as a condition for New Mexico's admission to the Union. That amendment was adopted in 1911.

SECTION 5

Revision of amendment provision restricted. The provisions of Section One of this article shall not be changed, altered or abrogated in any manner except through a general convention called to revise this constitution as herein provided.

This section requires that the amendment process provided for in the constitution can only be changed by a constitutional convention. The section, as presently worded, was the same in the constitution as originally adopted, but it was included in the required amendment of this article proposed by Congress and incorporated into congressional resolution, as a stipulation for the admission of New Mexico as a state. That amendment was adopted in 1911. Proposed amendments that would have repealed this section were rejected by the voters in 1965, 1970, and 1971.

Article XX

Miscellaneous

SECTION 1

Oath of office. Every person elected or appointed to any office shall, before entering upon his duties, take and subscribe to an oath or affirmation that he will support the constitution of the United States and the constitution and laws of this state, and that he will faithfully and impartially discharge the duties of his office to the best of his ability.

This provision requires that state officers take an oath of office before assuming their duties. The elements the oath should entail are presented here, but these are not presented to be the words required in such an oath. A newly appointed or elected official must take an oath and give bond where it is required, in order for the incumbent's term to come to an end (*Bowman Bank & Trust Company v. First National Bank*, 1914). Assistant attorney generals are not required to undergo the same formal swearing-in ceremony as the attorney general (*State v. Koehler*, 1981).

SECTION 2

Tenure of office. Every officer, unless removed, shall hold his office until his successor has duly qualified.

This section governs tenure and succession in office. This section continues an incumbent in office beyond his term until his successor has duly qualified (*State ex rel Rives v. Herring,* 1953). Officers appointed to fill the terms of elected officers are to serve until a successor is elected by the voters and duly qualified according to law (*State ex rel Walker v. Dilley,* 1974). The treasurer of the board of regents of a university may continue to serve in that capacity after a new board is appointed, until the new board elects a successor who is duly qualified by filing the proper bond (*Bowman Bank & Trust Co. v. First National Bank,* 1914).

"Removal" in this section contemplates statutory removals, and a trial court is without power to remove a state officer where no successor has qualified (*Haymaker v. State ex rel McCain,* 1917). Statutes which assign the district attorney the authority to suspend a public official pending investigation of an accusation looking to his removal do not violate this section (*State ex rel Harvey v. Medler,* 1914). If there is no statutory or constitutional provision requiring that notice and hearing be given before one is removed from office, neither a notice nor hearing is a necessary condition for a valid removal from office. And if the power of removal from office is vested in the governor and he assigns a constitutional cause for removal, his action must be accepted by the court (*State ex rel Ulrick v. Sanchez,* 1926). When a person is appointed to an office which is incompatible with an office then held, no vacancy is created in the first office, except for the purpose of supplying another person for the office; and the court, absent a qualified successor, has no power to remove the officeholder (*State v. Blancett,* 1918).

SECTION 3

Date terms of office begin. The term of office of every state, county or district officer, except those elected at the first election held under this constitution, and those elected to fill vacancies shall commence on the first day of January, next after his election.

The date terms of office begin is designated by this section. Article V § 5 and Article XX § 4 provide the specific provisions for those elected to fill vacancies. This section did not create district officers as a class of officers and relieve them of restrictions imposed on all other officials; district attorneys are state officers (*State ex rel Ward v. Romero,* 1912).

SECTION 4

Vacancies in offices of district attorney or county commissioner. If a vacancy occurs in the office of district attorney or county commissioner the governor shall fill such vacancy by appointment, and such appointee shall hold such office until the next general election. His successor shall be chosen at such election and shall hold his office until the expiration of the original term.

This section was amended in 1988 by substituting "Vacancy occurs" for "vacancy occur" near the beginning and deleting "judge of the supreme court or district court" following "district attorney." These changes reflected the method of judicial selection provided for in Article VI §§ 33, 34, 35, 36, and 37. A similar amendment was rejected by the people in 1982.

The first sentence of this section is self-executing The second sentence, however, is not; it needs legislation to provide for the manner of nomination and the conduct of the election (*State ex rel. Nobel v. Fiorina*, 1960). Except in the case of a vacancy resulting in the creation of a new district attorney position, the office of one filling an unexpired term of district attorney ends at the conclusion of that term (*State ex rel. Swope v. Mechem*, 1954).

SECTION 5

Interim appointments. If, while the senate is not in session, a vacancy occurs in any office the incumbent of which was appointed by the governor by and with the advice and consent of the senate, the governor shall appoint some qualified person to fill the same until the next session of the senate; and shall then appoint by and with the advice and consent of the senate some qualified person to fill said office for the period of the unexpired term.

This section provides that when the Senate is not in session, the governor may make interim appointments to fill vacancies in office which require the Senate's advice and consent. This section has not been the subject of judicial interpretation.

SECTION 6

Date of general elections. General elections shall be held in the state on the Tuesday after the first Monday in November in each even-numbered year.

This section established the date for holding general elections. The term "general election" is construed to refer to the statewide biennial election when all state and county officials are elected (*Benson v. Williams*, 1952).

SECTION 7

Canvass of returns for officers elected by more than one county. The returns of all elections for officers who are chosen by the electors of more than one county shall be canvassed by the county canvassing boards of each county as to the vote within their respective counties. Said board shall immediately certify the number of votes received by each candidate for such office within such county, to the state canvassing board herein established, which shall canvass and declare the result of the election.

This provision prescribes the process for tabulating the votes cast for officers elected by more than one county. It has not been the subject of court interpretation.

SECTION 8

First national election. In the event that New Mexico is admitted into the union as a state prior to the Tuesday next after the first Monday in November in the year nineteen hundred and twelve, and if no provision had been made by the state legislature therefor, an election shall be held in the state on the said Tuesday next after the first Monday in November in nineteen hundred and twelve, for the election of presidential electors; and such election shall be held as herein provided for the election upon the ratification of this constitution, and the returns thereof made to, and canvassed and certified by, the state canvassing board as herein provided in the case of the election of state officers.

This obsolete section made provision for the first election after statehood was achieved, in the event the legislature would not have sufficient time to do so. It was not the subject of litigation.

SECTION 9

State officers limited to salaries. No officer of the state who receives a salary, shall accept or receive to his own use any compensation, fees, allowance or emoluments for or on account of his office, in any form whatever, except the salary provided by law.

This section abolishes the fee system as a means of compensating officers of the state (*State ex rel. Delgado v. Romaro*, 1912). There are no legal services that can be rendered to a county board of commissioners by a district attorney for which he may exact extra compensation (*Hanagan v. Board of County Commissioners*, 1958).

Public officers are also prohibited from receiving extra compensation by Article IV § 27. Article X § 1 provides for the disposition of fees collected by county officers.

SECTION 10

Child labor. The legislature shall enact suitable laws for the regulation of employment of children.

The statutory provisions regulating child labor are found in Chapter 50, Article 6 NMSA 1978.

SECTION 11

Women as public officers. Women may hold the office of notary public and such other appointive offices as may be provided by law.

This obsolete section made provision for women to serve in appointive office; the drafters of the constitution did not contemplate women being eligible for elective office. This section has not been the subject of judicial interpretation.

SECTION 12

Publication of laws in English and Spanish. For the first twenty years after this constitution goes into effect all laws passed by the legislature shall be published in both the English and Spanish languages and thereafter such publication shall be made as the legislature may provide.

This section, like Article II § 5 and Article XII §§8 and 10, reflects the constitution-makers' sensitivity to the rights of the significant Spanish-speaking portion of the population. This section requires that the laws be published in the form of their enactment (*State v. Armstrong,* 1924). After the legislature appropriated money in 1915 to translate the code into Spanish, this section gives succeeding legislatures the authority to appropriate money to provide extra services not contemplated by the 1915 appropriation (*State ex rel. Sedillo v. Sargent,* 1918).

SECTION 13

Sacramental wines. The use of wines solely for sacramental purposes under church authority at any place within the state shall never be prohibited.

The constitution was written during the period when prohibitionists were beginning to manifest considerable political power. By this provision the drafters of the constitution sought to insure that the uses of sacramental wine would not be prohibited should prohibition be enacted. The constitution was amended in 1917 to prohibit intoxicating liquors, see Article XXIII. This section has not been the subject of judicial interpretation.

SECTION 14

Public officers barred from using railroad passes. It shall not be lawful for the governor, any member of the state board of equalization, any member of the corporation commission, any judge of the supreme court or district court, or any district attorney, any county commissioner or any county assessor, during his term in office to accept, hold or use any free pass; or purchase, receive or accept transportation over any railroad within this state for himself or his family upon terms not open to the general public; and any person violating the provisions hereof shall, upon conviction in a court of a competent jurisdiction, be punished as provided in Sections Thirty-Seven and Forty of the article on Legislative Department in this constitution.

This provision reflects the power of the railroads in the western United States in the nineteenth century. Its primary purpose was to eliminate graft upon the part of legislators and relieve them of any feeling of obligation toward a railroad company because they were given free passes. Article IV §§ 37 and 40 apply the prohibition specifically to legislators, provide that accepting such passes is a felony, and specify the punishment. This section has not been the subject of judicial interpretation.

SECTION 15

Penitentiary to be reformatory and industrial school; labor by inmates. The penitentiary is a reformatory and industrial school, and all persons confined therein shall, so far as consistent with discipline and public interest, be employed in some beneficial industry; and where a convict has a dependent family, his net earnings shall be paid to said family if necessary for their support.

This section requires that those confined to the state penitentiary be employed in beneficial work and that their earnings be paid to their dependents. Article XX § 18 forbids the state from leasing convict labor. This section has not been subjected to judicial interpretation.

SECTION 16

Railroad's liability to employees. Every person, receiver or corporation owning or operating a railroad within this state shall be liable for damages for injury to, or the death of, any person in its employ, resulting from the negligence, in whole or in part, of said owner or operator, or of any of the officers, agents or employees thereof, or by reason of any defect or insufficiency, due to its negligence, in whole or in part, in its cars, engines, appliances, machinery, track, roadbed, works or other equipment.

An action for negligently causing the death of an employee as above provided shall be maintained by the executor or administrator for the benefit of the employee's surviving widow or husband and children; or if none, then his parents; or if none, then the next of kin dependent upon said deceased. The amount recovered may be distributed as provided by law. Any contract or agreement made in advance of such injury with any employee waving or limiting any right to recover such damages shall be void.

This provision shall not be construed to affect the provisions of Section Two of Article Twenty-Two of this constitution, being the article upon Schedule.

This section insures that railroads will be liable to pay damages for injuries to or the death of employees. Under this provision the "fellow servant" common law doctrine is denied to railroads as a defense in suits for injury or death (*Morstad v. Atchison, T. & S. F. Railroad*, 1918).

This section should be understood in conjunction with Article XXII § 2. That section provides that the Federal Employers' Liability Act (45 U.S.C. §§ 51 to 60) shall have the same force it had in the Territory of New Mexico. The New Mexico courts have a mandatory duty to assume jurisdiction over the rights created by the Federal Employers' Liability Act; in such cases, what constitutes negligence is a federal question and does not vary according to differing conceptions of negligence in state law. Every vestige of the common law assumption of risk doctrine has been eliminated by the Federal Employers' Liability Act (*Bourguet v. Atchison, T. & S. F. Railroad*, 1959).

SECTION 17

Uniform system of textbooks for public schools—repealed on November 2, 1971. [This section is repealed.]

A 1971 amendment repealed this section which formerly read, "There shall be a uniform system of textbooks for the public schools which shall not be changed more than once in six years."

SECTION 18

Leasing of convict labor prohibited. The leasing of convict labor by the state is hereby prohibited.

Read Article XX § 15 in conjunction with this section. This section has not been subjected to judicial interpretation.

SECTION 19

Eight-hour day in public employment. Eight hours shall constitute a day's work in all cases of employment by and on behalf of the state or any county or municipality thereof.

This section was transplanted from the constitution of Oklahoma; it establishes an eight-hour work day as the normal work day of state and municipal employees. This section declares a policy as to the number of hours employees should work to be entitled to a day's wages, but it is not self-executing and requires enabling legislation to provide its effectiveness (*Jaramillo v. City of Albuquerque*, 1958).

SECTION 20

Waiver of indictment; proceedings on information. Any person held by a committing magistrate to await the action of the grand jury on a charge of felony or other infamous crime, may in open court with the consent of the court and the district attorney, be entered upon the record, waive indictment and plead to an information in the form of an indictment filed by the district attorney, and further proceeding shall then be had upon said information with like force and effect as though it were an indictment duly returned by the grand jury.

This section provides for formal criminal charges by information, rather than by grand jury indictment. Other provisions concerning information, indictment, and the rights of the accused are given in Article II § 14. Before the 1923 amendment of Article II § 14, there were so many safeguards associated with the permissive use of information that it was unlikely the framers could have expected that the requirements of Article II § 14 be waived except by this section (*State v. Chacon*, 1957).

The requirement of the Fifth Amendment for indictment by a grand jury is not applicable to the states (*State v. Holly*, 1968). Persons who are charged by criminal information are not entitled to demand indictment by a grand jury (*State v. Mosley*, 1968). Persons arrested before information is filed are not thereby entitled to a grand jury indictment, and subsequent filing of information does not violate this section (*State v. Reyes*, 1967).

SECTION 21

Pollution control. The protection of the state's beautiful and healthful environment is hereby declared to be of fundamental importance to the public interest, health, safety and general welfare. The legislature shall provide for control of pollution and control of despoilment of the air, water and other natural resources of this state, consistent with the use and development of these resources for maximum benefit of the people.

The maintenance of a beautiful and healthful environment in New Mexico is made a constitutional requirement by this section. The legislature is mandated to enact appropriate laws to control and limit the pollution and despoilment of natural resources. This section was added by a 1971 amendment.

SECTION 22

[The outcome of a 1994 vote to ratify the addition of this section was not certified.]

A proposal to amend this article by adding a new Section 22 that would have allowed the legislature to establish a state-operated lottery, and would have made wagering on video machines lawful statewide was declared to be a violation of Article XIX § 1 by the supreme court. The court ordered the State Canvassing Board not to certify the election. (*State ex rel Clark v. State Canvassing Board,* 1995).

Article XXI

Compact with the United States

PREAMBLE

In compliance with the requirements of the act of congress, entitled, "An act to enable the people of New Mexico to form a constitution and state government and be admitted into the union on an equal footing with the original states; and to enable the people of Arizona to form a constitution and state government and be admitted into the union on an equal footing with the original states," approved June twentieth, nineteen hundred and ten, it is hereby provided:

The act of Congress referred to in this preamble is the Enabling Act (June 20, 1910, 36 Stat. 557, ch. 310), which set out the requirements Congress imposed on the people of New Mexico in order to attain statehood. By including the provisions of this article the constitution-makers intended to insure compliance with those requirements. Provisions for amending the Compact with the United States are given in Article XIX § 4. A few of the provisions in this Article are obsolete or self-explanatory; therefore there is no commentary.

SECTION 1

Religious toleration; polygamy. Perfect toleration of religious sentiment shall be secured, and no inhabitant of this state shall ever be molested in person or property on account of his or her mode of religious worship. Polygamous or plural marriages and polygamous cohabitation are forever prohibited.

A 1953 amendment of this section deleted a provision at the end of this section that prohibited the sale, barter, or gift of intoxicating liquors to Indians or the introduction of such liquors into Indian country. Congress consented to the amendment (67 Statutes 586, ch. 502, § 3 [1953]). The section that was deleted is the same as Section 2A of the Enabling Act (*Tenorio v. Tenorio*, 1940).

In applying this section, whether a defendant's belief is "religious" is a determination to be made by the trial court. In making the decision the court may consider traditionalism and the nature of the belief; however, the lack of an organization espousing the belief should not be a factor in the decision. Where a defendant merely believes that marijuana is a gift of God, and therefore its use and distribution of marijuana is permitted, is not an intrinsic part of a religion (*State v. Brashear*, 1979). Other constitutional provisions guaranteeing religious freedom are found in Article II § 11, and Article XII § 9.

SECTION 2

Control of unappropriated or Indian lands; taxation of federal government, nonresident and Indian property. The people inhabiting this state do agree and declare that they forever disclaim all right and title to the unappropriated and ungranted public lands lying within the boundaries thereof, and to all lands lying within said boundaries owned or held by any Indian or Indian tribes, the right or title to which shall have been acquired through the United States, or any prior sovereignty; and that until the title of such Indian or Indian tribes shall have been extinguished the same shall be and remain subject to the disposition and under the absolute jurisdiction and control of the congress of the United States; and that the lands and other property belonging to citizens of the United States residing without this state shall never be taxed at a higher rate than the lands and other property belonging to residents thereof; that no taxes shall be imposed by this state upon lands or property therein belonging to or which may hereafter be acquired by the United States or reserved for its use; but nothing herein shall preclude this state from taxing as other lands and property are taxed, any lands and other property outside of an Indian reservation, owned or held by any Indian, save and except such lands as have been granted or acquired as aforesaid, or as may be granted or confirmed to any Indian or Indians under any act of congress; but all such lands shall be exempted from taxation by this state so long and to such extent as the congress of the United States has prescribed or may hereafter prescribe.

This section renounces forever any proprietary claims by the state over both unappropriated and ungranted federal lands and lands held by Indians or Indian tribes that lie within the boundaries of the state. It also sets limitations on the taxing power of the state over such lands, and prohibits the state from taxing the land of U.S. citizens who live outside of the state at a higher rate than the land of those who reside in the state. This section is the same as Section 2B of the Enabling Act (*Tenorio v. Tenorio*, 1940).

The immunity related to tax-exempt property granted the federal government by this section and by Article VIII § 3 is not available to one who holds a lease to construct housing on federal land; the lessee's interest may be taxed (*Kirtland Heights, Inc. v. Board of County Commissioners*, 1958).

Jurisdiction over Indians

The compact adds nothing to the authority of the United States over Indian lands as it existed under earlier congressional acts (*Martinez v. Martinez*, 1945). The disclaimer in this section over lands is a disclaimer of proprietary, rather than governmental, interests (*Sangre De Cristo Development Corp. v. City of Santa Fe*, 1972); civil jurisdiction over a suit against an Indian who does not live on the reservation is clearly a governmental interest; moreover, in matters not affecting either federal government or tribal relations, an Indian has the same status to sue and be sued in state courts as any other citizen (*Batchelor v. Charley*, 1965), and state courts have jurisdiction over an Indian living on the reservation, in matters concerning a contract that the Indian entered into while off the reservation (*State Security, Inc. v. Anderson*, 1973).

Indian tribes are distinct political entities with the right to self-government, and have exclusive authority within their territorial boundaries. The terms of this section leave no room for a state claim to governmental power over Indians or Indian lands except where such jurisdiction is specifically granted by an act of Congress or sanctioned by decisions of the United States Supreme Court (*Your Food Stores, Inc. v. Village of Espanola*, 1961). Congress, and not the state of New Mexico, legislates for the Indian pueblos of New Mexico (*Toledo v. Pueblo De Jemez*, 1954). The tribal affiliation of an Indian is unimportant in determining the status of a reservation Indian (*Fox v. Bureau of Revenue*, 1975).

Indian reservations are not completely separate entities existing outside of the political and governmental jurisdiction of New Mexico. The state has some jurisdiction, and there is not and never has been exclusive federal authority (*Montoya v. Bolack*, 1962), and even on reservations, state laws may be applied unless their application interferes with reservation self-government or impairs a right granted by federal law (*Mescalero Apache Tribe v. Jones*, 1973); the test of the validity of state action is whether such action interferes with the right of reservation Indians to make their own laws and be ruled by them (*Paiz v. Hughes*, 1966; and *Prince v. Board of Education*, 1975). But the state should not move into areas where Indian law and procedure have not achieved the degree of certainty of state law and procedure; to do so would deny Indians the opportunity to develop their own system (*Chino v. Chino*, 1977).

The criteria to be considered to determine whether or not application of state law would infringe upon the self-government of Indians are: (1) whether the parties are Indians or non-Indians, (2) whether cause of action arose within the Indian reservation, and (3) what is the nature of the interest to be protected (*Chino v. Chino*, 1977). Under these criteria the state may enforce support obligations because they arise from a marital relationship (*Natewa v. Natewa*, 1972). Likewise, state courts may exercise jurisdiction in criminal prosecutions against non-Indians for offenses committed on Indian lands, where no Indian property was involved, against non-Indians (*State v. Warner*, 1963). The state may also enforce compulsory school attendance laws against Indian children, if the tribal code has given consent to those laws and their enforcement (*Prince v. Board of Education*, 1975). Even though the federal government grants permission for the state to construct a highway across an Indian reservation, the beneficial title in the Indians' tribe is not extinguished, and the state does not gain criminal jurisdiction over Indians driving an automobile on such highways (*State v. Begay*, 1958).

The state's constitutional disclaimer of rights and title to Indian lands applies only to such lands and does not apply to state action involving a general right adjudication (*Jicarilla Apache Tribe v. United States*, 1979); nor does this section prohibit state adjudication of Indian water rights, since the state would not be asserting a proprietary interest in Indian lands (*State ex rel Reynolds v. Lewis*, 1976).

The Taxation of Indians

This section clearly precludes the state from levying an ad valorem property tax on Indian lands and Indian property on the reservation (*Prince v. Board of Education*, 1975), and taxing permanent improvements on the tribe's land is also prohibited (*Mescalero Apache Tribe v. Jones*, 1973). Neither can the state tax the income or gross receipts of Indians living on the reservation when the income and gross receipts involved are derived solely from activities within the reservation (*Hunt v. O'Cheskey*, 1973). Except in situations forbidden by Congress, New Mexico retains the right to tax all Indian lands and activities located or occurring outside the reservation (*Mescalero Apache Tribe v. Jones*, 1973), and taxing non-Indian activity on Indian land is not forbidden by this section (*G. M. Shupe, Inc. v. Bureau of Revenue*, 1976; and *Tiffany Construction Co. v. Bureau of Revenue*, 1981).

SECTION 3

Assumption of territorial debts. The debts and liabilities of the territory of New Mexico and the debts of the counties thereof, which were valid and subsisting on the twentieth day of June, nineteen hundred and ten, are hereby assumed and shall be paid by this state; and this state shall, as to all such debts and liabilities, be subrogated to all the rights, including rights of indemnity and reimbursement, existing in favor of said territory or of any of the several counties on said date. Nothing in this article shall be construed as validating or in any manner legalizing any territorial, county, municipal or other bonds, warrants, obligations or evidences of indebtedness of or claims against, said territory or any of the counties or municipalities thereof which now are or may be, at the time this state is admitted, invalid or illegal; nor shall the legislature of this state pass any law in any manner validating or legalizing the same.

This section requires that all debts and liabilities of the Territory of New Mexico will be assumed and paid by the state. This section is the same as Section 2C of the Enabling Act. The two cases that provide judicial interpretation of this section are no longer of any relevant application in law.

SECTION 4

Public schools. Provision shall be made for the establishment and maintenance of a system of public schools, which shall be open to all the children of the state and free from sectarian control, and said schools shall always be conducted in English.

The intention of Congress in Section 2D of the Enabling Act was to encourage the state to provide public education to its citizens, including Indians; that mandate is reflected in this section and Article XII § 1 (*Prince v. Board of Education*, 1975). Other provisions for a system of free public schools are found at Article XII § § 3, 8, and 10.

SECTION 5

Suffrage. This state shall never enact any law restricting or abridging the right of suffrage on account of race, color or previous condition of servitude.

This section was amended in 1912 by deleting provisions requiring that all state officers be sufficiently fluent in English, so as to conduct their duties without an interpreter. This amendment was authorized by Congress on August 21, 1911 (37 Statutes 39).

SECTION 6

Capital. The capital of this state shall, until changed by the electors voting at an election provided for by the legislature of this state for that purpose, be at the city of Santa

Fe, but no such election shall be called or provided for prior to the thirty-first day of December, nineteen hundred and twenty-five.

Santa Fe, the oldest capital established by Europeans, has remained the capital throughout New Mexico's statehood.

SECTION 7

Reclamation projects. There are hereby reserved to the United States, with the full acquiescence of the people of this state, all rights and powers for the carrying out of the provisions by the United States of the act of congress, entitled, "An act appropriating the receipts from the sale and disposal of public lands in certain states and territories to the construction of irrigation works for the reclamation of arid lands" approved June seventeenth, nineteen hundred and two, and acts amendatory thereof or supplementary thereto, the same extent as if this state had remained a territory.

SECTION 8

Allotted Indian lands subject to federal liquor control. Whenever hereafter any of the lands contained within Indian reservations or allotments in this state shall be allotted, sold, reserved or otherwise disposed of, they shall be subject for a period of twenty-five years after such allotment, sale, reservation or other disposal, to all the laws of the United States prohibiting the introduction of liquor into the Indian country; and the terms "Indian" and "Indian country" shall include the Pueblo Indians of New Mexico and the lands owned or occupied by them on the twentieth day of June, nineteen hundred and ten, or which are occupied by them at the time of the admission of New Mexico as a state.

This section is the same as the Enabling Act Section 2H (*Tenorio v. Tenorio*, 1940). The state has no expressed or implied grant of jurisdiction over liquor sales within the boundaries of reserved Indian lands (*U.S. v. New Mexico*, 1979).

SECTION 9

Consent to Enabling Act provisions. This state and its people consent to all and singular the provisions of the said act of congress, approved June twentieth, nineteen hundred and ten, concerning lands by said act granted or confirmed to this state, the terms and conditions upon which said grants and confirmations were made and the means and manner of enforcing such terms and conditions, all in every respect and particular as in said act provided.

This section again binds the state to the conditions of the Enabling Act concerning lands granted to New Mexico by Congress. For other provisions concerning public lands, see Article XIII. The Enabling Act became as much a part of New Mexico fundamental law as if it had been incorporated into the New Mexico Constitution (*State ex rel Interstate Stream Commission v. Reynolds*, 1963). By this section New Mexico accepted conditions imposed on the land grant trusts for the hospital for disabled miners (*United States v. New Mexico*, 1976).

SECTION 10

Compact irrevocable. This ordinance is irrevocable without the consent of the United States and the people of this state, and no change or abrogation of this ordinance, in whole or part, shall be made by any constitutional amendment without the consent of congress.

Even when Congress consents to a change in regard to the use of income from land granted to the state, the state must still adopt a constitutional amendment to carry this congressional consent into effect (*Bryant v. Board of Loan Commissioners*, 1922). Provisions for amendment of the compact with the United States are given in Article XIX § 4.

SECTION 11

Consent to exchange of lands. This state and its people consent to the provisions of the act of congress, approved June 15, 1926, providing for such exchanges and the governor and other state officers mentioned in said act are hereby authorized to execute the necessary instrument or instruments to effect the exchange of lands therein provided for with the government of the United States; provided that in the determination of values of the lands now owned by the state of New Mexico, the value of the lands, the timber thereon and mineral rights pertaining thereto shall control the determination of value. The legislature may enact laws for the carrying out of the provisions hereof in accordance herewith.

This section was added to the constitution by a 1932 amendment to put into effect the congressional act allowing such exchanges of public lands. The act provided for exchanges of state timberlands, scattered throughout the state, for larger tracts of federal grazing lands.

This section, which was added to the constitution by an amendment ratified in 1971, provides a constitutional duty for the legislature to enact environmental protection measures. It has not been the subject of judicial interpretation.

SECTION 12

[Amendment to add a section here not ratified.]

In 1990, the people rejected an amendment which would have added a Section 12 to this Article. It would have authorized the commissioner of public lands to exchange land under his control for lands held by the United States, a state agency or political subdivision, a public lands beneficiary, an Indian tribe or pueblo, or a private entity.

Article XXII

Schedule

That no inconvenience may arise by reason of the change from territorial to state form of government, it is declared and ordained:

SECTION 1

Effective date of Constitution. This constitution shall take effect and be in full force immediately upon the admission of New Mexico into the union as a state.

This article provides for New Mexico's transition from a territory to statehood. It generally defined how laws, rights, obligations, judicial cases, and records under the territorial government were to transfer to the state. It also provided for the elections necessary to ratify the constitution and to select the state's first officers. These provisions are obsolete. For the most part, any judicial interpretation of these sections is purely of historical interest; therefore the commentary for this article is minimal.

SECTION 2

Federal Employers' Liability Act. Until otherwise provided by law, the act of congress of the United States, entitled, "An act relating to liability of common carriers, by railroads to their employees in certain cases," approved April twenty-two, nineteen hundred and eight, and all acts amendatory thereof, shall be and remain in force in this state to the same extent that they have been in force in the territory of New Mexico.

The statute referred to is the Federal Employers' Liability Act (45 U.S.C. §§ 51 to 60); see Article XX § 16 for the substance of a railroad's liability to employees.

SECTION 3

Federal Mining Inspection Act. Until otherwise provided by law, the act of congress, entitled, "An act for the protection of the lives of miners," approved March three, eighteen hundred and ninety-one, and all acts amendatory thereof, shall be and remain in force in this state to the same extent that they have been in force in the territory of New Mexico; the words "governor of the state," are hereby substituted for the words "governor of the territory," and for the words "secretary of the interior" wherever the same appear in said acts; the chief mine inspector for the territory of New Mexico, appointed by the president of the United States, is hereby authorized to perform the duties prescribed by said acts until superseded by the "inspector of mines" appointed by the governor, as elsewhere provided by the constitution, and he shall receive the same compensation from the state, as he received from the United States.

The statute referred to is the Federal Mining Inspection Act (26 Statutes 1104, ch. 564); provisions regarding the state mine inspector are found in Article XVII § 1.

SECTION 4

Territorial laws. All laws of the territory of New Mexico in force at the time of its admission into the union as a state, not inconsistent with this constitution, shall be and remain in force as the laws of the state until they expire by their own limitation, or are altered or repealed; and all rights, actions, claims, contracts, liabilities, and obligations, shall continue and remain unaffected by change in the form of government.

As to fiscal affairs, the state is a mere successor of the territory (*State ex rel Lucero v. Marron*, 1912). The New Mexico wrongful death statutes were adopted from the territorial statutes, and the construction of those statutes by the territorial supreme court was also adopted with the statutes (*Mallory v. Pioneer Southwestern Stages, Inc.*, 1931).

One who asserts the inconsistency of the territorial laws with the constitution must show it (*Stout v. City of Clovis*, 1932). The reference in this section to conflict, if any, of the prior laws with the constitution, refers to the substance of the laws; territorial laws are not invalid under the constitution because they were enacted by methods valid at the time, but inconsistent with the constitution (*State v. Elder*, 1914). This section did not continue the fee and salary provisions of territorial law; such laws are inconsistent with Article XX § 9 (*Ward v. Romero*, 1912).

SECTION 5

Pardons for violation of territorial laws. The pardoning power herein granted shall extend to all persons who have been convicted of offenses against the laws of the territory of New Mexico.

SECTION 6

Territorial property vested in state. All property, real and personal, and all moneys, credits, claims and choses in action belonging to the territory of New Mexico, shall become the property of this state; all debts, taxes, fines, penalties, escheats and forfeitures, which have accrued or may accrue to said territory, shall inure to this state.

SECTION 7

Obligations due territory or subdivision. All recognizances, bonds, obligations and undertakings entered into or executed to the territory of New Mexico, or to any county, school district, municipality, officer or official board therein, shall remain valid according to the terms thereof, and may be sued upon and recovered by the proper authority under state law.

SECTION 8

Territorial judicial process and proceedings. All lawful process, writs, judgments, decrees, convictions and sentences issued, rendered, had or pronounced, in force at the time of the admission of the state, shall continue and remain in force to the same extent as if the change of government had not occurred, and shall be enforced and executed under the laws of the state.

A territorial supreme court justice, who was still holding office in January 1912, because his successor had not qualified for and taken office, had the authority to participate in deciding matters before the court (*Luna v. Cerrillos Coal R. R.* 1923).

SECTION 9

Territorial courts and offices; seals. All courts existing, and all persons holding offices or appointments under authority of said territory, at the time of the admission of the state, shall continue to hold and exercise their respective jurisdictions, functions, offices and appointments until superseded by the courts, officers or authorities provided for by this constitution.

Until otherwise provided by law, the seal of the territory shall be used as the seal of the state, and the seals of the several courts, officers and official boards in the territory shall be used as the seals of the corresponding courts, officers and official boards in the state; and for any new court, office or board created by this constitution, a seal may be adopted by the judge of said court, or the incumbent of said office or by the said board.

Under this section, territorial officers continued in power until their successors duly elected or appointed under statehood had qualified (*Luna v. Cerrillos Coal R. R.* 1923).

SECTION 10

Pending actions. All suits, indictments, criminal actions, bonds, process, matters and proceedings pending in any of the courts in the territory of New Mexico at the time of the organization of the courts provided for in this constitution shall be transferred to and proceed to determination in such courts of like or corresponding jurisdiction. And all civil causes of action and criminal offenses which shall have been commenced, or indictment found, shall be subject to action, prosecution, indictment and review in the proper courts of the state, in like manner and to the same extent as if the state had been created and said courts established prior to the accrual of such causes of action and the commission of such offenses.

SECTION 11

Execution and deposit of constitution. This constitution shall be signed by the president and secretary of the constitutional convention, and such delegates as desire to sign the same, and shall be deposited in the office of the secretary of the territory where it may be signed at any time by any delegate.

SECTION 12

Territorial obligations; names of political subdivisions. All lawful debts obligations of the several counties of the territory of New Mexico not assumed by the state and the school districts, municipalities, irrigation districts and improvement districts, therein, existing at the time of its admission as a state, shall remain valid and unaffected by the change of government, until paid or refunded according to law; and all counties, municipalities and districts in said territory shall continue with the same names, boundaries and rights until changed in accordance with the constitution and laws of the state.

This section was made necessary by the Enabling Act § 2C, which required the state to assume payment of debts and liabilities which were valid and subsisting on June 20, 1910. One purpose of this section was to provide for the validity of debts contracted by the territory after June 20, 1910 (*State ex rel. Lucero v. Marron*, 1912).

SECTION 13

Election to ratify constitution. This constitution shall be submitted to the people of New Mexico for ratification at an election to be held on the twenty-first day of January, nineteen hundred and eleven, at which election the qualified voters of New Mexico shall vote directly for or against the same, and the governor of the territory of New Mexico shall forthwith issue his proclamation ordering said election to be held on said day.

Except as to the manner of making returns of said election and canvassing and certifying the result thereof, said election shall be held and conducted in the manner prescribed by the laws of New Mexico now in force.

SECTION 14

Ballots for ratifying constitution. The ballots cast at said election in favor of ratification of this constitution shall have printed or written thereon in English and Spanish the words "For the Constitution"; and those against the ratification of the constitution shall have written or printed thereon in both English and Spanish the words "Against the Constitution"; and shall be counted or returned accordingly.

SECTION 15

Canvass of ratification election returns. The returns of said election shall be made by the election officers direct to the secretary of the territory of New Mexico at Santa Fe, who, with the governor and the chief justice of said territory, shall constitute a canvassing board, and they, or any two of them, shall meet at said city of Santa Fe on the third Monday after said election and shall canvass the same. Said canvassing board shall make and file with the secretary of the territory of New Mexico, a certificate signed by at least two of them, setting forth the number of votes cast as said election for or against the constitution, respectively.

SECTION 16

Submission of constitution to president and congress. If a majority of the legal votes cast at said election as certified to by said canvassing board, shall be for constitution, it shall be deemed to be duly ratified by the people of New Mexico and the secretary of state of the territory of New Mexico shall forthwith cause to be submitted to the president of the United States and to congress for approval, a certified copy of this constitution, together with the statement of votes cast thereon.

SECTION 17

Proclamation for first election of officers. If congress and the president approve this constitution, or if the president approves the same and congress fails to disapprove the same during the next regular session thereof, the governor of New Mexico shall, within thirty days after receipt of notification from the president certifying said facts, issue his proclamation for an election at which officers for a full state government, including a governor, county officers, members of the state legislature, two representatives to congress to be elected at large from the state, and such other officers as this constitution prescribes, shall be chosen by the people; said election to take place not earlier than sixty days nor later than ninety days after the date of said proclamation by the governor ordering the same.

SECTION 18

Conduct of first state election; certification of results to president Said last-mentioned election shall be held, the returns thereof made, canvassing and certified to by the secretary of said territory, in the same manner, and under the same laws, including those as to qualifications of electors, shall be applicable thereto, as hereinbefore prescribed for holding, making of the returns, canvassing and certifying the same, of the election for the ratification or rejection of this constitution.

When said election of state and county officers, members of the legislature, representatives in congress, and other officers provided for in this constitution, shall be held and the returns thereof made, canvassed and certified as hereinbefore provided, the governor of the territory of New Mexico shall immediately certify the result of said election, as canvassed and certified as hereinbefore provided, to the president of the United States.

SECTION 19

First state officers. Within thirty days after the issuance by the president of the United States of his proclamation announcing the result of said election so ascertained, all officers elected at such election, except members of the legislature, shall take the oath of office and give bond as required by this constitution or by the laws of the territory of New Mexico in the case of like officers of the territory, county or district, and shall thereupon enter upon the duties of their respective offices; but the legislature may by law require such officers to give other or additional bonds as a condition of their continuance in office.

SECTION 20

First legislative session; oaths of members; election of United States senators. The governor of the state, immediately upon his qualifying and entering upon the duties of his office, shall issue his proclamation convening the legislature at the seat of government on a day to be specified therein, not less than thirty nor more than sixty days after the date of said proclamation.

The members-elect of the legislature shall meet on the day specified, take the oath required by this constitution and within ten days after organization shall proceed to the election of two senators of the United States for the state of New Mexico, in the manner prescribed by the constitution and the laws of the United States; and the governor and secretary of the state of New Mexico shall certify the election of the senators and representatives in congress in the manner prescribed by law.

SECTION 21

Supplementary legislation. The legislature shall pass all necessary laws to carry into effect the provisions of this constitution.

A constitutional provision which is complete in itself needs no further legislation to put it in force; it is self-executing (*State v. Rogers*, 1926).

SECTION 22

Terms of first officers. The term of office of all officers elected at the election aforesaid shall commence on the day of their qualification and shall expire at the same time as if they had been elected on the Tuesday next after the first Monday of November in the year nineteen hundred and twelve.

This section was the end of the constitution as it was originally adopted. It closed with the following paragraph:

> Done in open convention at the City of Santa Fe, in the Territory of New Mexico, this 21 day of November, in the year of our Lord, one thousand nine hundred and ten.

This was followed by the names of the signers of the constitution.

Article XXIII

Intoxicating Liquors

ARTICLE XXIII IS REPEALED

Article XXIII §§1 and 2 was added to the constitution by a 1917 amendment. The Article prohibited the importation, manufacture, sale, barter gift, or offer of alcoholic liquors (except for scientific or sacramental purposes) after October 1, 1918, and provided for the punishment for violation of the prohibition. Article XXIII was repealed by a 1933 amendment.

Article XXIV

Leases on State Land

SECTION 1

Contracts for the development and production of minerals or development and operation of geothermal steam and waters on state lands. Leases and other contracts, reserving a royalty to the state, for the development and production of any and all minerals or for the development and operation of geothermal steam and waters on lands granted or confirmed to the state of New Mexico by the act of congress of June 20, 1910, entitled "An act to enable the people of New Mexico to form a constitution and state government and be admitted into the union on an equal footing with the original states," may be made under such provisions relating to the necessity or requirement for or the mode and manner of appraisement, advertisement and competitive bidding, and containing such terms and provisions, as may be provided by act of the legislature; the rentals, royalties and other proceeds therefrom to be applied and conserved in accordance with the provisions of said act of congress for the support or in aid of the common schools, or for the attainment of the respective purposes for which the several grants were made.

This article was added to the constitution by a 1928 amendment. In 1967, an amendment inserted "or for the development and operation of geothermal steam and waters" after "all minerals" near the beginning of the section. The act of

Congress referred to in this article is the Enabling Act for New Mexico (June 20, 1910, 36 Statutes 557, ch. 310). The state properly reserved the minerals and mineral rights in selling and issuing its patent to school and asylum lands granted to it by the Congress, and the patentee was not entitled to ejectment against the state's lessee of oil and gas rights (*Terry v. Midwest Refining Co.*, 1933).

■ BIBLIOGRAPHICAL ESSAY

Published works about New Mexico's constitution, government, and politics are relatively scarce. A good number of the works that do exist are either government reports or unpublished dissertations. Most of these can be found in the New Mexico State Library in Santa Fe, and the libraries at the University of New Mexico in Albuquerque and New Mexico State University in Las Cruces, but are seldom available in other libraries. The official edition of the Constitution of New Mexico is edited and published by the Secretary of State each time it is amended. An annually updated annotation of the constitution is included in the first volume of *New Mexico Statutes Annotated 1978* (Charlottesville, VA: The Michie Company). That volume also contains such useful primary sources as the Kearny Bill of Rights and Code, the Treaty of Guadalupe Hidalgo, the Organic Act Establishing The Territory of New Mexico, and the Gadsden Treaty. A more extensive collection of similar and later documents is found in Richard Ellis's *New Mexico Historic Documents* (Albuquerque: University of New Mexico Press, 1975). Several general works survey New Mexico's history from the pre-Columbian era to modern statehood; among them are Marc Simmons's *New Mexico: A History* (New York: W. W. Norton and Co., 1977); and his *New Mexico: An Interpretive History* (Albuquerque: University of New Mexico, 1988); and Myra Ellen Jenkins and Albert Shroeder's *A Brief History of New Mexico* (Albuquerque: University of New Mexico Press, 1974).

CONSTITUTIONAL POLITICS IN NEW MEXICO

In 1850, the year New Mexico became a territory, a constitutional convention drafted a constitution that was rejected by Congress. A record of that convention, *Journal and Proceeding of a Convention of Delegates Elected by the People of New Mexico,* was published in Washington, DC (Government Printing Office, 1850). The document itself was published as the *Constitution of the State of New Mexico, 1850* (Santa Fe: Stagecoach Press, 1965). Early accounts of constitutional politics are provided by L. Bradford Prince's *New Mexico's Struggle for Statehood: Sixty Years of Effort to Obtain Self Government* (Santa Fe: New Mexico Printing Co., 1910), and Ralph Twitchell's seven-volume *The Leading Facts of New Mexico History* (Cedar Rapids, Iowa: Torch Press, 1911). Both of these works reflect the Republican viewpoint of their strongly partisan authors.

I recommend as the most thorough account of the politics of gaining statehood Robert W. Larson's *New Mexico's Quest for Statehood: 1846–1912* (Albuquerque: University of New Mexico Press, 1968). The histories by three other scholars also provide useful information about New Mexico's struggle for statehood.

William A. Keleher provides twelve biographical sketches of territorial-period New Mexicans in *The Fabulous Frontier* (Albuquerque: University of New Mexico Press, 1963). A detailed examination of the struggle for land ownership in the late nineteenth century is presented in Victor Westphall's *The Public Domain in New Mexico* (Albuquerque: University of New Mexico Press, 1963). New Mexico statehood in the context of statehood for other territories is presented in Howard Robert Lamar's *The Far Southwest 1846–1912, A Territorial History* (New York: W.W. Norton and Co., 1970). Lamar presents a detailed analysis of resistance to statehood in "The Reluctant Admission: The Struggle to Admit Arizona and New Mexico to the Union," in *The American West: An Appraisal,* Robert G. Ferris, ed. (Santa Fe: Museum of New Mexico Press, 1963). The final roadblocks to statehood are examined in Marion Dargan's seven-part article "New Mexico's Fight for Statehood, 1895–1912," in the *New Mexico Historical Review:* "I: The Political Leaders of the Latter Half of the 1890's and Statehood," 14 (January 1939): 1–33; "II: The Attitude of the Territorial Press," 14 (April 1939): 123–142; "III: The Opposition Within the Party (1888–1890)," 15 (April 1990): 133–187; "IV: The Opposition Within the Territory During the Nineties," 16 (January 1941): 70–103; "V: The Silencing of the Opposition at Home," 16 (October 1941): 379–400; "VI: Advertising the Backyard of 'the United States,' " 18 (January 1943): 60–96; and "VII: The Part Played by the Press of the Southwest," 18 (April 1943): 148–175.

The official record of the 1910 Constitution is the *Proceedings of the Constitutional Convention* (Albuquerque: Press of the Morning Journal, 1910). The constitution as adopted by that convention can be found in *Annotated Constitution and Enabling Act of the State of New Mexico* (Santa Fe: A. S. Whittier, 1911). The leaders of its Republican and Democratic factions of the constitutional convention presented their political views on the constitution in speeches given during the campaign for ratification. Transcripts of two of those speeches were published as "Addresses on the Making of a Constitution by H. B. Ferguson and Frank W. Chancy," *Bulletin of the University of New Mexico, Sociological Series,* 1, no. 1 (1910). Several decades after the constitution's adoption, three other constitutional framers offered their insights about the 1910 convention: Thomas Mabry, "New Mexico's Constitution in the Making—Reminiscences of 1910," *New Mexico Historical Review* 19 (1944): 168–184; Reuben W. Heflin, "New Mexico Constitutional Convention," *New Mexico Historical Review* 20 (1946): 60–69; and Edward D. Tittmann, "New Mexico Constitutional Convention: Recollections," *New Mexico Historical Review* 27 (1952): 177–86.

A thorough analysis of the political influences on the drafting of the 1910 Constitution is Dorothy I. Cline's *New Mexico's 1910 Constitution, A Nineteenth Century Product* (Santa Fe: The Lightning Tree, 1984). In a more recent essay, she examines the deficiencies of the 1910 Constitution, and provides an overview of the political dynamics that led to the 1969 Constitutional Convention and to the drafting and rejection of the 1969 Constitution: "Constitutional

Politics in New Mexico," in Paul H. Hain, F. Chris Garcia, and Gilbert K. St. Clair, eds., *New Mexico Government,* third edition (Albuquerque: University of New Mexico Press, 1994). In the same book, in his essay "Recent Constitutional Activity," Richard H. Folmar provides an overview of the 78 constitutional amendments proposed between 1969 and 1990. The most comprehensive means of keeping abreast of the amendments to the constitution is the serial publication of the state legislature *Piecemeal Amendment of the New Mexico Constitution* (Santa Fe: Legislative Council Service, 1995), which is updated every two years or so.

In 1969, after calls for constitutional reform that spanned two decades, New Mexico held its only constitutional convention after becoming a state. Among the significant reports that called for reform and eventually for the constitutional commission are *Report: New Mexico State Reorganization Committee* (Santa Fe: The Capitol, June 30, 1952); *1964 Report of the Constitutional Revision Commission* (Santa Fe: The Capitol, September 29, 1964); and *Report of the Constitutional Revision Commission State of New Mexico, 1967,* adopted November 5, 1966, Harry L. Patton, Chairman (Santa Fe: The Capitol, 1967). The deficiencies of the 1910 Constitution were identified and outlined in a League of Women Voters of New Mexico publication, *What Have We Here: A Brief Look at the New Mexico Constitution* (Washington, DC: League of Women Voters Education Fund, 1968).

A number of the constitutional reforms recommended by the Constitutional Revision Commission's 1967 report are discussed by University of New Mexico School of Law students in a "Student Symposium: The New Mexico Constitutional Convention 1969," *Natural Resources Journal* 9 (1969): 422–480. In seven articles the symposium authors address (1) the reforms needed in the constitutional amendment process, (2) decreasing the number of elected officials in the executive branch, (3) the adoption of a merit system for selecting judges, (4) reform in the process for removing and disciplining judges, (5) eliminating the prohibition of state aid to private enterprise, (6) reform of constitutional provisions concerning Indians, and (7) reforms needed in the regulation of water rights.

The constitution drafted by the 1969 convention, and later denied ratification by the people, was published under the title *Proposed Constitution for the State of New Mexico* (Santa Fe: Governor's Committee on Reorganization of State Government, 1969). A brief description of the convention was written by Ernestine D. Evans, *New Mexico Constitutional Convention, August 5, 1969* (Santa Fe: Office of the Secretary of State, 1969). A comparison of the provisions of the new constitution with those of the 1910 Constitution can be found in Jeff Bingaman's *Comparison of Proposed and Present Constitution* (Santa Fe: Office of the Attorney General, 1969). An analysis of the new constitution prepared by legislative staff was published as *A New Constitution for New Mexico? An Analysis of Major Changes and Arguments For and Against* (Santa Fe: New Mexico Legislative Council Service, 1969).

NEW MEXICO GOVERNMENT AND POLITICS

Few scholars have examined the government and politics of New Mexico in great detail. A large amount of such study is the work of legislative commissions and legislative staff. Several general textbooks address New Mexican government and politics. Basic overviews of state politics are presented by Thomas C. Donnelly in *The Government of New Mexico* (Albuquerque: University of New Mexico Press, 1947); by Jack E. Holmes in *Politics in New Mexico* (Albuquerque: University of New Mexico Press, 1967); by F. Chris Garcia, Paul H. Hain, and Harold V. Rhodes in *State and Local Government in New Mexico* (Albuquerque: University of New Mexico Press, 1979); and by Maurilio E. Vigil, Michael Olsen, and Roy Lujan in *New Mexico Government and Politics* (New York: University Press of America, 1990). The most comprehensive work on the state's political system is the anthology edited by F. Chris Garcia, Paul H. Hain, and Gilbert K. St. Clair, *New Mexico Government,* third edition (Albuquerque: University of New Mexico Press, 1994). Particularly notable essays from this book are cited throughout this essay.

THE SEPARATION OF POWERS

Article III of the constitution provides explicitly for the separation of powers among the branches of New Mexico's government. This article has been the basis for a considerable number of court decisions. Law review articles that discuss the provisions of Article III include a discussion of the New Mexico Constitution's provisions for the separation of power by Thomas A. Garrity in "Separation of Powers Doctrine in New Mexico," *Natural Resources Journal* 4 (1964): 350–359. Albert E. Utton discusses the exercise of judicial and legislative functions by administrative agencies, and suggests that any constitutional dilemma created by this arrangement can be solved by distinguishing between judicial power and the mere exercise of judicial functions, and by insuring that executive agencies only promulgate regulations through the authority delegated to them by the legislature, "Constitutional Limitations of the Exercise of Judicial Functions by Administrative Agencies," *Natural Resources Journal* 7 (1967): 599–631. Michael B. Browde and M. E. Occhialino provide an extensive discussion of the legislature's role in making court rules in the context of a brief, comparative examination of judicial rule-making among the American states, "Separation of Powers and the Judicial Rule-Making Power in New Mexico: The Need for Prudential Restraints," *New Mexico Law Review* 15 (1985): 407–483.

THE LEGISLATIVE BRANCH

There is no single comprehensive study of the New Mexico legislature; however, several studies on various aspects of the legislative elections and coalition building in the legislature have been published in anthologies and journals. A good starting point to begin studying New Mexico legislature is Denny O. Ingram, Jr.'s "The Legislature," *Natural Resources Journal* 8 (1968): 148–168. He presents an overview of the legislature's authority and organization, and then suggests constitutional reform that he contends would improve the operation of the legislature.

Studies of the voting patterns in legislative elections discovered four major blocs: the urban, agricultural belt, little Texas, and Hispanic north. Harry P. Stumpf and T. Philip Wolf presented a summary of these findings in "New Mexico: The Political State," in Frank H. Jonas, ed., *Politics in the American West* (Salt Lake City: University of Utah Press, 1969). Cal Clark and Janet Clark explained the voting patterns in the 1978 elections in "New Mexico," in B. Oliver Walter, ed., *Politics in the West: The 1978 Elections* (Laramie, WY: Government Research Bureau, 1979). Christine Sierra examined the role of Hispanics in the 1988 election in "Hispanos in the 1988 General Election in New Mexico," in Rudolfo O. de la Graza, ed., *Latinos in the 1988 Election* (Austin: Center for Mexican American Studies, University of Texas, 1990). Unfortunately, more recent studies have not been published.

The voting patterns of New Mexican legislators have been examined by several scholars. Robert E. Esterly's study of the House of Representatives roll-call votes from 1961 through 1969 discerned three basic voting blocs: (a) mostly Hispanic Democrats from Bernalillo County and northern New Mexico, (b) mostly Anglo Democrats from eastern and southern counties, and (c) Republicans: "A Longitudinal Analysis of Legislative Roll Call Voting: Patterns of Stability and Change in the New Mexico House of Representatives, 1961–1969" (Ph.D. diss., Tucson: University of Arizona, 1971). An explanation of the coalition of conservative Democratic legislators and their Republican colleagues is presented in Maurilio E. Vigil's "The Mama Lucy Faction in the New Mexico Legislature: A Study of Chicanos in Legislative Politics," *New Mexico Highlands University Journal* 2(1) (1980): 50–59. The role of the Chicano political boss in legislative elections was examined in Maurilio E. Vigil's "The Patron: Tyrant or Benevolent Leader?" in *The Hispanics of New Mexico: Essays on History and Culture* (Bristol, IN: Wyndham Hall Press, 1985). A constitutional requirement for legislators' behavior is discussed in the comment by John M. Wells, "Legislative Bodies—Conflict of Interest—Legislators Prohibited from Contracting with the State," *Natural Resources Journal* 7 (1967): 296–303.

Legislative apportionment patterns in New Mexico before and after the U.S. Supreme Court's landmark decision in *Baker v. Carr* (369 U.S. 186 [1962]) were examined in Richard H. Folmar's *Apportionment in New Mexico: 1944–1966* (Santa Fe: New Mexico Legislative Council Service, August 1966).

THE EXECUTIVE BRANCH

New Mexico has a plural executive, the governor and nine other executive officials are chosen in statewide elections. This division of power within the executive branch as well as the jumble of agencies under the governor's authority have been criticized by scholars and political practitioners, and have been the target of various reform efforts. The structure of the executive branch is reviewed in the chapters "The Fragmented Executive System," by Alan Reed and Denise Fort, and "The Cabinet and the Bureaucracy," by Raymond W. Cox. Both essays are in F. Chris Garcia, Paul H. Hain, and Gilbert K. St. Clair, eds., *New Mexico Government,* third edition (Albuquerque: University of New Mexico Press, 1994). The organization and authority of the executive branch and the need for constitutional reform was surveyed by Denny O. Ingram, Jr., in "The Executive," *Natural Resources Journal* 7 (1967): 267–295. In 1951, the legislature created a reorganization committee to recommend a structure for the executive branch that would give the governor more authority over departmental affairs. Frequent calls for reform followed the publication of the committee's findings: *Report of the New Mexico State Reorganization Committee of 1952* (Santa Fe: State of New Mexico, 1952).

The most extensive reform of the executive branch was during the administration of Governor Jerry Apodoca. He proposed a reorganization that would increase accountability and provide more efficiency by reducing duplication and encouraging consistency in policy: *Responsive Government in New Mexico—1977: A Plan for the Reorganization of the Executive Branch of New Mexico State Government* (Santa Fe: Office of the Governor, 1977). The legislature enacted a package of statutes that structured most of the executive branch into a cabinet-based organization and brought independent agencies into the new structure. Apodoca summarized the new system in *Responsive Government 1978: Final Report of the Governor* (Santa Fe: Office of the Governor, 1978). A history of this reform effort is provided in Dorothy I. Cline's *Reorganization of the Executive Branch of State Government* (Santa Fe: State of New Mexico, 1978).

THE JUDICIAL BRANCH

The courts have been the focus of more investigation and analysis than the other institutions of government in New Mexico. Susan A. Roberts presented a comprehensive history of the state's highest court in "A Political History of the New Mexico Supreme Court, 1912–1972," *New Mexico Law Review* 5 (Special Issue 1975): 1–83. John N. Urtes examined and explained the difficulties and inefficiencies created by the supreme court's frequent use of three judge panels in his law review note "Courts: Numbers of Justices Concurring in Opinions—Some Dangers of New Mexico's Three-Judge Court," *Natural Resources Journal* 5 (1965): 403–407. Using voting-bloc analysis, George W. Kozeliski examined the court's influence on the development of state constitutional law in "The Impact of the New Mexico Supreme Court on the State Constitution and the Lower State Courts, 1912–1962" (Master's thesis, Las Cruces: New Mexico State University, 1974). My own Master's thesis examined the effect of the state intermediate appellate court on the caseload and policy making of the supreme court: Charles E. Smith, "The Effect of the New Mexico Court of Appeals on the State Supreme Court's Output" (Master's thesis, Albuquerque: University of New Mexico, 1989).

The twenty-fifth anniversary of the Court of Appeals was marked by the publication of its history by Thomas A. Donnelly and Pamela B. Minzner, "History of the New Mexico Court of Appeals," *New Mexico Law Review* 22 (1992): 595–619. The Court of Appeals adopted a prehearing mechanism designed to reduce the increasing workload resulting from criminal appeals. The effects of the system were described and evaluated as being beneficial in Simpson Mahlum's "Court of Appeals Prehearing Division: An Introduction," *State Bar Appellate Practice Section Newsletter* 1 (Summer 1991): 4, and in Thomas B. Marvell's "Abbreviate Appellate Procedure: An Evaluation of the New Mexico Summary Calendar," *Judicature* 75 (1991): 86–88.

The need for reform of the court system in New Mexico was emphasized in several studies and commission reports. The most important of these, *The Courts of New Mexico: A Report to the Twenty-fifth Legislature of New Mexico* (State Judicial Systems Study Committee, Santa Fe: State of New Mexico, 1961), provided an extensive review of the problems in the justice of the peace courts and the serious appellate caseload problem and called for a restructuring of the courts. Such criticisms and recommendations were repeated in other reports, such as the *1964 Report of the Constitutional Revision Commission* (Santa Fe: The Capitol, September 29, 1964); and *Expediting Appeals: A Study of the Supreme Court of New Mexico* (Santa Fe: Institute of Judicial Administration, 1963). These studies contributed to the reform that culminated in the ratification in 1965 of constitutional amendments which created the New Mexico Court of Appeals, and the 1966 constitutional amendments which abolished the justice of the peace courts and created the magistrate and metro court systems.

THE STATE SCHOOL SYSTEM

A good starting point for examining New Mexico's educational policy is David L. Colton and Luciano Baca's excellent essay "Governing New Mexico's Schools," in Paul H. Hain, F. Chris Garcia, and Gilbert K. St. Clair, eds., *New Mexico Government,* third edition (Albuquerque: University of New Mexico Press, 1994). They presented a brief history of the school system, then explained the structure for educational policy making and administration, and finally, the influence of education interest groups on the educational policy was reviewed by presenting case studies on the politics of setting curriculum, equity in funding, and externally imposed standards.

The need for reform of the school finance system in order to insure equitable spending across districts was recognized early in New Mexico. The role of non-local funds in such equalization was examined by Jose A. Perea in "A Comparison of the Equalization Effects of Federal and State Public School Fund Distribution in New Mexico" (Ph.D. diss., Albuquerque: University of New Mexico, 1971). William F. Carr examined the inequities in the New Mexico system in light of the landmark California Supreme Court school finance decision and argued that the New Mexico system would not meet the standard set in that case: "Note: *Serrano v. Priest* and Its Impact on New Mexico," *New Mexico Law Review* 2 (1972): 266–268. Jo Ann Krueger examined the 1974 legislative enactment designed to provide across-districts equality in per student funding in her article "The Politics of School Finance: New Mexico Passes a State Funding Formula," *Journal of Educational Finance* 1 (1975): 86–95.

Several legal challenges to the state's compulsory school attendance policy have failed in court. The judiciary's rationale in upholding the policy is discussed in Nancy Scanlan Neary's "Compulsory School Attendance—Who Directs the Education of a Child? *State v. Eddington*" *New Mexico Law Review* 14 (1984): 453–465.

Claims of a mandate for a far-reaching right to a bilingual educational system based in the constitutional provisions protecting the rights of Spanish-speaking students have been rejected by the courts. Law review articles that discuss this issue are Ray R. Montez's "Education and the Spanish-Speaking—An Attorney General's Opinion on Article XII, Section 8 of the New Mexico Constitution," *New Mexico Law Review* 3 (1973): 364–380, and Joseph M. Holmes's "Bilingual Education: *Serna v. Portales Municipal Schools*," *New Mexico Law Review* 5 (1975): 321–333.

LAND AND WATER USE REGULATION

Disagreements about land use or water use frequently become points of political and legal contention in New Mexico. This is reflected by the number of law review articles that address such questions. An extensive survey of these articles is outside of the scope of this essay. I present here some of the more significant discussions.

A large proportion of the land in New Mexico is owned by federal, state, or Indian governments, which results in legal and constitutional questions about land use. The range and flavor of these disputes can be found in these articles: Clarence E. Keys, "Note: Administration of Grazing Lands in New Mexico, A Breach of Trust," *Natural Resources Journal* 15 (1975): 581–601; Forrest S. Smith, "Note: Forest Fire Protection on Public and Private Lands in New Mexico," *Natural Resources Journal* 4 (1964): 374–397; and Richard A. Marquez, "New Mexico's National Forests and the Implied Reservation Doctrine," *Natural Resources Journal* 16 (1976): 975–1002.

The right to water has been the subject of extensive litigation in New Mexico. An excellent foundation for understanding water rights law is Ludwik A. Taclaff's, "What You Have Always Wanted to Know About Riparian Rights, But Were Afraid to Ask," *Natural Resources Journal* 12 (1972): 30–55. Constitutional questions concerning the allocation of water rights is discussed in Walter R. Parr's "Water Rights—Failure to use—Forfeiture," *Natural Resources Journal* 6 (1966): 127–134; R. E. Clark's "Water Rights Problems in the Upper Rio Grande Watershed and Adjoining Areas," *Natural Resources Journal* 11 (1971): 48–56; Kevin J. Bliss's "Protection of the Means of Groundwater Diversion," *Natural*

Resources Journal 20 (1980): 625–651; Gail Gottlieb's "New Mexico's Mine Dewatering Act: The Search for Rehoboth," *Natural Resources Journal* 20 (1980): 653–690; Zachary A. Smith's "Centralized Decisionmaking in the Administration of Groundwater Rights: The Experience of Arizona, California and New Mexico and Suggestions for the Future," *Natural Resources Journal* 24 (1984): 641–688; and Shannon A. Parden's "The Milagro Beanfield War Revisited in *Ensenada Land & Water Ass'n. v. Sleeper*: Public Welfare Defies Transfer of Water Rights," *Natural Resources Journal* 29 (1989): 861–876.

The allocation of water rights is complicated by the treaty and statutory rights of Native Americans. Extensive New Mexico case law addresses these complications. Representative discussion of such law can be found in these articles: David Brookshire, James Merrill, and Gary Watts, "Economics and the Determination of Indian Reserved Water Rights," *Natural Resources Journal* 23 (1983): 749–765; Rondolyn R. O'Brien, "Indian Pueblo Water Rights Not Subject to State Law Prior to Appropriation," *Natural Resources Journal* 17 (1977): 341–344; Charles DuMats and Helen Ingram, "Congressional Quantification of Indian Reserved Water Rights: A Definite Solution or a Mirage?" *Natural Resources Journal* 20 (1980): 17–43; James L. Merrill, "Aboriginal Water Rights," *Natural Resources Journal* 20 (1980): 45–70; William Douglas Black and Jeffery S. Taylor, "Navajo Water Rights: Pulling the Plug on the Colorado River," *Natural Resources Journal* 20 (1980): 71–90; and Judith E. Jacobsen, "The Navajo Indian Irrigation Project and Quantification of Navajo Water Rights," *Natural Resources Journal* 32 (1992): 825–853.

Questions of water use are also the subject of contention between New Mexico and its neighboring states. The flavor of such interstate disagreements can be gained from Nancy E. Hetrick's article "Recent Developments in the El Paso/New Mexico Interstate Groundwater Controversy—The Constitutionality of New Mexico's New Municipality Water Planning Statute," *Natural Resources Journal* 29 (1989): 223–249. An extensive study of the impact of federal use of the interstate commerce clause to regulate the use of water among the states was commissioned by the legislature in 1983. The report of the Water Study Committee was published as "The Impact of Recent Court Decisions Concerning Water and Interstate Commerce on Water Resources of the State of New Mexico," *Natural Resources Journal* 24 (1984): 688–744.

AMENDING THE CONSTITUTION

The 1910 constitutional convention drafted a document that, for all practical purposes, was impossible to amend. Congress required that a more realistic amendment process be adopted before it would allow statehood; therefore, the "Blue Ballot" amendment changed the constitution before New Mexico became a state. Still some provisions in the constitution have more stringent amendment requirements than others; this is explained by Dorothy I. Cline, "Constitutional Politics in New Mexico," in Paul H. Hain, F. Chris Garcia, and Gilbert K.

St. Clair, eds., *New Mexico Government,* third edition (Albuquerque: University of New Mexico Press, 1994). Theoretical difficulties and limitations presented by the amendment requirements of the constitution are also discussed in Hellene Simpson's "Procedural Problems in Amending New Mexico's Constitution," *Natural Resources Journal* 4 (1964): 151–159. The problems that Simpson postulates, however, have not developed or been resolved by court decisions; see the discussion of these decisions in *State ex rel Clark v. Canvassing Board* (1995).

TAXATION AND FINANCE

A thorough discussion of New Mexico's tax and expenditure policies is provided by M. Brian McDonald and Juliana Boyle's essay "The Fiscal Structure of New Mexico," in Paul H. Hain, F. Chris Garcia, and Gilbert K. St. Clair, eds., *New Mexico Government,* third edition (Albuquerque: University of New Mexico Press, 1994). Particular taxation policies are discussed by Hugh B. Muir, "Ad Valorem Tax Status of a Private Lessee's Interest in Publicly Owned Property: Taxability of Possessory Interests in Industrial Projects Under the New Mexico Industrial Bond Act," *New Mexico Law Review* 3 (1973): 135–151; and in Robert L. McGeorge's "Approaches to State Taxation of the Mining Industry," *Natural Resources Journal* 10 (1970): 156–170.

■ TABLE OF CASES

A

Abeytia v. Gibbons Garage, 195 P. 515, 26 N.M. 622 (1920), **53**
Adams v. Tatsch, 362 P.2d 984, 68 N.M. 446 (1961), **85**
Albuquerque Metropolitan Arroyo Flood Control Authority v. Swinburne, 394 P.2d 998, 74 N.M. 487 (1964), **168**
Allen v. Allen, 194 P.2d 270, 52 N.M. 174 (1948), **110**
Amador v. State Bd. of Education, 455 P.2d 840, 80 N.M. 336 (1969), **148**
American Trust & Savings Bank v. Scobee, 224 P. 788, 29 N.M. 436 (1924), **158**
Ammerman v. Hubbard Broadcasting, Inc., 551 P.2d 1354, 89 N.M. 307 (1976), cert. denied 436 U.S. 906 (1978), **89**
Anaconda Co. v. Property Tax Department, 608 P.2d 514, 94 N.M. 202 (Ct. App. 1979), cert. denied 614 P.2d 545, 94 N.M. 628 (1980), **112**
Apodaca v. Wilson, 525 P.2d 876, 86 N.M. 516 (1974), **133**
Atlas Corp. v. DeVilliers, 447 F.2d (10th Cir. 1971), cert. denied 405 U.S. 933 (1972), **55**

B

Batchelor v. Charley, 398 P.2d 49, 74 N.M. 717 (1965), **193**
Beauchamp v. Campbell, Civ. No. 5887 (D.N.M. 1966), unreported, **62**
Benson v. Williams, 246 P.2d 1046, 56 N.M. 560 (1952), **183**
Black Hawk Consolidated Mines Co. v. Gallegos, 191 P.2d 996, 52 N.M. 74 (1948), **67**
Board of Commissioners v. District Court, 223 P. 516, 29 N.M. 244 (1924), **109**
Board of County Commissioners v. Harris, 366 P.2d 710, 69 N.M. 315 (1961), **55**
Board of Education v. Jennings, 651 P.2d 1037, 98 N.M. 602 (Ct. App. 1982), **148**
Board of Education v. Maloney, 477 P.2d 605, 82 N.M. 167 (1970), **124**
Board of Education v. Robinson, 259 P.2d 1028, 57 N.M. 445 (1953), **124**
Board of Trustees v. Montano, 481 P.2d 702, 82 N.M. 340 (1971), **54**
Bourguet v. Atchison, T. & S. F. Railroad, 334 P.2d 1112, 65 N.M. 65 (1959), **187**
Bourne v. Board of Education, 128 P.2d 733, 46 N.M. 310 (1942), **148**
Bowman Bank & Trust Co. v. First National Bank, 139 P. 148, 18 N.M. 400 (1914), **181, 182**
Bryant v. Board of Loan Commissioners, 211 P. 597, 28 N.M. 319 (1922), **197**
Bryant v. State Office Building Commission, 120 P.2d 453, 46 N.M. 58 (1941), **122**
Bureau of Revenue v. Dale J. Bellamah Corp., 474 P.2d 499, 82 N.M. 13 (1970), **64**
Buzbee v. Donnelly, 634 P.2d 1244, 96 N.M. 692 (1981), **50**

C

Cannon v. First National Bank, 291 P. 924, 35 N.M. 193 (1930), **96**
Carlile v. Continental Oil Co., 468 P.2d 885, 81 N.M. 485 (Ct. App. 1970), **48**
Casuse v. City of Gallup, 746 P.2d 1103, 106 N.M. 571 (1987), **133**
Catron v. Marron, 142 P. 380, 19 N.M. 200 (1914), **114, 121**

D

E

F

J

K

L

M

S

T

U

V

W

Y

Z

■ INDEX

About the Author

CHUCK SMITH, Assistant Professor of Political Science, West Virginia State College, has done considerable research on constitutional and judicial issues and on state government in New Mexico.

www.ingramcontent.com/pod-product-compliance
Ingram Content Group UK Ltd.
Pitfield, Milton Keynes, MK11 3LW, UK
UKHW020924170926
475595UK00031B/52

9 780199 779154